AN
AMERICAN CRISIS
Congress and Reconstruction
1865-1867

BY

W. R. BROCK

Fellow of Selwyn College, Cambridge
University Lecturer in American History

LONDON
MACMILLAN & CO LTD
NEW YORK · ST MARTIN'S PRESS
1963

MACMILLAN AND COMPANY LIMITED
St Martin's Street London WC2
also Bombay Calcutta Madras Melbourne

THE MACMILLAN COMPANY OF CANADA LIMITED
Toronto

ST MARTIN'S PRESS INC
New York

PRINTED IN GREAT BRITAIN

For
ANNA
and
JAMES

PREFACE

It may seem presumptuous in a foreigner to enter the American family quarrel over Reconstruction; my excuse for doing so is that the problem transcends its domestic context. The present status of the United States in the world makes their history the concern of all peoples, and the contemporary preoccupation with racial questions makes every attempt to answer them of general significance. Nor is the problem of Reconstruction that of the negro alone, for it raises crucial questions about American institutions, about American political philosophy, and about assumptions which are not confined to Americans. It is the behaviour of American politicians, and the American political system in a time of crisis, that I have sought to study in this book. Because I have tried to see the problems mainly through Northern eyes I shall be accused of taking sides against the South, for it is a tragedy of modern American historical writing that one cannot discuss this central episode in American history without appearing to be involved in sectional bitterness. Though I have tried to suggest that the authors of congressional Reconstruction were human beings — and that a few of them were human beings with exceptional qualities — I do not imply that Southerners had no case against the North. I do, however, believe that this 'case' has been poorly presented when Southern polemics stop with the statements that Thaddeus Stevens was wicked, that Charles Sumner was fanatical, and that carpetbag rule saw the 'black out of honest government'. The true fact about congressional Reconstruction was that it became law by a succession of two-thirds votes in both Houses of Congress, and that in mid-passage the Republicans won a resounding electoral victory. This kind of sustained solidarity is exceptional in American political history, and one must infer that there were powerful forces at work in the Northern society which produced this measure of support for an extremist policy. Reconstruction was not imposed upon the South by a few bad men but by democratic processes in the victorious Northern society; it was not the outcome of petty spite or vindictiveness but of deep-seated emotions which drew upon the experience of war and upon political slogans sanctified since 1776. Reconstruction may have been unwise, but if so it was not the folly of a few but of a whole society and its traditions. Moreover this folly — if folly it be — is riding high in the contemporary world.

In describing Northern attitudes I may well be accused of placing too much faith in the utterances of Northern politicians, and, though historians may have drawn away a little from the convention that all words must be searched for their ulterior meaning, it may still be perilous to suppose that men meant what they said. I believe that most Republicans did mean what they said when they touched upon idealistic themes, but in fact their sincerity is often irrelevant to my argument. The politicians live in a public world and they say what they hope will be publicly acceptable; they speak not only with their eyes upon their immediate hearers but also upon the unseen audience of newspaper readers. When a politician makes an idealistic statement its significance lies not so much in the speaker as in the extent to which others respond and accept it as an expression of their own aspirations. The significance of Sir Winston Churchill's wartime speeches would not be destroyed by proving that he had a personal vendetta against Hitler or that he stood to lose if the Germans invaded Great Britain. In the same way Thaddeus Stevens (though a lesser man) made statements about equality and rights which do not become insignificant because he was 'vindictive', or because he owned an ironworks in Pennsylvania, or because he had a club-foot and kept a mulatto mistress; their significance lies in the fact that, when spoken, they seemed to be charged with wisdom and compulsive in their rhetoric. The many Radical utterances which are quoted in the following pages are not there to whitewash the individuals, but to discover something about the character of the society in which they were accepted as valid and important.

An English scholar engaged upon American history is probably unable to emulate his American colleagues in their meticulous and comprehensive use of unpublished material. Visits are necessarily short and infrequent, and microfilms are only a poor substitute for first-hand acquaintance with the documents. While making this apology and explanation I must, however, express a doubt whether my argument would have been altered in any important respect if I had been able to spend a longer time in American libraries. It is my impression that the story of Reconstruction at the national level has been so exhaustively covered that no new documentary discovery is likely to alter it to any significant degree. Additional light will doubtless be thrown upon the motives of individuals as new papers come to light, but the primary task in Reconstruction history is now to ask new questions of familiar material and not to expect a discovery which will put the whole episode in a new light. There ought, however, to be a further stage in exploring Reconstruction history below the national level and in discovering what forces and ferments were at work in Northern society; in my sixth chapter I have suggested the kind of picture which I think will emerge, but the investigation of local sources is a task which can only be undertaken by the men on the spot.

Much of the basic research for this book was done during a semester spent at Johns Hopkins University, and my thanks are due to the authorities of that university, and in particular to the members of the Department of History, who made my stay there pleasurable and, I hope, profitable. In common with most other British colleagues I owe a debt to the Commonwealth Fund of New York not only for making two trips to the United States financially possible, and for personal assistance on every occasion, but also for a lively interest in the promotion of American Studies in Great Britain.

W. R. BROCK

Selwyn College,
Cambridge

CONTENTS

CHAPTER   PAGE

       PREFACE   vii

       ABBREVIATIONS   xii

       I   *The Nature of the Crisis*   I

       II   *Policies and Possibilities*   15

       III   *Men in Congress*   49

       IV   *First Congressional Reconstruction*   95

       V   *Second Congressional Reconstruction*   153

       VI   *The Forces behind Reconstruction*   212

       VII   *Reconstruction and the Constitution*   250

       VIII   *The Waning of Radicalism*   274

       BIBLIOGRAPHICAL NOTE   305

       INDEX   307

ABBREVIATIONS USED IN THE NOTES

References to the *Congressional Globe* appear in this way:

C.G. 39.1.752 = Congressional Globe. Thirty-
ninth Congress. First Session.
Page 752.

References to papers in the Library of Congress appear in this way:

L. C. *Stevens Papers.*

· I ·

The Nature of the Crisis

Reconstruction presented the United States with a probing challenge to their institutions and political beliefs, and it cannot be understood at the superficial level of recrimination and apologetics. It followed upon the greatest failure in American history, and it is intimately bound up with the subsequent failure to solve the problems of a bi-racial society or to produce real harmony between the North and the South. It has been tempting to find scapegoats to bear the responsibility for failure and there has been a tendency to blame individuals and groups rather than to appreciate the character of the Reconstruction crisis. Books have been written upon the assumption that a little good-will and a little good sense could have combined reconciliation with justice to all, while ignoring the fact that after April 1861 nothing could ever be the same again. When war broke out the argument over constitutional obligations, the rights of States or the extension of slavery, ceased; thereafter the question was simply which side would gather enough force and show sufficient pertinacity to win. When the South surrendered the Northern force remained in command of the situation, and with the power to act went the necessity of decision. Whatever happened in the South — whether it were a resumption of the old life or a revolutionary departure — must be the result of Northern decision. Responsibility lay with the power which had won the military victory, and it could not be avoided by pretending that the page could be turned back to 1861. It is the purpose of this book to examine the nature of that responsibility, the interpretations placed upon it by those who had to act, and the arguments

I

which produced the decision reached by the Northern people
through their elected representatives.

It is a great error to suppose that the ideals enunciated by people
during war are insincere and that their force evaporates when the
fighting ends. The catastrophe of war had cut deeply into the
emotions and forced men to decide for themselves why, how, and
with what objectives it was necessary to fight. Ideas which had
been dimly perceived before the war emerged as clear-cut propositions, and views which had been held by small minorities suddenly
became great national convictions. It was a war to preserve the
Union, and a good many men hoped that it need be no more than
that; but the political and material ascendancy of the Union was
too cold a cause to sustain the will and enthusiasm of a people
trained in idealistic modes of thought. Two years after the end of
the war a sober Northern journal, catering for educated opinion,
could assert editorially that 'if there be anything which the
press, the pulpit, the prayers, the hymns, the conversations of
the North have been emphatic in affirming during the last six
years, it is that the late war was not merely a contest for empire,
as Earl Russell called it, not merely a struggle to settle a political difference, but a struggle between moral right and moral
wrong. . . . We took a far higher than political ground. We
said that the rebellion was an immoral enterprise, conceived and
carried out not by mistaken men, but by bad and unscrupulous
men, animated by corrupt and selfish motives, and determined to
gain their ends at whatever cost or suffering to others'.[1] It is
impossible to understand the crisis of Reconstruction unless one
also understands the depth, extent and sincerity of feelings such
as these; and whether they were justified or unjustified it is an idle
hypothesis to suppose that people who had fought through a
soul-searing war would calmly abandon ideals which had been so
loudly proclaimed. The war had been started to preserve the
Union, but for the majority in the victorious North it had become
a war to create a more perfect Union.

In July 1861 Lincoln had described the war as 'essentially a

[1] *The Nation*, IV, 414.

people's contest' to preserve that form of government 'whose aim was the betterment of mankind'.[1] The idea of defending a form of government was easily translated into the need to eradicate those elements in American society which had threatened American government with failure. At the end of the war there might be malice towards none, but in the meantime Northern propaganda had sown deep in the Northern mind a picture of all the evils propagated and preserved by the leaders of the South. It was not only a political clique but a whole system of society which fell under the axe of condemnation; the South had to be fought not only because it had broken the Union but because 'aristocracy' and forced labour were incompatible with American aims. It was not only necessary to defeat the South but also to democratize it, and of all needs the first was the abolition of slavery. In a famous letter Lincoln told Horace Greeley that his sole object was to save the Union, and that if he could save it without touching slavery he would do so; but when this letter was written Lincoln had already drafted the Emancipation Proclamation and was waiting only for an expedient opportunity to issue it.[2] The process by which the character of the war was changed was described in oversimplified but illuminating terms by Senator Stewart of Nevada: 'We commenced to force the Southern people to obey the Constitution. We said they had no right to secede. That was the first proposition. In the progress of the war it was ascertained that the negro had become an element of strength to the South ... and President Lincoln, patriotically and properly, thank God, had the boldness to issue his proclamation and strike a blow at the war power. We then declared, and the nation's honour was pledged, that we would maintain for the negro his freedom. Then the issue became the Union and the freedom of the negro.'[3] Indeed the end of slavery came to assume ever greater significance in Northern eyes; if the passions of war looked less happy as

[1] Message to Congress, 4 Jul. 1861, Richardson (ed.), *Messages and Papers*, VI, 20 ff.

[2] Lincoln to Greeley, 22 Aug. 1862. Lincoln had read a draft of the Emancipation Proclamation to the Cabinet on 22 Jul. 1862. Roy P. Basler (ed.), *The Collected Works of Abraham Lincoln*, V, 336–7; David Donald (ed.), *Inside Lincoln's Cabinet: The Civil War Diaries of Salmon P. Chase*, 99.

[3] C.G. 39.1.297. For Senator Stewart see p. 117.

enthusiasm cooled, if the 'democratization' of the South was too
elusive and too much in conflict with treasured notions of local
self-government, the abolition of slavery stood forth as a single,
simple and essential contribution to the betterment of mankind.
But was the achievement a simple one? If the negro was not a
slave, what was he? And who would decide?

Leslie Stephen once attacked the London *Times* for its attitude
towards the Civil War by saying that 'a foreigner looking on at a
cricket match is apt to think the evolutions of the players mysterious; and they will be enveloped in a sevenfold mystery if he
has a firmly preconceived prejudice that the ball has nothing to do
with the game. At every new movement he must invent a new
theory to show that the apparent eagerness to pick up the ball is a
mere pretext; that no one really wants to hit it, or to catch it, or to
throw it at the wickets: and that its constant appearance is due to
a mere accident. He will be lucky if some of his theories do not
upset each other. As, in my opinion, the root of all the errors of
The Times may be found in its views about slavery, which lay
as is now evident, at the botton of the whole quarrel'.[1] Stephen's
interpretation of the Civil War is one upon which Americans
will never agree amongst themselves, but his remarks can be
applied to those historians who have written about Reconstruction
with the firmly preconceived prejudice that the question of race
had nothing to do with the game and that any concern for the
civil rights of negroes must be ignored or explained away. In fact
negro status stood at the heart of the whole Reconstruction problem and presented a devastating challenge to American civilization.
In October 1867 *The Nation* summed it up by saying that 'We
boast of having gone beyond others in social and political science,
but we have at last come to a place where the claim is to be most
solemnly tested. This question of race is put before us as stone of
stumbling, or a rock of exaltation. It is for the rising or falling of
our Israel. . . . Over and over again, in every form but one, have
we set forth the principle of human equality before the law. We

[1] *'The Times' on the American War. A Historical Study by L. S.* [*Leslie Stephen*],
(London 1865), 19.

have boasted of our land as the free home of all races. We have insulted other nations with the vehemence of our declamation. And now we are brought face to face with a question that will test it all. . . . Is the negro a man? Say what we will, this is the real issue in the controversy respecting him'.[1]

If one preoccupation of Reconstruction was with the poorest in the land, the other was with the men who were to fill the highest offices and provide government for the people. The Confederate leaders were the avowed enemies of the Union and countless Northerners held them personally responsible for the war and all its losses. It was a perfectly proper question to ask whether these men could be allowed to continue to rule in their States and to resume their old power in the national government. Yet side by side with this problem was the indubitable fact that the war had been fought to force the Southern States to remain as States in the Union and, if States in the Union were to be denied the right to place in office those whom their people chose, a traditional bastion of American Federal government would have fallen. Many Northern Americans believed that State rights had been the cause of the war, but few emerged from the war with any clear idea of the way in which the rights of States could or ought to be modified. Were the States to be denied the right to do wrong, to elect the wrong people, or to commit whatever folly the local majority might sanction? Again it was idle to suppose that these questions could be ignored, or answered by reference back to the Constitution as it was in 1861. The words of the precious document might remain unaltered but the people for whom it provided had changed.

To Charles Sumner 'the problem of reconstruction did not appear perplexing at all'.[2] He believed that the Declaration of Independence was the charter document incorporating the American nation and that the Constitution must be interpreted in the light of its assertion of self-evident equality and inalienable rights. On the other side Democrats became frantic when confronted with the suggestion that the work of their great Founding Father

---

[1] *The Nation*, IV, 520, 26 Oct. 1867.
[2] Carl Schurz, *Eulogy on Charles Sumner* (Boston, 1875), p.50.

could be invoked to justify an attack upon the rights of States.[1] The right to amend was, of course, a part of the Constitution, and the principles of the Declaration could well be added in this way, but it might be argued that the Constitution could not be amended without the participation of all the States. Many Republicans were inclined to agree that there was no power in the Declaration to control interpretation of the Constitution, and were troubled by the thought that an amendment made only by the loyal States might be legally invalid. Yet everyone knew that any proposed amendments must affect adversely the Southern States and that once in Congress they would have power to block them for ever. It might have been simplest to do what Thaddeus Stevens wished: to regard the Constitution as suspended, to alter it as might be necessary to guarantee the results of the war, and to present the amended document as the Constitution to which 'rebels' must swear allegiance. But in a world governed by lawyers the idea of suspending the Constitution seemed to offer far more difficulties than remedies, and the majority of Republicans preferred to get the illogical best of both worlds by excluding the Southern States from participating in the making of amendments, but by asking them to ratify, and then making ratification an explicit or implicit condition for re-admission to Congress. This constitutional tangle, and the other means by which the Republican majority sought to keep within the Constitution while breaking it, has been made a standing reproach by those who wish to discredit congressional Reconstruction. It might be fairer to ask whether the Constitution itself was not responsible for many of the difficulties and whether an instrument of government which had failed deserved the veneration which a subsequent generation bestowed upon it.

Within the national government the problems of Reconstruction imposed a severe strain upon the system of checks and balances. The outstanding political novelty of the crisis was the solidarity of the Republican party. At no other period did an

---

[1] *World*, 5 April, 1872. 'In the revolution we have gone through, the Declaration of Independence has been substituted for The Constitution; in other words the political equality of man has been substituted for the equality of sovereign states.'

American party stand together with such consistency. The Fourteenth and Fifteenth Amendments both obtained the necessary two-thirds in both Houses of Congress. Of President Johnson's seven vetoes of major Reconstruction bills only the first failed — by one vote in the Senate — to win re-passage by the requisite two-thirds. In addition the Republicans won a resounding electoral victory in 1866 half-way through the Reconstruction controversy. It has sometimes been customary to dismiss this record with a sneering reference to 'strict party votes' though it is never explained how the party whip was applied or why party loyalty should be regarded as discreditable. In fact the Republicans could hardly fail to be conscious of the weight of opinion behind them, and it was not unexpected that they should have spoken of themselves as national representatives of the national will, and regarded a President who had been repudiated and a Supreme Court which represented no one and still contained members who had concurred in the notorious Dred Scott decision as their inferiors in the scales of popular government. Legislative supremacy looked more logical, more desirable and more just than executive encroachments or judicial usurpations. If this view was challenged, as Johnson challenged it, by stating that a Congress which excluded eleven States was no Congress, it could be claimed that a Congress which had had authority to fight the war must have equal authority to decide the conditions of peace. Indeed the President's argument seemed so absurd and so insulting that it added weight to the theory of legislative supremacy and helped to reduce the Presidency to a point at which its power to initiate disappeared and its power to check survived as mere obstruction. The Supreme Court having made a major raid upon the preserves of the legislature in *ex parte Milligan* was tied by restraints upon its appelate jurisdiction, threatened with major changes in its right to review congressional statutes, and saved its power only by a timely retreat. It is easy to see these conflicts in an unfavourable light, and most historians of Reconstruction have been ready to add unconstitutional behaviour to the long list of indictments against the Republicans;

but what was at stake was not the reputation of individuals but the ability of a government of separate powers to deal with a crisis. As on other occasions the American system of government helped to confuse policy, to foster harmful delays, and to prevent anyone from making an effective decision.

The political controversies over Reconstruction took place at a significant moment in American economic history. The war had distorted and in some cases retarded the development of the Northern economy and it had ruined the economy of the South but, as it ended, the United States were on the threshold of a great age of expansion. The first benefits of growth were enjoyed by the economy of the Northeast, the middle Atlantic and the Midwestern States; the less-developed regions of the South and West were certain to feel the impact of this vigorous society mesmerized by the benefits to be gained from entrepreneurial activity. In a sense political Reconstruction reflected the economic tension between developed and under-developed societies, but it would be an error to oversimplify the relationship between economic and political aims. The great political upheaval which lay behind congressional Reconstruction is not to be explained by the aims of comparatively small business groups. The Republican party was predominantly the party of the small entrepreneur — both in farming and in manufacturing — and of the small towns. Its heartland was the Midwestern rural region where everyone was interested in economic betterment and small towns were established with amazing rapidity as commercial, marketing and manufacturing centres. On specific economic issues there was, however, little agreement within the party. Leading Radicals professed currency heresies which were equally shocking to old Jacksonian hard money men and to banker adherents of the gold standard. The tariff tended to divide Eastern from Western Republicans, and among the Easterners there was often a sharp difference of opinion upon what should be protected. Many Republicans carried on the old anti-monopoly theme which was most unpleasing to railway promoters and operators, and some Radicals were beginning to interest themselves in labour causes such as the eight hour day. Disagreement upon these economic questions was muted because men felt that the political questions of Reconstruction were more urgent and more important. It was the crisis of Reconstruction which gave solidarity to the Republican party not the economic aspirations of business.

At a more profound level it is possible to seek a reconciliation between political and economic aims of the Northern and Midwestern society. If men differed about the incidence of economic policy, they agreed upon the great benefits to be expected from economic enterprise, and the South had a long record of obstruction to railway land grants, homestead laws, internal improvements and tariffs. The Northern and Midwestern society was not united in its opposition to the Southern economic policy, but almost every part of it had reason to regard the former policy of the South as having been, at some point, harmful and obstructive. The picture of the South as the enemy of economic progress completed the picture of the South as opposed to that government whose object was the betterment of mankind. Like their English contemporaries, the Gladstonian Liberals, the Republicans saw moral and material progress as two aspects of the same great movement, and the crisis of Reconstruction was a part of the world-wide crisis of the nineteenth-century liberal tradition.

To the majority of Northern people the problems of Reconstruction took their place in an historic process which had been unfolding since the origin of the American nation. The immediate past assumed a forbidding aspect as the shadow of the slave power was seen in retrospect with ever greater intensity. Thaddeus Stevens reminded congressmen of the days when 'the mighty Toombs, with his shaggy locks, headed a gang who, with shouts of defiance on this floor, rendered this a hell of legislation. . . . It was but six years ago when they were here, just before they went out to join the armies of Catiline, just before they left this hall. Those of you who were here then will remember the scene when every Southern member, encouraged by their allies, came forth in one yelling body, because a speech for freedom was being made here: when weapons were drawn, and Barksdale's bowie knife gleamed before our eyes'.[1] Elihu B. Washburn recalled in milder terms the time 'when the slaveholders, in the pride and insolence of their power, undertook to "crush out" in the Senate every aspiration for liberty and every noble and elevated sentiment for freedom; when treason upheld by a perfidious and treacherous Executive, stalked through the Senate Hall with brazen impudence, and when the galleries roared their applause of traitors'.[2] In this dark past the anti-slavery men had held aloft the lamp of reason and humanity; they had been 'the little band of courageous and patriotic men who resisted with unsurpassed ability and eloquence the repeal of the Missouri compromise';[3] they had been the despised prophets of the new age, and now with honour at last in their own country they were held up as shining examples to their fellow countrymen.

If the past had been fearful the old abolitionists felt that they were now riding the crest of the wave of history. 'For nearly ten years past', exclaimed Ben Wade, 'no man has won any considerable promotion unless he has won it at the hands of those who are called radicals. The radical men are the men of principle; they are men who feel what they contend for. They are not your slippery politicians who can jigger this way, or that, or construe a thing any way to suit the present occasion. They are the men who go deeply down for principle, and have fixed their eyes upon a great principle connected with the liberty of mankind or the welfare of the people, and are not to be detached by any of your higgling. The sternness of their purpose has regenerated as it were this whole continent, has revolutionized it, at any rate.'[4] Henry Wilson of Massachusetts took Radical history back to the original settlers who 'ran away from conservatism and became radicals in America', and then to the revolution, the Declaration of Independence, and the Constitution ('made by those same radicals who carried us through the fire and blood of the Revolution and founded a nation!'). The task was now to 'accept the living truths of the present, and ... incorporate into the fundamental law of

---

[1] C.G. 39.1.2544.   [2] From remarks upon the death of Senator Foot. C.G. 39.1.1923.
[3] Ibid.   [4] C.G. 38.2.165.

the land what is necessary to make the country what its founders intended it should be'.[1] What was never quite clear was the relationship between this epic struggle for principle and the democratic processes of American government. In 1869 Henry Wilson resisted the suggestion that the Fifteenth Amendment, enacting negro suffrage, should be submitted to the people in the form of a referendum and not for ratification to the State legislatures. He explained that 'The struggle of the last eight years to give freedom to four and a half millions of men who were held in slavery, to make then citizens of the United States, to clothe then with the right of suffrage, to give them the privilege of being voted for, to make them in all respects equal to the white citizens of the United States, has cost the party with which I act a quarter of a million votes. There is today not a square mile in the United States where the advocacy of the equal rights and privileges of those coloured men has not been in the past and is not now unpopular'.[2] This gave Radicalism a curiously uncertain attitude towards popular government; at one time they would be speaking of the will of the people as the supreme and sovereign authority, at another they spoke of the need to enshrine their policy in constitutional amendments beyond the reach of the people, and they could never for long remain unconscious of the threatened Democratic majority of the future.

The political interpretation of the past as a contest between the darkness of slavery and the light of anti-slavery was reinforced by an apocalyptic view of the war. A people trained in the language and imagery of the Bible turned naturally to think of the war as the vengeance of God and one did not have to seek far to discover the sins which had incurred His displeasure. 'Struggle and long agony were needful to this nation,' wrote one Northerner, 'Frivolous, worldly, imitating other nations; nourishing in the very bosom of the Republic the serpent of a barbarous despotism; in our heedlessness and hurry giving no ear to the cries of the oppressed; we needed the baptism of blood and the awful lessons of loss to bring us back to sanity and soberness.'[3] The war had

---

[1] C.G. 39.1.114.   [2] C.G. 40.3.672.   [3] J. T. Trowbridge, *South* (New York, 1866), 86.

been the wage of sin, but with the shedding of blood came the promise of remission. It was not military prowess or industrial might but repentance and retribution which had turned away the wrath of God, and men remarked that the turn of the tide for Northern arms had come with the Emancipation Proclamation and that the final collapse of the South followed immediately upon the passage of the Thirteenth Amendment.[1] This religious interpretation of the war was particularly obnoxious to Democrats who strove to confine the war to its first objective — the preservation of the Union — and looked forward to political alliance with a restored South. Writing upon Lincoln's second inaugural the *World* remarked that 'instead of regarding God as the author or abettor of this horrible war, it would seem more consistent with humility, at least, to ascribe it to the unhallowed sectional passions and the accursed personal ambitions which were the visible agencies in bringing it on'.[2] It was a politicians' war insisted one Democratic congressman 'and of politicians who were faithless to the obligations of the Constitution of their country',[3] and another did not 'believe that this war is an instrument of God for the purpose of working out His design with reference to the institution of slavery. I do not believe that God writes His decrees in the blood of brother shed by brother'.[4] Rational though these protests might be, the apocalyptic vision had caught firmly hold of many Northern minds and reinforced their determination not to restore the past.

The sense of moving with the great tide of history was a lively one. A Republican senator asked those who argued that the objects of the war had been achieved if they were 'utterly oblivious to the grand results of four years of war? Are we not in the midst of a civil and political revolution which has changed the funda-

---

[1] In January 1865, when speaking in support of the Thirteenth Amendment, Thaddeus Stevens said, 'Those who believe that a righteous Providence punishes nations for national sins believe that this terrible plague is brought upon us for our oppression of a harmless race of men inflicted without cause and without excuse for ages. I accept this belief. . . . We are about to ascertain the national will by another vote to amend the Constitution. If the gentlemen opposite will yield to the voice of God and humanity and vote for it, I verily believe the sword of the destroying angel will be stayed and this people reunited.' C.G. 38.2.124.

[2] *World*, 6 Mar. 1865.   [3] C.G. 38.2.167.   [4] C.G. 38.2.215.

mental principles of our government in some respects?'[1] 'Each hour has its duties', declared Sumner in 1867, 'and this hour has duties as few others in our history has ever presented. Is there anyone who can question it? Are we not in the midst of a crisis? It is sometimes said we are in the midst of a revolution. Call it if you will simply a crisis. It is a critical hour having its own peculiar responsibilities.'[2] As men looked to the future they could see the same demands for present action. 'History is not repeating itself,' declared William D. Kelley in a striking speech, 'we are unfolding a new page in national life. The past has gone forever. There is no abiding present; it flies while we name it; and as it flies it is our duty to provide for the thick coming future. . . . We are to shape the future. We cannot escape the duty; and "conciliation, compromise and concession" are not the methods we are to use.'[3] A few Radical Republicans saw the anti-slavery movement merging into a wider struggle for human rights. G. W. Julian of Indiana saw abolition as 'simply the introduction and prelude to the emancipation of all races from all forms of servitude. . . . The rights of men are sacred, whether trampled down by Southern slave-drivers, the monopolists of the soil, the grinding power of corporate wealth, the legalized robbery of a protective tariff, or the power of concentrated capital in alliance with labor-saving machinery'.[4] Wendell Phillips transferred his whole enormous and erratic energy to labour agitation, and Ben Butler ended his extraordinary career as the Greenback-Labor candidate for President in 1884. These welling springs of optimism, idealism, conscious achievement and determination to carry forward the revolution thus begun beat fiercely upon established institutions, modes of thought, and hopes for an easy peace.

At the heart of the Reconstruction crisis was a momentous question about the character of national existence. It was framed most often with reference to the vexed question of loyalty. What did it mean to be a loyal American? Was it enough to give formal allegiance to the Constitution, or did it mean acceptance of a once

---

[1] Senator Morrill. C.G. 39.1.570. [2] C.G. 39.2.525. [3] C.G. 38.2, 16 Jan. 1865.
[4] G. W. Julian, *Political Recollections* (Chicago, 1884), 322.

despised but now triumphant political doctrine? In February 1865 a respected Republican senator, Jacob Collamer of Vermont, asked when Congress ought to admit the Southern States back into full membership of the Union, and answered that 'It is not enough that they should stop their hostility and are repentant. They should present fruits meet for repentance. They should furnish us by their actions some evidence that the condition of loyalty and obedience is their true condition again'.[1] This typical Republican comment confused the loyalty of individuals with the loyalty of States, substituted a vague concept of a change of heart for precise and legal tests, and left unspecified the conditions of real loyalty. But if there was no such 'loyalty', how could the nation ever be reunited and safe from its enemies? If the Southerners of 1865 had been ready, like the Germans of 1945, to repudiate their leaders and their past, it might have been possible to solve the problem in political terms; as they were not, all that could be done was to ask for 'guarantees' of Southern good behaviour and to treat their formal professions of loyalty as insufficient.

A new concept of national existence demanded a new construction of the Union. Once it had been defended as an expedient; then it had gathered symbolical power; now it must have an ideological core. It must be dedicated to a belief in equal rights, and the faithless could not be considered as true Americans. It seemed self-evident that anything less would be a betrayal of those who had died, and this was not the mere rhetoric of politicians but the profound reaction of millions who had been touched by the agonies of war. The restoration of the Southern States was not enough without a reconstruction of Southern minds. On the one hand was an unshakable confidence in the justice and morality of the Northern cause, and on the other a deep-seated and popular conservatism sustained by traditional modes of life. Reconstruction was an ideological struggle, and the crisis must be understood in emotional terms and not merely as a record of personal rivalries, conflicting interests and political manoeuvre. This was the true crisis of Reconstruction.

---

[1] C.G. 38.2.591, 4 Feb. 1865.

· II ·

Policies and Possibilities

Three questions lay at the heart of the Reconstruction controversy: who was to control the South, who was to govern the nation, and what was the status of the negro? Like many simple questions they demanded intricate answers and it was an error of Northern opinion to expect easy ones. In May 1865 Sam Wilkinson, of the firm of Jay Cooke, gave a picture of Northern opinion distilled from the reports of some 4,000 loan agents. 'The feeling is now general', he wrote, 'that the war must be prosecuted until the Rebels lay down their arms and submit to the Government. To the poor deluded soldier in the ranks, pardon — if repentant. To the leaders and their accomplices in Treason, the justice that is due to *Traitors! !* No peace until it can be made a permanent peace — and the feeling is, that peace cannot be permanent with Slavery in the country.'[1] This statement was typical of much Northern opinion, and its various elements were to recur again and again with countless variations. Submission and a return to allegiance was the first requisite, and once the Southern armies had laid down their arms this was not difficult to obtain. Indeed the willingness of Southerners to take an oath of allegiance to the United States as the price of amnesty became a source of embarrassment to Northerners who concluded that the formal oath of loyalty was being taken by large numbers who remained at heart enemies of the United States. Allegiance as a legal concept was not enough, but how could it be defined in such a way that it would include those who were loyal at heart and exclude all others? This question was to plague and weaken every Northern plan of Reconstruction. A possible escape from the

[1] L.C. *Butler Papers*, 3 May 1865.

dilemma seemed to be indicated by Wilkinson's second point, for it might be possible to achieve a workable solution by distinguishing between the mass of the Southern people and their leaders. The North had evolved a convenient theory that the real will of the Southern people had always been in favour of the Union and against secession, but that they had fallen under the selfish domination of their aristocratic leaders. There might be ardent secessionists among the men in the ranks, and there might be true Unionists among the leaders, but they did not form the majorities in their respective classes; though some of the wicked might flourish and some of the innocent might suffer, discrimination by class might be the most equitable way of distinguishing the secessionist goats from the deluded sheep. This argument made it necessary to define a leader and here the difficulties began. Every plan of Reconstruction proposed by the two Presidents and by Congress included some scheme for discriminating against Confederate leaders, but the proposals ranged from a narrow schedule which would penalize only those who had held high executive or military rank and members of legislatures to the exclusion of all who had supported the Confederacy. The more far-reaching the proposal for penalization the more difficult it became to provide for law and order in the South, and the more restricted the discrimination the more likely was the South to fall into 'disloyal' hands.

The difficulties in devising a programme for penalizing the leaders of secession did not alter the invincible repugnance of Northerners to the idea that Confederate leaders should resume their places of authority in the nation. This was indeed one of the pivots upon which the crisis of Reconstruction turned, and it was one of the common strands which bound together the diverse elements of the Republican party.

The problem was complicated by the myth of Southern Unionism. The favourite belief that many, perhaps the majority, of those fighting for the Confederacy were 'deluded' and not true secessionists was supplemented by a persistent conviction that there were large numbers of faithful Unionists in the South, suppressed and persecuted during the war, but ready to step forward and assume the lead. Again it was a common feature in all plans of Reconstruction that power should be transferred to this hard core of real Unionists. Lincoln's ten-per-cent plan implemented this idea, and so, for that matter, did Andrew Johnson while war governor of Tennessee. This transference of power might be effected in Tennessee and Arkansas, where considerable districts had remained Unionist during the war, and might just work in Louisiana if the Unionists could capture the commercial interests of New Orleans; elsewhere in the South it was unlikely to succeed because the Unionists were scattered and drawn from the least educated portions of the population. And even if the Unionists could be placed in power by the authority of the national government they were unlikely to win from former Confederates that degree of respect and consent without which government would be impossible. Was it better to entrust civil government to a despised minority with the support of Federal troops, or to allow the suspect majority to resume or continue the functions of civil government, or to continue unqualified military rule until loyalty had grown deeper roots in the South? And if the South was held in tutelage was this more likely to lead to reconciliation through a change of heart or to permanent alienation? Again the simple expectation led into a bewildering maze of speculation.

The myth of Southern Unionism was but one aspect of Northern ignorance about Southern society. One way or another Northerners had accumulated a good deal of information about the South but much of it came through partisan channels. The pictures drawn by abolitionists, by wartime propaganda, and by genuine Southern loyalists, were unlikely to present the whole truth about the society or the men whom they condemned. A great many Northerners, including some of the politicians, had been in the South as soldiers, but the impressions gathered by armies of occupation are notoriously unreliable as sources of information about conquered peoples. Northern journalists and writers who went South after the war visited it as alien territory — to discover the facts which reinforced preconceived notions about the Southern character — and saw a demoralized and partially ruined society in which it was difficult to distinguish between the effects of war and the consequences of defects in the social system. For most of the time, therefore, Northerners were not only feeling in the dark but in a darkness which they had been taught to despise and attributed to slavery and 'aristocracy'. Northern congressmen had, however, their own sources of information and during the winter of 1865–6 their desks were being piled high with letters from the South which spoke of secessionism revived, of Unionists ostracized or even persecuted, of negroes denied their rights as free men, and of a bitterness which seemed incompatible with formal professions of allegiance to the United States.

*   *   *   *

Of all Republican propositions the easiest to state was the obligation to end slavery, and it was not difficult to demonstrate that this was not fulfilled with the formal act of abolition. If the negro was no longer a slave he had still to be made a citizen, and this carried Northern aims into the heart of Southern society. As Carl Schurz observed in his report on the South which President Johnson commissioned and rejected: 'The General Government of the republic has, by proclaiming the emancipation of the slaves, commenced a great revolution in the South, but has as yet not completed it. Only the negative part of it is accomplished. The slaves are emancipated in point of form, but free labor has not yet been put in the place of slavery in point of fact. And now, in the midst of this critical period of transition, the power which originated the revolution is expected to turn over its whole future development to another power which from the beginning was hostile to it and has never yet entered into its spirit, leaving the class in whose favor it was made completely without power to protect itself and to take an influential part in that development.'[1] In course of time President Johnson was to evolve a theory of Reconstruction by which the whole of congressional policy was

[1] F. Bancroft (ed.), *Speeches, Correspondence and Political Papers of Carl Schurz*, (New York, 1913), I, 355.

the outcome of a Radical conspiracy to force negro suffrage upon the South, and modern writers have added to this a corollary that the motive behind negro suffrage was the wish to fasten the economic domination of the North upon the South. In a sense the Johnson theory was true because abolitionists saw negro suffrage as a necessary element in Reconstruction, but on no point did they find it harder to convince the bulk of the Republican party. Even among the Radicals there was hesitation, and rank and file Republican politicians showed no eagerness to commit themselves. At the close of the war the Republicans could be divided into three main groups: those who carried on with varying degrees of sincerity and enthusiasm the abolitionist quest for racial equality, those who believed in the biological inferiority of the negro and were conscious of the dislike of the negro among their constituents especially in the Midwest, and those who believed in racial equality as an abstract proposition but thought that any attempt to give the negro all the rights of citizens was inexpedient and premature. Most members of the party were, however, able to subscribe to the general proposition that the rights of the negro must be protected against his former masters. Like other simple statements this concealed a multitude of snags and difficulties.

What were the rights which ought to be protected? The majority of Republicans, shirking the difficulties of full equality under the law, attempted to compromise by distinctions between the various kinds of right. There were, ran the theory most popular among moderate Republicans, three kinds of right — civil, political and social. The first ought to be secured to all citizens, the second lay within the discretionary power of State legislatures, and the third — being mainly affected by the private decisions of individuals — was beyond the reach of any law. Civil rights were confined to equal status in courts of law and equal protection outside; political rights included suffrage and the laws for such matters as public transport and public education; social rights were those which individuals could freely accord to or withhold from their fellow citizens when receiving them into their homes, giving them equal participation in business or equal status as labour, or welcoming them into private associations or private schools. Some Republicans could make and adhere to these distinctions to their own satisfaction; others were troubled from the start by the illogicality of declaring that a man was an equal citizen while allowing 'political' and social discrimination against him; Radicals such as Sumner and Thaddeus Stevens believed from the start that equal right was an indivisible concept though the latter was prepared to temporize in order to gain a point. Behind the theory of equal right, however subdivided, was a further and major difficulty, for the protection of negro rights was an implicit recognition of his inferiority in society. The Radical answer was that this inferiority was an artificial condition imposed by the slavery, and that once the negro was armed with the rights of a citizen he would raise himself to economic and educational equality; others were not so sure. It was an act of faith to believe in the unproven assumptions of racial equality, and circumstances alone could produce the admission that they were worth a trial. Opportunism brought more men to an acceptance of equal rights than faith in the principle, but it would be an error to discredit the cause because some men came to support it because they believed that it was necessary before they believed that it was right. Few great movements of reform would not be open to the same accusation.

The many variations upon the Republican attitude were in sharp contrast to the theory of State rights. The key doctrine was that the States were indestructible and retained under all circumstances rights which were guaranteed to them under the Constitution. These rights could be changed only by an amendment to the Constitution, and an extreme version of the State rights theory could maintain that even an amendment was unconstitutional if it subtracted from the essential reserved rights of States.[1] Paradoxically the upholders of State rights seized avidly upon the equally mystical doctrine that the Union was indissoluble. Secession was void and must be treated as a nullity; individuals had renounced their allegiance to the United States and had gone

[1] Cf. C.G. 38.2.222 and p. 266 below.

into rebellion, but the States could not do this as the war had been fought to prove, and it followed that once individuals had ceased their resistance to lawful authority the rights of States, which were a part of that authority, were resumed without alteration or diminution. The only Reconstruction which was necessary and lawful was for the people in the States to choose a new government and this government would then have exactly the same rights in the Union as loyal States and neither the President nor Congress could impose any conditions which were not already in the Constitution. This theory had a superficial logic for a people accustomed to believe that law was superior to events, but a close examination of its arguments will show an even deeper confusion than that which existed on the Republican side. It pretended that events which were legally void had never happened. It confused the State as a geographical entity, as a government, and as a community of people, and assumed that when the government and people had fought the United States there remained some quality inherent in the land of a State which was different from the will of its people. It failed to recognize that the initiative in remaking the States had to come from somewhere, and that in most of the Southern States there was no effective authority save the occupying armies of the national government. It imagined that a legalistic theory could compel a government with the power to act to acquiesce in chaos or in what its supporters believed to be wrong.

There was moreover one entering wedge which weakened the State rights position, and which appeared to have great force. Emancipation had automatically terminated the provision of the Constitution under which slaves counted as three-fifths of a man in making the count upon which congressional representation was based. If the law took its course without amendment the Southern States, when restored, would find themselves with a handsomely increased congressional apportionment. At the same time it was evident that, if left to themselves, no Southern States would give the vote to any negroes. It could be argued that the Northern States counted unnaturalized foreigners for the purpose

c

of apportionment, but there was a difference between counting those who would probably become qualified voters before the next census and counting those who were considered by their States to be permanently debarred from the suffrage. Calculations varied but it seemed that the South might expect between twelve and twenty additional seats in the House of Representatives, and therefore in the electoral colleges, because of abolition. This was a prospect which even sympathetic Northerners were disposed to regard with alarm.

In point of fact no plan of Reconstruction accepted the State rights theory as its starting-point. Lincoln ignored it and attempted to deal with things as they were. Johnson ignored it when he imposed his own conditions on the South, but invoked it to prevent the Republicans from imposing their conditions. Yet in a sense State rights did lie at the end of every Reconstruction road, for sooner or later the Southern States must be back in the Union with the same rights as all other States. Johnson believed that this must come soon; Radicals believed that it must be delayed until a revolution had been consummated in the South; but both accepted the eventual equality of all States in the Union. This gave a particular flavour to the great debate over Reconstruction because everyone knew that the Southerners must return to Congress (and perhaps with Northern Democrats to control the national government) and that even if they remained there as an isolated group they would have the power to resist amendments to the Constitution. If Republicans could see this danger only too clearly, the sad fragment of the once invincible Democratic party looked eagerly to the promised land; the future of both parties was at stake, and this gave an added bitterness and a frantic urgency to the debates over Reconstruction. The constitutional deduction for Republicans was that any programme which they enacted must be enshrined in amendments to the Constitution and not left at the mercy of future congressional majorities, and thus moderates were driven towards constitutional changes which might otherwise have alarmed them. Whatever policy was agreed would also have to be enacted before the Southerners returned, because future Congresses might be unwilling or unable to pass the necessary laws. The main casualty was any programme of staged development which might lead the negroes from their depressed condition towards full citizenship.

* * * *

This is the background for the various Reconstruction policies from Lincoln to the Reconstruction Acts. In his Proclamation of 8 December 1863 Lincoln offered a full pardon to all who had participated in the rebellion on condition that they would take an oath of allegiance to the United States and undertake to observe all presidential proclamations respecting slaves. This general amnesty was qualified by a long list of exceptions which excluded from its provisions all who had held positions of authority under the Confederacy or left offices under the United States to join the rebellion. When the loyal portion of the State, so defined, amounted to ten per cent of the votes cast in 1860, this minority could then set up a government which would be recognized by the President as the lawful government of the State. The President would not object to laws affecting the freedmen which 'shall recognize and declare their permanent freedom, provide for their education, and which may yet be consistent as a temporary arrangement with their present condition as a laboring, landless, and homeless class'.[1] Critics noticed in this the lack of any specific requirement that the freedmen should be given civil rights (though it was recognized that it was difficult to be more precise so long as emancipation depended solely upon a proclamation issued under the war power), and they were disturbed by the President's deliberate sanction to the continuance of pre-war State constitutions and legal codes which had included discriminatory treatment of free negroes. The most striking fact about this ten-per-cent plan was, however, its role in war strategy. In the midst of a war it was extremely useful to set up, in secessionist States, governments which could claim to be loyal; puppet

---

[1] Proclamation of Amnesty and Reconstruction, 8 Dec. 1863. Richardson (ed.), *Messages and Papers*, VI, 213 ff.

Unionist administrations could give a show of legality to Northern rule in occupied areas, might serve to attract waverers back
into the Union fold, and would encourage Unionists still under
Confederate rule. These arguments were, however, no longer
applicable once the South had surrendered. If the ten-per-cent
governments acted as magnets to attract the support of lapsed or
defeated Confederates their future might be assured, but they
were far more likely to be treated as governments dependent upon
Federal arms and composed of discreditable men who had
abandoned the cause in the hour of need. Thaddeus Stevens made
a cogent criticism of the ten-per-cent plan, as a means of Reconstruction, when he said that 'the idea that the loyal citizens,
though few, *are the State*, and in State municipalities may over-
rule and govern the disloyal millions, I have not been able to
comprehend. . . . When the doctrine that the *quality* and not the
number of voters is to decide the right to govern, then we no
longer have a Republic but the worst form of despotism. The
saints are the salt of the earth, but the "salt of the earth" do not
carry elections and make governments and presidents'.[1]

The Wade-Davis Bill of July 1864 is usually contrasted sharply
with Lincoln's plan, though Lincoln described himself as 'fully
satisfied with the system for restoration contained in the bill as one
very proper plan for the loyal people of any State choosing to
adopt it,' and was prepared 'to give the Executive aid and assistance
to any such people . . .'.[2] Lincoln vetoed the bill because he did
not wish to be committed to any one scheme of Reconstruction
and because it included a clause emancipating the slaves in the
Confederate States which he thought must be done by constitutional amendment. The Wade-Davis plan operated in three
stages. The first required an oath to support the Constitution of
the United States, and when a majority of white males in a State
had taken this oath the next stage of Reconstruction could begin.

[1] 22 Jan. 1864. C.G. 38.1.317.
[2] Proclamation of 8 Jul. 1864, Richardson (ed.), *Messages and Papers*, VI, 222. The
Wade-Davis Bill was sponsored by Ben Wade (cf. p. 82 above) and by Henry Winter
Davis. The text of the bill can be found in Richardson (ed.), *Messages and Papers*, VI,
223 ff.

In the second stage a convention was to be elected by loyal white male citizens who could take the 'iron clad' oath of 2 July 1862 which excluded all who had given any aid or support to the rebellion; this convention was to make a Constitution which would exclude from voting for the State legislature or governor all persons who had held 'any office, civil or military, except offices merely ministerial, and military offices below the grade of colonel, state or confederate, under the usurping power', to abolish slavery and to repudiate debt incurred under the Confederacy. This Constitution was then to be ratified by a majority of the legal voters as already defined. The third stage was the recognition by the United States (i.e. by President and Congress) of the State government as republican in form. It was specifically stated that the State should then be re-admitted to representation in Congress, but the right of Congress to accept or reject individual senators or representatives was tacitly assumed. The laws of the State, other than slave codes, in force before the rebellion would remain in force except that 'the laws for the trial and punishment of white persons shall extend to all persons' and the qualification for jurors should be same as that for voters. The bill then emancipated slaves in the rebel States and imposed penalties upon persons who restrained the liberty of freedmen with the intention of reducing them to involuntary servitude or labour. Looked at in reverse this procedure meant that in taking an oath of allegiance to the United States the majority of former Confederates would give assent to the remaking of the State by the Unionists, to the emancipation of the slaves, to civil rights for the freedmen, and to congressional control over the process of Reconstruction. Once the process of Reconstruction was complete all white males, with the exception of the disqualified classes, would be able to vote though nothing would prevent the convention from imposing restrictions beyond those which were mandatory in the bill.

It was expected that the process laid down in the Wade-Davis Bill would be a slow one, and in no Southern State would the white majority surrender constitution-making power to the Unionists so long as a hope of Confederate victory or of a negotiated peace remained. In the eyes of many Republicans this delay was a merit of the bill. 'These States', said Wade, 'must remain under military dominion, but I hope with all the equities that can be extended to a people thus unfortunate, until such time as they manifest to the people of the United States that they are able to govern themselves properly and subject to the laws of the General Government. . . . The only sensible plan is to leave these communities until in some way we can have at least reasonable evidence to show that a majority of them are loyal, and in a condition to maintain a free republican government of their own.'[1] 'Reasonable evidence' would be a willingness on the part of the majority to assent to the procedure laid down by the Wade-Davis Bill. The Bill would have prevented the institution of puppet ten-per-cent governments during the war, but it might not have worked too badly when defeat persuaded a majority of Southerners to agree to any conditions as the price of a return to normal political relations within the Union. It would also have satisfied the Northern demand for the exclusion from public life of the Confederate leaders and for a guarantee of negro civil rights. It did not introduce negro suffrage which was the ultimate abomination in Southern eyes. The least which can be said of the Wade-Davis Bill is that it would have been better than no plan at all which was what the United States had when Lincoln was assassinated and the war ended.

Lincoln was like a good poker player who had kept his hand concealed, and it will never be known whether it contained a straight flush or a single pair. His last public utterance gave little away, and he had confided in none of his cabinet ministers. The last public address was concerned largely with the question of Louisiana, which had established the most stable of the ten-per-cent governments. Lincoln did not give an unequivocal undertaking to support that government; 'as to sustaining it,' he said, 'my promise is out . . . but, as bad promises are better broken than kept, I shall treat this as a bad promise and break it, whenever I shall be convinced that keeping it is adverse to the public

[1] C.G. 38.2.560.

interest; but I have not yet been so convinced.' This might be taken as a veiled threat to the Louisiana government that it would have to conform to the wishes of the President in order to keep his support. He seemed then to admit that the Louisiana government was not all that might be desired, but argued that it was probably better to keep it in being as the twelve thousand voters who had supported its constitution would be better encouraged than repelled and demoralized. 'We encourage the hearts and nerve the arms of twelve thousand to adhere to their work, and argue for it, and proselyte for it, and fight for it, and feed it, and grow it, and ripen it to a complete success.' Whatever the present deficiencies of the Louisiana government it was the best which could be obtained, and might prove to be the nucleus around which the State could re-form as a loyal and acceptable member of the Union.[1] Lincoln's advice was therefore purely empirical, devoted largely to the affairs of one problem child which had advanced a small way along the road to Reconstruction, and offered no solution for those States in which even a ten-per-cent government still lay beyond the range of practical politics. It is untrue to say that Lincoln had a 'plan' of Reconstruction; he had certainly announced no method of dealing with the new situation created by the collapse of the South.

In this new situation two plans, poles apart, were to emerge. There was a Radical plan, associated particularly with Thaddeus Stevens, and a conservative plan which was put into operation by President Johnson. Stevens wanted to give the former Confederate States Territorial status without any statement of the conditions under which they would be readmitted to the Union.[2] This would have had some advantages. The status of a Territory was familiar

---

[1] *Writings of Abraham Lincoln*, Constitutional ed., VII, 362 ff.

[2] Thaddeus Stevens tried to steer clear of the complex argument over that status of the States. Cf. C.G. 39.1.697. 'It has several times been said in the course of debate that I hold that States that were engaged in the rebellion are dead. Now, I have never said anything of that kind. In my speech on this subject, I argued that, whether they are out of the Union, or dead, lying about in the Union, it amounts to practically the same thing. But I have never pretended that those States are dead; I insist that they have never been dead, that they have always lived as States. The only difference in my position from that of some other gentlemen who have spoken is that I affirm that during the war they were States under the Confederate government, and not under the Government of the Union.'

to law and opinion in the United States, it would give to the Territories local self-government with their own legislatures, but with governors and officials appointed by the President with the consent of the Senate, while reserving to Congress power to make general laws affecting them. It provided a procedure by which the Territories would submit their constitutions to Congress when applying for statehood. There is no doubt that Stevens intended the period of Territorial status to be employed to reconstruct Southern society; he intended to destroy the power of the Southern ruling class by imposing political disabilities, by confiscating their estates, and by distributing their land among the freedmen to provide the economic basis for a free negro peasantry. Stevens did not favour immediate negro suffrage because he believed that in their present condition the freedmen would fall under the influence of their former masters, but when they had been made economically secure he expected them to be given the vote and assume a Jeffersonian role as cultivators of the soil and bulwarks of political virtue. 'This is not a "white man's Government",' he said, 'this is a man's Government; the Government of all men alike.' He did not expect any but white men to be elected to office for 'long ages to come' because 'the prejudices engendered by slavery would not soon permit merit to be preferred to color. But suffrage would still be beneficial to the weaker races. In a country where political division will always exist, their power joined with just white men, would greatly modify, if it did not entirely prevent, the injustice of majorities'.[1] Reconstruction in the South would thus create a new political interest which would act as a safeguard for the Union and a pillar of support for the party of the Union. The plan proposed by Stevens had the advantage of letting everyone know where they stood; its disadvantage was that it had not the slightest chance of being enacted.

President Johnson succeeded at a moment which could hardly have been more awkward. As the news of the surrender of the remaining Southern forces came in he had to make decisions which

[1] C.G. 39.1.74.

would affect the whole future of the United States, and he had to do so with all the handicaps of inexperience in an atmosphere charged with emotion. The first decision was whether to call Congress into special session to consider the problems of the peace. It is known that Lincoln had not intended to anticipate the normal session of Congress in December 1865, but it was probably a mistake for Johnson not to do so. Lincoln had behind him a triumphant re-election, he was closely acquainted with leading men of all shades of opinion in the Union party, and he had spent the whole of his political life in the climate of opinion of the Northern and Midwestern States; he knew from experience and political instinct what was or was not possible and he knew how to defeat ardent friends without making enemies. Johnson was an accidental President; everyone knew that he could not have reached even the Vice-Presidency except on the Lincoln ticket. His personal prestige had suffered from his unfortunate lapse during the inauguration. He was a Southern Unionist and had very little idea of the way in which the Northern mind worked. He was not on familiar terms with leading men in the Republican party. It was therefore urgently necessary for him to establish the kind of relation with Congress which is necessary for a successful President; it was necessary for him to know Congress and for Congress to know him and if he intended to continue the wartime ascendancy of the Presidency the way to do so was by understanding the co-ordinate branch of government and not by appearing to slight it. Failing an early call to Congress Johnson should have made an effort to impress his views upon congressional leaders and to hear their views in return, for these were men who would ultimately come to sit in judgment upon his policy. Yet though several congressional leaders called upon Johnson most of them found the experience singularly unsatisfying and Johnson himself made no overtures towards the men who, whatever their merits or demerits, were the chief movers among the representatives of the people.[1]

[1] At one time there was a chance that the Radicals might get a representative into the Cabinet, and Ben Butler believed that he was the man. Before Lincoln's death he told Wade that he was willing and thought that the Radicals might succeed if they backed him. (L.C.

At his succession to the Presidency the career of Andrew Johnson formed one of the great success stories of American history. From humble origins in a small country town and handicapped by early illiteracy he had made his way to the supreme position in the United States. His great assets had been honesty, fixity of purpose, and a command of the kind of oratory which was so popular with rural American audiences. Lacking subtlety he met attacks by attacking vigorously himself. He had become the spokesman of the small farmers of Tennessee in their running fight with the large planters who dominated the Mississippi valley in the State, and epitomized the aspirations of Jacksonian democracy in the West. At the outbreak of the Civil War he had earned fame as the only Southern senator to oppose secession (though he was as bitter against abolitionists as against secessionists), and in the war years he became the most distinguished representative of the elusive Southern Unionists and thus a key figure in the nation. This won him the vice-presidential nomination in 1864 at a time when it was particularly important to prevent the slave States in the Union from going sour on the war effort. Before that he had been a severe and successful governor of occupied Tennessee, introducing emancipation, and standing no nonsense from former Confederates. In spite of his Democratic antecedents his war record led him well into the fold of the Union party and it seemed that there was little to distinguish him from many Republicans. Indeed the Radicals rather than the moderates took comfort from the fierceness of his denunciations of Southern traitors. As President he was to prove

Butler Papers, Butler to Wade, 1 Mar. 1865.) Soon after Lincoln's assassination Butler was told that all but five or six of the Massachusetts State senators had signed a petition in his favour, and Wade took this to the President (ibid., Wade to Butler, 9 May 1865). In July a further petition was stimulated from New Hampshire urging Butler's appointment, and again Wade took it to the President. On this occasion he 'did not hesitate to say to him that . . . I believed it to be his bounden duty to call around him the ablest men in the nation and those in whom the public had most confidence'. The President seemed responsive, but Wade was no longer hopeful and explained that 'were it not for the experience we have both had in regard to the impressions made upon his mind (which the event has shown up to have been entirely mistaken) I should have but little doubt that you would soon be called into the public service' (ibid., Wade to Butler, 19 Jul. 1865). Butler was perhaps the most eligible of the Radicals; he had been chairman of the Breckinridge Democratic Convention in 1860, was then a Union Democrat, and had carried a substantial element of the Massachusetts Democracy with him into Radical Republicanism.

a good administrator (much better than the somewhat casual Lincoln) and he had a natural dignity which made him a much more impressive figure than such predecessors as Pierce and Buchanan. He earned the respect and loyalty of the majority of those who worked closely with him in the administration, and there can be little doubt that in happier times he would have made a successful President.

Yet with all his qualities Johnson had limitations which were to be disastrous for his own policies. General Richard Taylor, son of the former President, who saw a good deal of him during the period of controversy, found 'that he always postponed action, and was of an obstinate, suspicious temper. Like a badger, one had to dig him out of his hole; and he was ever in one except when on the hustings addressing a crowd. . . . He had acquired much knowledge of the principles of government, and made himself a fluent speaker, but could not rise above the level of the class in which he was born and to which he always appealed. He well understood the few subjects laboriously studied, and affected to despise other knowledge, while suspicious that those possessing such would take advantage of him. . . . Compelled to fight his way up from obscurity, he had contracted a dislike of those more favoured of fortune, whom he was in the habit of calling "the slave aristocracy", and became incapable of giving his confidence to any one, even to those on whose assistance he relied in a contest . . . with Congress'.[1] These comments may be discounted as those of a Southern gentleman and old Whig but the points made are corroborated too frequently to be dismissed: initial indecision, followed by a decision which was then adhered to with great obstinacy, a kind of defensive arrogance towards those who were better endowed by birth or nature, a fear of betraying his thoughts, and a confirmed reluctance to take counsel with those who might give him unwelcome advice, were all characteristics which unfitted him for the delicate tasks which the President was called upon to perform. Men who went to see him

---

[1] Richard Taylor, *Destruction and Reconstruction*, (Edinburgh and London, 1879), 326–7.

on business often found him apparently receptive and went away with the impression that they had made their points; when they discovered, from his later actions, that they might never have spoken, they were apt to conclude that they had been intentionally deceived.

Johnson hoped to surprise the country, and to win over public opinion, by the striking success of his Southern policy. Unable to admit that he had ever been wrong, he treated all criticism as betrayal or as the work of a malignant and frustrated minority. His perseverance in a policy which was obviously running into difficulties has often been described as 'courageous'; but his was not a courage illuminated by understanding, and never for one moment would he consider an escape from the lonely rock upon which his own logic had stranded him. This loneliness is perhaps the most evident symptom of Johnson's personal tragedy. With an invalid wife and a drunken son, working enormously long hours at his desk, and seeing the world as a succession of faces which appeared before him for brief interviews, he created the self-portrait of a man of the people who could interpret their wishes without listening to what they were saying. This withdrawal from the real world of politics became disastrous when the people whose wishes would decide policy were those of the Northern and Midwestern States whose opinions Johnson never had understood and never would.

*   *   *   *

During the five weeks after he became President Johnson reached the decision from which he never afterwards withdrew, and on 29 May 1865 he issued a Proclamation of Amnesty and a Proclamation on North Carolina which was to be the model for others issued to all those Southern States which had not already set up governments under the Lincoln plan. The amnesty promised a pardon to all those who would take an oath of allegiance to the United States and of obedience to the proclamations affecting the emancipation of slaves. A very long list of exceptions to the general amnesty included all those already made by Lincoln and added men with taxable property of over $20,000 who had taken part in the rebellion; but these drastic exclusions from pardon (and thus from public life and a valid title to property) were qualified by a promise that special application could be made for pardon by all members of the excepted classes and 'such clemency will be liberally extended as may be consistent with the facts of the case and with the peace and dignity of the United States'.[1] The Proclamation on North Carolina laid the constitutional foundations for the President's action by stating his duty to take care that the laws be faithfully executed and inferring that it therefore became necessary and proper for him to carry out and enforce the obligation of the United States to secure to the States a republican government. The claim to act without the participation of Congress was sound in logic but weak in application: the President might be bound to enforce the law but he was operating in a new situation in which the supreme legislature of the United States had been given no opportunity to say what the law should be. The proclamation went on to appoint a provisional governor 'whose duty it shall be, at the earliest practicable period, to prescribe such rules and regulations as may be necessary and proper for convening a convention composed of delegates to be chosen by that portion of the people ... who are loyal to the United States, and no others'. Loyalty was defined as willingness to take the oath prescribed in the amnesty proclamation. This convention was to draw up a new Constitution and either it or the new legislature 'will prescribe the qualification of electors and the eligibility of persons to hold office under the constitution and laws of the State — a power the several States composing the Federal Union have rightfully exercised from the origin of the Government to the present time'.[2]

The Reconstruction proclamations came like a tonic to the demoralized South. The mass of the people were unconditionally pardoned, and their leaders were led to expect a favourable consideration if they made personal application for presidential pardons. All except the unpardoned could take part in Recon-

---

[1] Richardson (ed.), *Messages and Papers*, VI, 310.   [2] Ibid., 312.

struction if they took a simple oath to the United States, which was no more than a recognition of the situation following Southern defeat. The vital power of fixing the qualifications for office and suffrage was specifically given to the States, and the claim of Congress to exclude leaders of the rebellion from State office or to alter the suffrage was denied. The whole process was unencumbered with conditions, and though Johnson was later to insist upon ratification of the Thirteenth Amendment abolishing slavery and repudiation of the Confederate debt, and to suggest limited negro suffrage, he did so only when Southern hopes of 'home rule' had so far revived that they felt able to reject advice or to accept it on conditions. The hope which dawned for the majority of Southerners with Johnson's proclamations was a mortal blow to Southern Unionists. They had enjoyed a brief spell of influence so long as it seemed that they might be given a special role to play in remaking the Southern States and their subsequent plight is epitomized in the frantic plea to Ben Butler of a humble loyalist, who claimed to have broken through the lines at Richmond to bring intelligence to the Northern armies: 'I am out of employment and get nothing to do. The rebels won't employ me because I went to the Yankees, and I went to Gen. Terry but he had nothing to give me to do; all the positions he had to fill were filled, and most of them by rebels — young men who served in the rebel army. My most noble Patron, I tell you such treatment is almost enough to make a man curse his Government.'[1] At the end of the year, when Johnson had issued pardons in profusion, another reported a conspiracy amongst ex-Confederate soldiers in Louisiana to renew the struggle for secession or at least to prescribe Union men. 'All this is nonsense you may say in the North, but it is death or ruin to the Union men of the South. And

---

[1] L.C. *Butler Papers*, D.D. Bulmer to Butler, 14 Nov. 1865. There were complaints of this nature as early as May 1865, cf. General J. W. Turner to Butler, *Private and Official Correspondence of Benjamin F. Butler*. V, 616, 7 May 1865. 'It is not satisfactory to us to see a dozen or more Major Generals of the rebel service headed by General Lee, drawing their rations daily of the Government, and then ostentatiously displaying their uniforms on the streets and in public places. The way matters look now, we don't quite understand what we have been fighting for. A rebel uniform today in Richmond carries a man where a Federal uniform will not. It takes him into all our own public offices and further into society.'

what is the real cause of all this new Southern movement? In our opinion, it is the too early granted pardons to them. No one is punished as the law directs. The sovereignty of the law is not enforced — no it is made a perfect nullity. The rebels are courted and flattered instead of reproved.'[1]

Southern exuberance was the natural consequence of restored hope and unexpected freedom of action, but they used their opportunities with a singular lack of wisdom. They should have realized that the final word on their readmission would lie with Congress, and wisdom would have counselled a cautious respect for Northern opinion. One difficulty was that their only channel of communication with the North was through the President. Few Northern newspapers circulated in the South except the New York *World* which was emphatically pro-Southern, and it was said that even Federal officials found it impossible to obtain newspapers such as *Tribune* and other influential Northern papers.[2] Southerners believed that the President was on their side, and they may have seen him as a new Andrew Jackson come to judgment, who would overawe Congress and force through his policy. They overlooked the fact that while Jackson had stood upon the strong ground of popular support in the North and West Johnson represented nobody. Johnson himself was singularly hesitant in the advice which he offered and did not exploit to the full the enormous influence which he could have exerted upon Southern actions.[3] Even his famous telegram to Governor Sharkey advising the extension of suffrage to negroes on some literacy or property test was offered as a tentative suggestion on grounds of expediency because it 'would completely disarm the adversary'. His pardons seemed often to follow rather than to anticipate Southern movements and were given not infrequently to those who had already been chosen for office; nor does he seem

[1] L.C. *E. B. Washburn Papers*, anon. to E. B. W., 1 Dec. 1865.
[2] L.C. *E. B. Washburn Papers*, D. Richards to Washburn, 21 May 1866 (from Florida). 'I have subscribed for the N. Y. Tribune, Washington Chronicle, and N. Y. World, but they have all stopped coming. They would undoubtedly let the World come through if they could know what paper it is without tearing off the wrapper.'
[3] E. L. McKitrick, *Andrew Johnson and Reconstruction* (Chicago, 1960), Ch. 7, section IV passim.

to have used the pardon as an instrument by which men of influence could be bound to the national government.[1]

Under these circumstances, the people of the South followed their natural preferences and chose for State offices the respected leaders of the Confederacy. More discretion might have been expected in the choice of senators and representatives for Congress, but the delegations which presented themselves at Washington in December — and included several Confederate congressmen and members of State legislatures under the Confederacy, four generals and five colonels of the Confederate army, and Alexander H. Stephens sometime Vice-President of the Confederate States — seemed to epitomize in Northern eyes the unchastened spirit of rebellion. More grievous and provocative was the passage by the new Southern legislatures of 'black codes' for the emancipated negroes. That some form of regulation was necessary could hardly be denied though the States might have been justified in leaving responsibility for the time being to the Federal Freedmen's Bureau. The Southern States did give formal recognition to the legal rights acquired with freedom, allowing negroes the right to hold property, to sue and be sued, to make contracts and to marry, but in some States the conferment of these rights was accompanied by apprenticeship and vagrancy laws which made it clear that the negroes were to be treated as a subordinate caste assigned to labour. The code of Mississippi laid down that labour contracts should be in writing and that 'every civil officer shall, and every person may, arrest and carry back to his or her legal employer any freedman, free negro or mulatto who shall have quit the service of his or her employer before the expiration of his or her term of service without good cause'. Louisiana laid down conditions of labour and added, 'Bad work shall not be allowed. Failing to obey reasonable orders, neglect of duty, and leaving home without permission will be deemed disobedience; impudence, swearing, or indecent language to or in the presence of the employer, his family or agent, or quarreling and fighting with one another will be deemed disobedience. . . .

[1] Ibid., 149 ff.

All difficulties arising between the employers and laborers . . . shall be settled by the former; if not satisfactory to the laborers, an appeal may be had to the nearest Justice of the Peace and two freeholders, citizens, one of the said citizens to be selected by the employer and the other by the laborer.' Mississippi had an elaborate apprenticeship law under which negroes under the age of eighteen who were orphans or whose parents had not the means or will to support them were apprenticed to employers; the law laid down conditions for humane treatment and for teaching those under fifteen to read and write, but any apprentice could be ordered to return to his or her master by any justice of the peace and severe penalties were provided for not doing so. Negroes over the age of eighteen without lawful employment or business, and all white persons 'usually associating' with them, were deemed vagrants and subject to heavy fines. It was an old Southern belief that the negro would not work without compulsion and it was reasonable to maintain that coercion was necessary to revive the Southern economy, but a system under which negroes were forced to make labour contracts under the penalties of the vagrancy laws, then held strictly to the conditions of service — with grievances determined by employers in the first instance and then by white officials whose interests were likely to be those of the employing class — was not free labour as understood in the North.[1] If the codes did not re-enact slavery they might well make the condition of the negro worse in some respects than it had been under slavery, for the machinery of the State was now brought in to enforce obligations which had hitherto been the responsibility of the master. 'This arbitrary and inhuman act', said the Radical Henry Wilson of the code of Mississippi, 'makes the freedmen the slaves of society, and it is far better to be the slave of one man than to be the slave of arbitrary law.'[2] Exaggeration was to be expected from Radical critics, but no one aware of the sensitivity of Northern opinion to the negro question could have expected approval. What was perhaps more shocking than anything else was the

[1] The Black Codes of Mississippi and Louisiana are given in H. S. Commager (ed.), *Documents of American History*, II.
[2] C.G. 39.1.39.

D

assumption that the negro was condemned by nature to a dependent status; as the compiler of a collection of South Carolina laws remarked, 'These two great classes, then, are distinctly marked by the impress of nature. They are races separate and distinct: the one the highest and noblest type of humanity, the other the lowest and most degraded.' He believed that to mingle the social and political existence of the classes more closely 'would surely be one of the highest exhibitions of treason to the race'.[1]

President Johnson himself was probably unhappy about the trend of events in the South, and Gideon Welles, who of all the Cabinet was nearest to him in temperament and opinion, wrote in his diary on 1 August 1865, 'The tone of sentiment and action of people of the South is injudicious and indiscreet in many respects. I know not if there is any remedy, but if not, other and more serious disasters await them, and us also perhaps, for if we are one people, dissension and wrong affect the whole.'[2] Johnson, however, regarded the indiscretions of Southerners as irritating but irrelevant to the main issue of Reconstruction. Fundamentally he agreed with them about the place of the negro in society, though sufficiently humane not to close the door of opportunity to those who could deserve it. The strong expressions of gratitude which he was receiving from the South convinced him that he was on the right lines in overcoming as rapidly as possible the feelings of resentment and hatred in the South. Nor was he without support in the North from quarters in which a man of his antecedents was least likely to expect it. Merchants in the Eastern cities tended to favour a policy which would lead to an early resumption of normal commercial relations, and on 20 October Adam Badeau wrote to E. B. Washburn, 'Everywhere I hear warm commendation of Mr Johnson's policy; in New York as well as at Washington — just as at Galena, all the sober substantial men seemed to support him. The attempt of foolish impractical men to foist their notions upon the country has met

---

[1] Quoted by Louis M. Hacker, *The Shaping of the American Tradition* (New York 1947), 628 ff. from H. Melville Myers, *Stay laws and . . . Freedmen's Code* (Charleston 1866).

[2] H. K. Beale (ed.), *Diary of Gideon Welles* (New York, 1960), III, 347.

with no success, so far as I can judge.'[1] The comment was not without significance for Adam Badeau was secretary to General Grant who was susceptible to the opinions of sober substantial men. By the middle of December Johnson had on his desk a concise report from the General himself on conditions in the South in which he said that 'the citizens of the Southern States are anxious to return to self-government, within the Union, as soon as possible; that whilst reconstructing they want and require protection from the government; that they are in earnest in wishing to do what they think is required by the government, not humiliating them as citizens, and that if such a course were pointed out they would pursue it in good faith'.[2] Warmed by the gratitude of Southerners, supported by his Cabinet, Johnson believed that his policy of restoration was a success, that its opponents were troublemakers and hollow men, and that Congress would respond to the arguments of the first annual message which he had commissioned George Bancroft to cast in literary form. Beyond Congress were the people of the Northern and Western States, a shadowy entity conceived perhaps as a vastly enlarged audience of Tennessee farmers who had always been so responsive to his oratory.

There were, however, indications of dissent which Johnson might have taken more seriously. There was for instance the report of Carl Schurz which reached him before the meeting of Congress. Schurz was the most distinguished of German Americans; a refugee from Germany inspired by the liberalism of the mid-century he had seen in the Republican party an American version of the universal movement for freedom; he had had much to do with winning Midwestern Germans from their Democratic affiliations, and had gone on to a distinguished career in the army reaching the rank of Major-General. He had made no secret of his Radical leanings, and he was therefore surprised to receive in July a request from the President accompanied 'with many flattering assurances of his confidence in my character and judgment' to

---

[1] L.C. *E. B. Washburn Papers*, 20 Oct. 1865.
[2] *Senate Executive Documents*, 39th Congress, 1st Session, No. 2, 107 ff.

undertake a tour in the South and to report upon conditions. By his own account he told the President that 'so far as I was then informed, I considered the reconstruction policy ill-advised and fraught with great danger, but that if my observations should show this view to be erroneous, no pride of opinion would prevent me from saying so'. The President repeated his expressions of confidence and sent him on his way.[1] Schurz was not a rich man and he was receiving only nominal pay for his mission; with something less than complete discretion he allowed some Northern friends to pay the premium on a life insurance and during his tour contributed anonymous articles to Northern newspapers on conditions in the South. The real cause of his offence to Johnson was, however, a well-meant effort to interfere in a dispute between Governor Sharkey of Mississippi and General Slocum, commanding the Federal troops, in which the latter attempted to stop the arming of the State militia. Johnson sustained Sharkey and rebuked both Slocum and Schurz. It was probably this incident (in which most fair-minded men would admit that the President was wrong) which convinced Johnson that Schurz was intriguing against him.[2] Whatever the explanation Schurz received on his return the coldest possible reception from the President, who informed him that there was no need for him to submit a report.[3] Schurz nevertheless wrote one, though it is doubtful whether Johnson read it and because of its Radical authorship it has been largely ignored by historians. This neglect has been unfortunate for the report was the work of a humane and unusually intelligent man who had immersed himself for six months in the problems of the South.

Schurz was able to appreciate the tragedy of the South and left it 'troubled by great anxiety'. 'No fair-minded man could have had my experiences in the Southern country without conceiving and cherishing a profound and warm sympathetic feeling for the Southern people, white as well as black.' He respected the gallantry of the South though lamenting that it had been 'wasted

---

[1] *The Reminiscences of Carl Schurz* (New York, 1908), III, 157 ff.
[2] McKitrick, op. cit., 163–4, 193–4. *Reminiscences of Carl Schurz*, III, 189 ff.
[3] *Reminiscences of Carl Schurz*, III, 201–2.

upon a hopeless cause — the cause of slavery — which, while held sacred by the white people of the South, was abhorred by the moral sense and enlightened opinion of the century'.[1] He wasted no words in pointless accusations of treason, but emphasized the magnitude of the Southern crisis: 'Now the South found precipitated upon it a problem of tremendous moment and perplexing difficulty — the problem of abruptly transforming a social organism based upon slave labor into a free labor society.' Southerners, true to their traditions, tried to avoid the implications of abolition, and attempted to combine a professed willingness to accept the results of the war with a true purpose which was 'to use the power of the State Governments, legislative and executive, to reduce the freedom of the negroes to a minimum and to revive so much of the old slave code as was thought necessary to make the blacks work for the whites'. These were the facts of the case as he saw them, and the true remedy was not to indulge in frantic denunciations of the Southerners but to take action if a different result was desired. On the vital question of Southern loyalty his report was illuminating and his separation of Southern leaders into various groups demonstrated how easy it was to draw different conclusions according to one's Southern company: first there were men, mostly of mature age and experience — planters, merchants and professional men — who 'have a clear perception of the irreversible changes produced by the war, and honestly endeavour to accommodate themselves to the new order of things' (these were the men with whom Grant talked on his brief visit, and in this class one might also include some of the Confederate military leaders); then there were those who wanted at all costs to restore their States to influence in the Union and would make any concession which did not threaten their own control at home — these were mainly the professional politicians and all were strong supporters of Johnson and bitter opponents of the Freedmen's Bureau; the third group was composed of the irreconcilables, mainly young men who continued to talk of eventual Southern independence and were actively suppressing

[1] Ibid., 199.

negroes and Unionists, but of whom many had taken the oath of
allegiance and worked temporarily with the politicians; finally
there was the mass of the people 'whose intellects are weak, but
whose prejudices and impulses are strong'.[1] Reviewing the whole
problem he believed that there were great dangers in 'home rule'
without national protection for negroes and Unionists, nor did he
believe that danger threatened the blacks alone for there was no
knowing what savage impulses might not be released if the promise
of negro freedom remained unfulfilled.

*   *   *   *

Throughout the summer and autumn the storm clouds
gathered on the Radical front. A few days after the North
Carolina Proclamation Sumner was writing to Ben Wade asking
whether he could give him 'any comfort with regard to the policy
of the President. *He has missed a golden opportunity*, and is entail-
ing upon the country trouble, controversy and expense. *He cannot
prevent the triumph of the cause*. This is certain. But he may delay
it'.[2] In July Ben Butler was telling one correspondent that he still
had faith in the President's 'integrity and desire to do right' and
that he expected him to change his policy when he saw it to be
wrong,[3] but was writing to Wade that 'all is wrong. We are losing
the just results of this four years struggle'.[4] Wade told the
President frankly that 'the policy he was pursuing with regard to
reconstruction was filling many of our best friends with alarm'
and that he ought to add some Radical representation to his
Cabinet, but thought that his advice would be ignored.[5] He then
wrote to Sumner that 'all appears gloomy. The President is
pursuing, and I believe is resolved to pursue a course in regard to
reconstruction that can result in nothing but consigning the great
Union, or Republican party, bound hand and foot, to the tender
mercies of the rebels we have so lately conquered in the field and
their copperhead allies in the north. . . . We have in truth already

---

[1] Bancroft (ed.), *Speeches, Correspondence and Political Papers of Carl Schurz*, I, 285.
[2] L.C. *Wade Papers*, 12 Jun. 1865
[3] L.C. *Butler Papers*, draft reply to J. Ogden Smith, 1 Jul. 1865.
[4] L.C. *Wade Papers*, 26 Jul. 1865.   [5] L.C. *Butler Papers*, Wade to Butler, 19 Jul. 1865.

lost the whole moral effect of our victories over the rebellion and the golden opportunity for humiliating and destroying the influence of the Southern aristocracy has gone forever'.[1] In October the influential though erratic Wendell Phillips was saying the same thing to Butler: 'It seems to me that the Administration is handing us over, bound hand and foot, into the power of the rebels.'[2] He added that 'the Administration needs to be defied or overawed by such an exhibition of popular sentiment as you and Sumner and one or two others could easily start. To be effectual this should be attempted before Congress meets'.

To men who believed that Reconstruction must be drastic to be just the future seemed bleak, for the majority of the Republican party might be swayed to an easy acceptance of Johnson's restoration.

Ben Butler wrote to Henry Wilson, with a copy to Thaddeus Stevens, suggesting a preamble to a Reconstruction Act which would declare the negroes entitled to the rights of citizens, and that Congress, acting upon the second section of the Thirteenth Amendment, should declare void all discriminatory State legislation, and adding that 'the whole preamble seems to be necessary in order to hold the weak kneed brethren of the Republican party, who are troubled upon the question whether the States are in or out of the Union will be carried by the claim that they ought to vote to admit some States so as to have ratified the Constitutional Amendment by the requisite majority'. He hoped to force the wavering majority to commit themselves 'to give life and effect to the Constitutional Amendment and in favor of liberty and equal rights not raising however any question of the rights of suffrage'.[3] But it is difficult to demonstrate a Radical plot in the rising tide of disquiet in the Northern Press, and the most disturbing influence was emanating not from Radical quarters but from the South itself with its choice of Confederate leaders, its black codes, its reviving arrogance, its open contempt for the moralistic ideas of the North, and its clear determination to rescue

[1] L.C. *Wade Papers*, Wade to Sumner (draft), 29 Jul. 1865.
[2] L.C. *Butler Papers*, Phillips to Butler, 24 Oct. 1865.
[3] L.C. *Butler Papers*, 20 Nov. 1865.

as much as possible from the past. Most alarming of all was Johnson's apparent tolerance of these things, and his failure to indicate that the South was not going to have everything its own way.

* * * *

At the end of November the mild-mannered Schuyler Colfax, speaker designate of the new Congress, came to town and made a little speech which attracted considerable notice. He praised the President warmly, but warned against haste. He did not think that Congress ought to be in a hurry about the admission of Southerners. He was not satisfied with Southern behaviour because the States had quibbled about ratifying the abolition amendment, about repudiating their debts and about nullifying secession, because of their hostility to Unionists and because they had not made proper laws for the freedmen. The government had given the slave his freedom and meant to maintain it. He did not, however, believe that these doubts meant a rupture with the President and thought that 'the executive and legislative departments of government, when they compare views together, will cordially co-operate in this great work before us all, and so act that the foundations of our Union, wisely and patriotically reconstructed, shall be eternal as the ages, with a hearty acceptance by the South of the new situation'.[1] This speech — with its temperate statement of Northern doubts, its expressed willingness to work with the President and its belief in harmony with justice — was widely welcomed in the North. The speech did, however, indicate that Congressional leaders intended to take the initiative and this was sheer Radicalism to a man who believed that 'restoration' was complete. Johnson did not expect to alter or enlarge his policy to comprehend Northern anxieties which were, he was convinced, the work of a few troublemakers. He was, however, about to meet Northern opinion in the form of a Congress chosen at the same election as that which had raised him

[1] McKitrick, op. cit., 185–6. Willard H. Smith, *Schuyler Colfax* (Indianapolis, 1952), 222.

to the Vice-Presidency, and the meeting was to prove a shock for both.

Some Radicals wished to scrap the whole presidential plan, but a majority in the party were ready and willing to allow the President credit for his work in restoring the normal machinery of government and to believe that he would readily accept the additional 'guarantees' proposed by Congress. These guarantees were aimed to protect the Union against its enemies and the negro against those who would deprive him of civil rights. According to temperament or interest men stressed one danger or one remedy more than another. Roscoe Conkling said later that the one binding tie amongst all Republicans was a conviction 'that the destinies of the nation should never be yielded up to men whose hands and faces are dripping with the blood of murder'[1] and Schuyler Colfax had written privately to a friend, 'I remember very well that last day I was in Congress, they were fighting us and killing our soldiers, and had their members in the Rebel Congress. It would be rather pleasant for them to take their seats the first day of the next session; but I am a little too old fogyish for that. I want to be very certain that a majority of their voters are — not merely whipped back into the Union, as they say — but heartily devoted to the Union and ready to fight with us against all its enemies at home and abroad, now and in the future.'[2] Other Republicans saw negro rights as the dominant and binding issue. 'The Union party are agreed', said Senator Stewart (who wanted a general amnesty), 'that all men are entitled to life, liberty and the pursuit of happiness, and they will endorse any reasonable means to secure these inalienable rights to every American citizen. . . . The President's plan of restoration was unsatisfactory because it ignored the rights and excluded from constitutional liberty four million loyal citizens guilty of no offence but fidelity to the Government . . . because it placed the State government of the South in the hands of the very men who plunged the country into war for secession, and the extension of slavery, and because it admitted into Congress an increased representation of the disloyal

[1] C.G. 39.1.4272.   [2] Smith, *Schuyler Colfax*, 221.

elements of the rebellion.'[1] Nearly all Republicans felt the force of one or other of these criticisms, and even Henry J. Raymond, who clung to the President long after other Republicans had abandoned him, and who wished to accept the restoration of the Southern States as suggested by him, wished also to 'provide by law for giving to the freedmen of the South all rights of citizens in courts of law and elsewhere', to exclude from Federal office 'the leading actors in the conspiracy which led to the rebellion', to make such amendments to the Constitution as might seem appropriate, and to use troops to prevent the overthrow of Southern governments which were Republican in form.[2]

Public opinion in the North had been bewildered by the course of events, and there was no clear determination as the year 1865 drew to its close upon the policy which should be followed. But in a negative sense there was a growing consensus of opinion that not enough had been done. Anyone could have predicted that Radical attacks would be made, but the new factor in the situation was the response which they aroused. Many moderate Republicans were sincerely anxious for a generous peace and were likely to be extremely cautious of any commitments on the racial problem, but even they felt that further guarantees were necessary. Thaddeus Stevens declared that the Southern States ought 'never to be recognised as capable of acting in the Union, or being counted as valid States, until the Constitution shall have been so amended as to make it what its framers intended; and so as to secure perpetual ascendancy to the party of the Union; and so as to render our republican government firm and stable for ever'.[3] Though expressed by the sternest of Radicals this assertion united rather than divided the party. Equal rights in the Constitution and perpetual union proved to be the two hinges upon which congressional policy turned, and the doom of Johnson's policy lay in the discovery that the party could be united upon the need for certain 'guarantees' which he had failed to provide.

The Republican consensus was as yet limited in scope and it

[1] C.G. 39.1.2798.   [2] C.G. 39.1.491.   [3] C.G. 39.1.74.

did not extend to any advanced propositions about racial equality. For many Republicans the sticking-point was the question of suffrage. A good many were prepared to see the vote given to negroes with property and education, and even the Democrat Reverdy Johnson was ready to admit that many of the negroes were 'capable of as much and as high a civilization as the white race' and that if protected by the paramount authority of the Constitution 'they will ere long become valuable citizens of the country'.[1] But there was a long gap between this kind of statement and a commitment to immediate and unqualified suffrage. On the one hand many Republicans were aware of the racial prejudice in their own constituencies — several Northern States excluded negroes from the suffrage and were to reaffirm this during the Reconstruction controversy — and on the other some Republicans were alarmed by the idea of indiscriminate suffrage extended to the illiterates of either race. Privately Horace Greeley proposed that the suffrage should be given to all who had voted prior to 1861 and to such others 'as shall have read understandingly the Constitution of the United States, and have paid a State tax during the year preceding'.[2]

Though no agreement on negro suffrage was likely in the immediate future, the case for it was being made. Speaking for the negro to the annual meeting of the Massachusetts Anti-Slavery Society in 1865 in a lecture called 'What the Black Man Wants' Frederick Douglass explained that they wanted suffrage 'because it is our *right* first of all. No class of men can, without insulting their own nature, be content with any deprivation of their rights. We want it again as a means of educating our race. . . . Again I want the elective franchise, for one, as a colored man, because ours is a peculiar government, based upon a peculiar idea, and that idea is universal suffrage. If I were in a monarchical government, where the few bore rule and the many were subject, there would be no special stigma resting upon me, because I did not exercise the elective franchise'. He concluded that if the negro 'knows as much when sober as an Irishman knows when he is drunk, he

<hr/>

[1] C.G. 39.1.373.   [2] L.C. *Butler Papers*, 24 Aug. 1865.

knows enough to vote, on good American principles'.[1] The abstract case for negro suffrage was, however, being powerfully reinforced by a purely political argument. In March 1865 Sumner, whose sincerity in the cause of racial equality cannot be doubted, was writing to Bright that without negro votes 'we cannot establish stable government in the rebel States . . . without them the enemy will reappear, and under forms of law take possession of the governments, choose magistrates and officers, and in alliance with the Northern democracy, put us all in peril again'.[2] It could also be argued that negro suffrage must be the keystone for any policy of guarantees and when Congress met, the Radical George Boutwell argued that restoration without negro suffrage 'opens the way to the destruction of this government from which there is no escape' while rights without suffrage were illusory for 'with the right of voting everything that a man ought to have or enjoy of civil rights comes to him. Without the right to vote he is secure in nothing'.[3] Thus stood the question of negro suffrage at the end of the year 1865: with strong advocates, encountering many doubts, drawing upon the stock of traditional American beliefs, and provided with arguments arising from the political situation and increasing in cogency as men pondered upon the future distribution of power in the United States. For those who believed that negro suffrage in the South would be a disaster the best tactics would have been to settle with the moderate Republican majority before they were forced to choose between the negro vote and the abandonment of what they deemed to be essential. Such would have been the wisdom of political calculation, but in times of stress politicians are, perhaps, no more likely than other men to calculate correctly. Johnson, his supporters, and the South were set upon the surest road to colour-blind democracy but they remained oblivious of the direction in which they were heading and adhered instead to their belief that 'restoration' could be achieved without 'guarantees'.

[1] Frederick Douglass. Speech at the Massachusetts Anti-Slavery Society, 1865. Issued as a pamphlet, *What the Black Man Wants*, Boston, 1865.
[2] E. L. Pierce, *Memoirs and Letters of Charles Sumner* (Boston, 1877–94), IV, 229.
[3] C.G. 39.1.309.

· III ·

Men in Congress

The men who gathered in Washington in December 1865 as members of the Thirty-ninth Congress were faced with the need to make decisions which were to be as important as any in the history of the United States, but the historian who seeks to understand them is hampered at the outset by the habit of denigration into which Americans fall when they deal with politicians. As Lord Bryce observed, a few years after Reconstruction, they 'are fond of running down Congressmen. The cultivated New Englanders and New Yorkers do this out of intellectual fastidiousness, and in order to support the role which they unconsciously fall into when talking to Europeans. The rougher Western men do it because they would not have congressmen seem to be in any way better than themselves, since that would be opposed to Republican equality'.[1] Congress had never had the opportunity given to representative assemblies in monarchical countries of winning repute by opposition to arbitrary government, and congressmen of this period, who saw themselves as playing this part in opposition to presidential usurpation, had no strong traditions to exploit. Twentieth-century Americans have become accustomed to the strong Presidency with its claim to represent the people against the factiousness and local interests of Congress, and view with suspicion the claim of Reconstruction majorities to represent the will of the people against an obstructive President. It is also unusual to find Congress formulating a policy without the aid and against the wishes of the Executive, while maintaining the cohesion necessary for the enactment of controversial laws. Party loyalty has become an accepted part of repre-

[1] Lord Bryce, *The American Commonwealth*, 3rd ed. (New York and London, 1900), I, 147.

sentative government in most democratic countries but in the United States the phrase 'strict party vote' has become a term of abuse. Thus the men of the Thirty-ninth Congress start with a heavy handicap and the tendency has been to condemn them unheard.

In spite of the criticisms which he had heard from Americans Bryce did not find them supported by his own observations. As men of business he did not find congressmen inferior to the House of Commons and he noted a welcome absence 'of two classes hitherto well represented in the British Parliament, the rich dull parvenu who has bought himself into public life, and the perhaps equally unlettered young sporting or fashionable men who, neither knowing nor caring anything about politics, has come from a county or a small borough on the strength of his family estates'.[1] There was indeed no short cut to political eminence in the United States, or none which was likely to keep a man at the top for very long. The American politician fought his way forwards in a hard and rough world; he owed his success to his position in his party in his State, and this in turn he owed to ability gauged to the needs of the situation, to determination and to a facility for winning political friends. His continued success depended upon the degree to which he was able to make national influence serve local interests. The logic of his situation demanded that he would seek to win favours at Washington for those upon whom he depended, that he would be constantly on guard against measures damaging to his district or his State, that in the party he would be anxious to increase the influence of the faction or group which had made him or which he had made. Yet it would be unfair to say that congressional success depended solely upon services rendered, and in a period of crisis he could not afford to ignore the swirling tides of public opinion on national questions in which local interests might well be submerged. It would be unwise to assume at the outset that Reconstruction must be explained in terms of material advantage to the victors or that the crisis was made by politicians and forced upon

[1] Ibid.

the people. The real independence of the congressman was often slight; he had to play the game according to the rules of the system which made him, his political future depended upon the good-will of his constituents and he could afford to ignore neither their interests nor their prejudices nor their ideals.

E. L. Godkin, the expatriate Englishman who explained Americans to themselves in *The Nation* and to the British public in the London *Daily News*, wrote in the latter newspaper that Congress contained a sprinkling of highly educated and a large number of plain sensible men 'wanting all polish, but accustomed to business, with a tolerably strong hold on a few leading principles of government which they make serve as guides in everything which comes before them'. He thought that they blundered a good deal 'but in great lines of policy they are very seldom wrong'.[1] Most members of Congress had some education beyond the secondary stage and in the Senate a majority had attended the better known universities. In many cases the higher education to which a majority of the remainder could claim was received in some remote rural college or a law school of doubtful merit, but a surprisingly small number confessed to no formal education or to one which ended at the elementary stage.[2] The great gateway through which most had entered public life was the practice of law, and even those who had carried on other trades or professions had often had early legal experience. The Senate especially could be described as a body of lawyers though then as now a successful lawyer could pick up a wide range of business associations; a few senators were connected with manufacturing but only one was a manufacturer on a large scale; some were connected with banking though usually with small local banks and none with great

---

[1] Rollo Ogden, *Life and Letters of E. L. Godkin* (New York, 1907), II, 319. From a letter to the *Daily News*, 7 Sep. 1867. In 1874, in a private letter, he was less complimentary: 'I think what strikes one most about the members of the House is the cleanness of their shirts. There is a kind of man, you know, whom clean linen gives an odd Sunday look to, and most of these men belong to it. I think we under-rate their honesty, but we over-rate their intelligence. Their ignorance is awful, and it is not tempered and restrained as the ignorance of the corresponding class is in Europe by contact with foreign nations.' Ibid., 311.

[2] These statements are based upon information contained in the *Biographical Directory of the American Congress, 1774–1949* (81 Cong., 2 Sess. House Doc. No. 609).

Eastern financial houses; a handful of senators were interested in newspapers but most of them as a sideline rather than as a principal activity and there was no editor of a great urban daily. The background of members of the House of Representatives was similar though usually with less distinction. In both Houses the predominant characteristic was service in State governments as legislators, judges or holders of executive offices, and most senators had sat at one time in the House of Representatives. This apprenticeship in State and national public life is worth remembering for it meant that most of them had had to master and to expound some of the vast questions which perplexed the Union during the prolonged emotional crisis of the preceding twenty years; whatever their other limitations the leaders of Congress were not political novices who were likely to blunder into traps set by ignorance or emotion.

In a country which was still predominantly rural, and had been even more so within recent memory, most congressmen were country bred. The focal points of their lives were not great cities but small country towns in which they were known to everybody and could gather the threads of local opinion by walking down main street. Next to the small town on which his operations were based the most important social group for the congressman to consider were the local politicians who acted as his aides and agents. At this period few possessed the economic stature to give them a ready-made local ascendancy and none possessed the kind of territorial influence which was the birthright of the British landed class. They did depend upon something not unlike the 'connection' of British eighteenth-century politics though without the nucleus of family and consisting of a group of friends and aides, who would keep in touch with what was going on in his State, play on his behalf the complex and unending game of manipulation, and start working for the next election as soon as the last was over. The congressman could be regarded either as the head of a gang of professional politicians who were attached to him for the favours which he could bestow, or as the centre of a group of friends who had projected him into public life to serve a cause in which they all believed; it would be wrong to assume that either picture was wholly correct or that both could not co-exist, perhaps in the same person.

Senators were conscious of their own importance and dignity. A senatorship was the legitimate object of ambition for most politicians, and the man who had attained it usually knew that he was at the top of his particular tree. As a senator he might become a nationally known figure with a place in history, or he might sink into obscurity. As a senator his place in the world would depend upon the man himself and upon his fellow senators, for whatever his constituents might think of him it was in the Senate that he must make or mar his reputation. It would not matter greatly whether he came from a small or a great State, whether he was a local dictator or had come to Congress as a result of a compromise between rival factions, whether he distinguished himself by party regularity or by independence; what really counted was the positive contribution which he made to the life and work of the Senate. It was still possible to establish a reputation by oratory, but a close attention to business and speeches which were practical rather than rhetorical won more respect. Charles Sumner could command attention by the fluency, passion and erudition of his enormously long speeches, but he drafted no bills, paid little attention to committee work, made erratic interventions in debate, and in the years after 1865 wasted away his enormous influence by failing to play the game according to the rules which a businesslike and undramatic assembly evolved for itself. Ultimately more influence was wielded by the quiet grey men who steered committees and reduced tension with speeches which were weighty rather than spectacular. To those who could remember Clay, Webster and Calhoun the Senate might seem dull, and Bryce was to describe it as 'modern, severe and practical', but more business was transacted than in the great but frustrating golden age of the Senate.

Senators sat for a longer term than representatives and were more likely to be re-elected; they sat in a smaller body and tended to display the kind of cohesion, which one finds among

E

groups of men who have known each other for a long time and whose mutual exasperation is mitigated by familiarity. It was this rather than anything else which offset the anarchic rules which placed no limit on debate or on the length of speeches. Perhaps the one abiding, unwritten rule was that the Senate must not appear ridiculous. While senators were very jealous of their freedom of speech they also knew that laws must pass if the country was to be governed, and the day of the filibuster had not yet dawned. As one might expect, the main burden of steering business through the Senate was carried by a small number of men: William P. Fessenden was perhaps the most influential of these with J. W. Grimes of Iowa as his faithful friend and ally; others who seemed to have belonged to the inner group of Republican 'men of business' were Jacob M. Howard of Michigan, Timothy M. Howe of Wisconsin, John Sherman of Ohio, Lyman Trumbull of Illinois, Ben Wade of Ohio, George H. Williams of Oregon and perhaps Zachariah Chandler of Michigan and Henry Wilson of Massachusetts.[1] Sumner, though influential because of his anti-slavery record and because of his position as keeper of the New England conscience, stood somewhat apart. James R. Doolittle of Wisconsin might have joined such a group but his vehement support of Johnson's policy cut him off from other Republicans. Among the Democrats Reverdy Johnson of Maryland was moderate, experienced and constructive in his criticisms, and Thomas A. Hendricks of Indiana was the most weighty representative of the former 'peace' Democrats; Garrett Davis of Kentucky spoke frequently in Reconstruction debates but with such exaggeration that he did his cause more harm than good.[2]

---

[1] For Chandler, Grimes, Howard, Howe, Wade, Williams and Wilson see pp. 82 ff. below; for Fessenden see pp. 125 ff. and for Trumbull pp. 104-5 below.

[2] Reverdy Johnson, though classed as a Democrat, was really an old Southern Whig who failed to find a natural home in any party. He was a man of considerable distinction, one of the most successful lawyers of his day, and a leading authority on constitutional law. He was born of a legal family at Annapolis in 1796, became a Whig senator in 1845, and was appointed Attorney-General by President Taylor in 1849. In this office he was not very successful and did not continue after Taylor's death. He drifted towards the Democratic party, and took a moderate pro-Southern line in the controversies of the 1850's; but he strongly opposed secession and took an active part in keeping Maryland in the Union. After the war he supported Johnson's Reconstruction policy, but, when these proved to be politically impracticable, he tried to use his influence to persuade Southerners

The forum in which the leaders explained policy to their fellow party members was the caucus, and a caucus meeting was also the occasion when a restive senator could challenge the leadership. Votes were taken and were usually binding; but nothing could gag a senator who was determined to have his public say.

The House of Representatives was a less orderly and less impressive assembly than the Senate. It was, of course, much bigger and any Congress would contain a large number of men sitting their first term; it also contained a surprisingly large number who would not be re-elected. There was a fairly clear division in the House between the old hands, who had sat in several Congresses, and rank and file who were destined to serve for no more than one or two terms. Between the two were the younger aspirants to a permanent political career who were already marked down as the 'old hands' of the future. In the past the bulk of the old hands had come from the South and, as a representative from New York explained, 'under our Northern miserable system of representation, every two or four years, after a man has been educated to a place in this body, after he has come to know its rules, and understand his duties, after he has been trained and educated as a statesman, then at that hour the political wheel rolls him out, and a green man comes here to meet the Representatives of the South who have been here ten, twenty, thirty and even forty years.'[1] It was therefore upon a sea of inexperience that the men of business, helped by the young men of ambition who had no intention of leaving public life, had to impose some kind of order, and the rules were necessarily harsh and restrictive.

Discipline was imposed by caucus, the gag rule and the previous question. The caucus of party members met frequently

to accept Northern conditions; thus, though a frequent speaker against the majority policy, he supported the four key Reconstruction measures: the Wade-Davis Bill, the Thirteenth Amendment, the Fourteenth Amendment, and the First Reconstruction Act. Despite this Johnson appointed him Minister to Great Britain in 1868. When he relinquished this post in 1869 he returned to the law and died while still in active practice. Good manners, good temper and good sense make Reverdy Johnson one of the most attractive personalities of the period.

[1] James Brooks, C.G. 38.2.148, 6 Jan. 1865. His assertion of the length of Southern service was exaggerated but this did not invalidate the point.

during sessions in the same way as the Senate caucus; measures were explained (with far greater brevity than on the floor of the House) and the order of business was outlined; sometimes there was discussion and nearly always a vote after which a majority decision was binding upon the members present. The gag rule limited speeches to one hour, and though permission was frequently given by unanimous consent to extend time when a member had something to say, the bore and the obstructionist could not expect this indulgence. Another form of the gag was the allocation of a limited time to a motion for debate. The chairman of the committee reporting the bill had charge of the time and could allocate it to members at his discretion; he might well take the major portion himself, then yield to two or three supporters of the measure, allow a fair share to a leading minority spokesman and end with some insultingly short allocations to lesser minority speakers. At the tail end of such a debate most of the time would probably be consumed by complaints from the minority that their time was too short. A skilful committee chairman could therefore ensure that the main arguments for a measure were well presented, do a good turn to friends who wished to speak, preserve the appearance of fair discussion, and perhaps allow to the floor those minority spokesmen whom he judged would most irritate any waverers whom he wished to convince. The previous question was the most powerful instrument of all: the man in charge of a bill could move that 'the main question be now put', on which motion there could be no debate, and if carried it was followed immediately by a vote on the bill under discussion. In addition to these procedural checks upon freedom of debate, which would usually be announced in advance at the caucus meeting, there was a pressure for party regularity and an impatience of minor criticism which were characteristic of a period of emotional stress. 'We seem to have fallen upon strange times,' said a Republican who hankered after greater freedom, 'heretofore independence of thought and action has been permitted in this honorable body on the part of its members; but now it seems as if every difference of opinion amounted to a desertion of the Republican ranks in the

opinion of some.'[1] Pressure of this kind increased as soon as it
became apparent that majority policy would have to be carried
over presidential vetoes and every man who showed signs of
weakening the necessary two-thirds would be regarded as an
enemy of his party.

Given these rules it is not surprising that comparatively few
men participated in the more important debates, but rank and file
congressmen might hope for a chance to speak on Saturday
mornings when thin houses listened to elaborately prepared
speeches which members intended for the newspapers in their
home towns and, with the use of congressional franking privileges,
for circulation to important constituents. Occasionally a man who
was thwarted in his attempts to obtain the floor could get leave
from the House to print his speech without having delivered it.
When a member had obtained possession of the floor of the House
his troubles had only begun; it was the custom of the House for
members to 'yield for a question' even when in the full spate of
their oratory. Old hands could occasionally get away with a curt
refusal to yield until their arguments had been completed,
but even they could not do this frequently unless they had the
sympathy of the House and the novice hardly dared to do so.
Questions could come from friends, who wished to bring out a
particular point, but more frequently from enemies who wished
to expose an error in fact, a fault in logic or an inconsistency in the
speaker's record, and the sight of a man trying to evade the issue
or refusing an answer would almost certainly rouse the fighting
instincts of the professional spoilers of whom there were always
several in the House. 'I have been here three years,' said one
exasperated congressman, 'and in witnessing the manner in which
debates are carried on upon the floor of this House it has occurred
to me that if some members of this House had been present when
our Saviour delivered the Sermon on the Mount they would have
asked him to yield for a question.'[2]

In spite of the rules of debate observers were struck by the

[1] R. G. Spalding, C.G. 39.2.290, 5 Jan. 1867.
[2] C.G. 41.2.984. Knott of Kentucky speaking in Feb. 1870.

noise and bustle of the House. It was 'like that of short sharp waves in a Highland loch,' said Bryce, 'fretting under a squall against a rocky shore. Conversation, shuffling papers, scratching pens, calls for pages (usually made by clapping the hands), and errands made by these pages from one part of the House to another formed the background of debate, and the hall was so large that even when a speaker commanded attention he had difficulty in making himself heard.'[1] In the Senate a man could command respect with quiet and orderly delivery, but in the House the few who rose firmly above the rank and file had to be men of commanding personality. 'There is no place where so little deference is paid to reputation previously acquired, or to eminence outside; no place where so little consideration is shown for the feelings or the failures of beginners,' said James G. Blaine, and added with a touch of self-satisfaction (for he was himself an outstandingly successful congressman), 'What a man gains in the House, he gains by sheer force of his own character and if he loses and falls back he may expect no mercy and will receive no sympathy.'[2] Yet some men did establish themselves: James A. Garfield was to win his way to the Presidency, and so in later years did William McKinley; Rutherford B. Hayes was a member of the Thirty-ninth Congress, though a silent one, and James G. Blaine made his reputation there. The twentieth-century House has produced no men of similar presidential calibre. Among those who did not rise to quite this eminence John A. Bingham, William D. Kelley, Henry J. Raymond, Samuel Shellabarger, Elihu B. Washburn and James F. Wilson were all men of considerable ability;[3] there were several others of equal attainments, and there was always the indefatigable and dominating Thaddeus Stevens who was, for a short spell, the most important man in the nation. The Speaker was a man of considerable influence and much depended upon him. He appointed members of committees, acted in effect as majority leader in the arrangement of business, recognized or

[1] Bryce, op. cit., I, 143.
[2] Theodore C. Smith (ed.), *Life and Letters of James A. Garfield* (New Haven, 1925), I, 363.
[3] For Kelley, Washburn and J. F. Wilson see pp. 86 ff. below.

failed to recognize would-be participants in debate, interpreted the rules of the House, and dealt with the numerous points of order. Schuyler Colfax was a bland and efficient Speaker, and a good deal of the success of Republican party management was due to his unobtrusive and unflurried control of the House.[1]

In both Houses the business was largely managed by a relatively small group of men, but it would be misleading to exaggerate their cohesion. They were linked together by experience, by common enjoyment of the satisfaction which comes from an assured position, and by mutual respect; but they had no formal collective responsibility and they remained individualists prepared at any time to take independent decisions. They had neither the power nor the responsibility of ministers in the British House of Commons, and they were usually unable to take the initiative as a policy making group. A good deal of power rested with the chairmen of committees, though perhaps less than in more recent times, and much of the real work of both Houses was done behind closed doors. The normal work of an important committee was to consider the broad lines of policy affecting its sphere of activity, and the lines of its discussion were usually determined by the relevant passage in the President's annual message; it could request further information from the executive departments and this might come to it in the form of detailed proposals; it considered and digested the numerous bills which had been proposed in Congress and immediately referred to the appropriate committee, and occasionally it might have referred back to it bills which had reached an advanced stage in Congress; and out of all these considerations it was supposed to report to its House what legislation it might deem to be necessary. A committee report was usually drafted in the form of a bill and

[1] Schuyler Colfax was born in New York City in 1823 and moved with his family to Indiana in 1836. He studied the law but did not practice and while still a very young man became a leader of the Whigs in his State. He helped to organize the Republican party in Indiana, came to Congress in 1855, and was Speaker from 1863-9. He then became Vice-President but supposed sympathies with the Liberal Republicans prevented his re-nomination in 1872. He was implicated in the Credit Mobilier scandal though his guilt was not proven. Until this disaster, which put an end to his political career, he was regarded as a representative and spokesman of religious interests in the Midwest; he himself was an active Methodist leader.

presented by the chairman, and here the measure would enter into the deliberations of the informal inner group. In the Senate there was not much more to do than to decide its place in the congressional timetable. In the House it would be necessary to decide upon its allocation of congressional time, when it would be called up, and whether it should be allowed to take its chance in debate or forced through under the previous question. At this stage of negotiation the personality of the committee chairman and the importance which he attached to the proposed measure would obviously have great effect. A bill which was allowed to take its chance in debate (as most of them were) might well be mangled by amendment, might be referred back to the originating committee or occasionally to another committee, and if it eventually reached the statute book might do so in a form which differed in important points from that which it had been given by the committee. Committee bills were not often killed by a direct vote but there were many other ways of stifling a measure which was unwelcome to a considerable number of the majority party; debate might be prolonged by numerous amendments or the bill might be referred back at a late stage in the session when it was unlikely to re-emerge unless the congressional leaders attached great importance to it. Bills were read three times, of which the first two readings were formal; but custom had decreed what was virtually a fourth reading on a motion to reconsider a vote which had been taken. The man in charge of a bill had the privilege of moving to reconsider and this could be used tactically: if a bill had been passed handsomely he would probably move immediately for reconsideration and obtain a confirmatory vote while a favourable majority was in the chamber; if the bill had been defeated or passed by an uncomfortably small majority he might defer the motion for reconsideration to another day when he might expect to find more friends present. Occasionally decisive debates could take place on motions to reconsider which led to the reversal of earlier votes.

It can be seen that the procedure was complex and that the outcome could be uncertain; no one could predict at the beginning of a Congress what measures would be passed, and if a small group of 'old hands' tried to press forward and facilitate the passage of legislation an equally small number of individuals could often divert and delay the outcome of their efforts; nor was it uncommon for a born obstructionist to find himself among the old hands where he could exert his influence to the utmost and probably ensure that nothing which he actively disliked became law. The nature of Congress ensured that a great many different points of view would be represented in the course of legislation, and those which were well presented or pressed by able and persistent men might have a substantial effect upon the laws produced or the proposals which were suppressed, but it was not a body which could ordinarily initiate policy or in which it was easy to carry through a broad, consistent and well co-ordinated legislative plan. When the President was in harmony with the majority and on familiar terms with the congressional leaders these handicaps might be overcome by the judicious use of executive influence, but when the President and the majority were at loggerheads a stalemate might well result as the experience of the Whigs with John Tyler had demonstrated. The success of the Republicans in seizing the initiative in Reconstruction policy and in forcing it through Congress was therefore abnormal and requires special investigation.

Leaders in Congress controlled no patronage, and once they had broken with the President the patronage which they might expect to influence was denied to them. Moreover when a majority had broken with a President chosen by their own party executive influence could be used against them in a particularly insidious way; a President belonging to the minority party would naturally use his influence to sustain that party but the influence of Johnson could be used to break up the Republican party itself. The rank and file of Republican politicians would be faced with the choice between winning executive favour and enjoying the rewards, or following their own leaders at the sacrifice of the patronage upon which professional politics usually depended. Unusual pressure was thus placed upon the party organization and unusual counter-pressure was necessary to preserve it from disintegration.

The difficulty was increased by the divisions within the party on important questions of policy; it was for instance impossible to carry measures affecting the tariff, currency or land grants to railroads with a 'strict party vote', and it was only on Reconstruction measures that party solidarity was obtained. It is not possible to explain this by attributing to the leaders any mystical powers of persuasion or coercion, for when all was said the leaders could do little against individuals whose political lives depended upon local party organizations. The really unusual fact about Reconstruction was the way in which, on this question, the local organizations tended to move along the same lines and to press upon their men in Congress the same kind of action which their leaders demanded. To a certain extent politicians were driven together by Johnson's threat to the party, but their solidarity would have had little effect if Johnson had not become unpopular with the Republican voters. Something too depended upon the prospect of party advantage, but the dire consequences for the Republican party if Johnson's restoration policy succeeded was an effective argument only if a majority of the electors believed the party worth preserving. An attempt to interpret Reconstruction policy solely in terms of partisan passion and material interest is likely to fail, for the great moving power behind Reconstruction was the conviction of the average Republican that the objectives of his party were rational and humane.

For its adherents the Republican party was no ordinary political association: it was the party which had stood firm against the expansion of slavery, saved the Union, and represented all which the age regarded as enlightened. Socially it was diverse, ranging from the educated upper class of New England to recent settlers on the Great Plains; it embraced genuine fanatics and cautious practical men; it united the Northern intelligentsia with professional politicians trained in the toughest of schools; its appeal was directed equally to large employers and to industrial labour. Nearly every man who joined the party before the war had had to make a personal decision to cut adrift from traditional party organizations, and for some the decision to join the new party had aroused the same intense emotions as a religious conversion.[1] To the frustrated eighteen-fifties it had seemed to bring a new sense of dedication and purpose, and unlike most American parties it was able to convince its supporters that its doctrines were worth a war. By the end of the war the party had acquired a momentum which could have carried it through a slack period, and a period of crisis which seemed to bring in question its basic convictions stimulated enthusiasm and fostered the conviction that it must be preserved.

Something of the Republican character can be understood from that of the rival party. 'The old Democratic doctrine was to permit the town to do nothing which the school district could not as well do; the county nothing which the town could do; the State nothing which the county or city could do; and the federal government nothing the State could as completely and safely accomplish.'[2] In this sentence the New York *World*, which was the most influential Eastern Democratic newspaper, summed up the political philosophy of the party. Or, another occasion, it declared that 'We plant our standard boldly on the great cardinal doctrine of State Rights. . . . The State Rights principle stood foremost in the Democratic creed, and next to that a Metallic Currency and Free Trade'.[3] And when making a defence of the two-thirds rule in Democratic Nominating Conventions the *World* explained that it rested 'upon the principle that the minority has rights which the majority is bound to respect . . . a safeguard against rash innovations, and against the premature adoption of reforms to which the party has not been fully educated'.[4] In 1871 the same newspaper was still declaring that there had always been 'but two parties — the one which sought to extend the sphere of Federal government, the other which sought to confine its power to their exact, specified boundaries'.[5] Thus the Democrats claimed that the theory of State rights, which many Republicans regarded

[1] Carl Schurz recalled the impact made upon by the Republican campaign in 1856. 'The Republican platform sounded to me like a bugle-call of liberty, and the name of Frémont, "the Pathfinder", surrounded by a halo of adventurous heroism, mightily stirred the imagination. Thus the old cause of human freedom was to be fought for on the soil of the new world. The great final decision seemed to be pending.' *Reminiscences*, II, 67.
[2] *World*, 7 Mar. 1865. [3] Ibid, 18 Mar. 1867. [4] Ibid, 2 July 1868. [5] Ibid, 2 July 1871.

as a prime cause of the war, was the cardinal doctrine of their party and this was linked with the kind of conservatism which permitted any minority (so long as it was defined geographically) to veto the wishes of the majority. To Republicans this was simply an excuse for tolerating established wrong and preventing moral progress. 'This party', wrote Ignatius Donnelly, 'is the captive of our bow and spear; and as we drag it forward by the heels see how it fights against progress. . . . A year ago its efforts were to preserve slavery; today they are made to preserve legalized oppression. A year ago it struggled against the war and for peace at any price; today it seeks to hand over the nation, bound hand and foot, to those who were defeated in the mighty conflict.'[1] Northern Democrats apart from the copperheads had foresworn the doctrine of secession, but had made this denial the ground for demanding an automatic resumption of State rights when the South surrendered.

Democratic ideas stood therefore directly athwart the main objectives of Republican policy, and Republicans regarded Democrats with a contempt which outran the normal rivalry of party politics. In 1871 Carl Schurz told a Southern audience that Republicans felt the Democratic party to be 'essentially a party of the past', and though he then believed that many Republicans were dissatisfied with their party leadership 'they do not go over to the Democrats because they feel it would be like jumping into yesterday, and a yesterday too which they do not like'.[2] Republicans knew, of course, that many Democrats had supported the war and that on any rational calculation half of those who had fought in the Union armies must have been Democrats, but they were inclined to believe that the sincere Union Democrats had been absorbed into the Republican party and that the rump of the Democratic party was dominated by Peace Democrats and

---

[1] Minnesota State Historical Society, Ignatius Donnelly, *Diary*. This diary, to which some further references will be made, exists in two forms. The first is in Donnelly's hand-writing and was written at the time of the events to which it refers; the second is a type-script prepared from the original in 1891. In the 1891 version there are a number of altera-tions in the text and additional notes and comments (it was evidently prepared with the prospect of publication in view). Donnelly, then in his Populist phase, made no alteration in the judgments upon Reconstruction politics which he expressed as a Radical Republican.

[2] From a speech at Nashville, 20 Sep. 1871. Bancroft (ed.), *Correspondence and Political Papers of Carl Schurz*, II, 298.

copperheads, and that control of the party was thus shared between those who had had the courage to avow openly their secessionist sympathies and those who preferred to undermine the Union cause from within. If proof of this were required the damning peace platform of 1864 could be produced, while in the Union border States the true character of the Democrats was being shown in the welcome extended to returning Confederates. At the other end of the Northern Democratic party was the blatant corruption of New York's Tammany ring which apparently enjoyed the blessing of such respectable citizens as Horatio Seymour and Samuel Tilden. Indiana copperheadism, Kentucky negrophobia and city corruption seemed to be three legs of the Democratic edifice which only wanted a fourth — rebel restoration — to make it complete and perhaps invincible. In retrospect the animosities may appear exaggerated and the images upon which they depended may seem to be drawn in lurid and deceptive colours; but the depth of party feeling must be appreciated in order to understand the controversies of Reconstruction.

In contrast the Republicans saw themselves as the champions of everything which was enlightened, patriotic and progressive. 'This is not the old Whig party,' exclaimed Henry Wilson, 'that never professed to have an idea on earth, a party that simply advocated tariffs and banks and moneyed measures; nor is it the Democratic party corrupted by slavery. . . . It is a party that plants its foot on the rock of ages, and has all the measureless moral force of the universe to sustain it.'[1] An Irish-Canadian living in Omaha wrote that 'I as a Canadian reformer must be a Republican, for Reform and Republicanism are identical and I assure you it grieves me to see the poor ignorant Irishmen upholding a miserable conservatism which has always kept them in bondage'.[2] Many years later a Republican who entered Congress in 1869 reflected that 'The Republican party, whatever its faults, since it came to power in 1860 has been composed of what is best in our national life. . . . On the other hand their antagonist has been, is, and for an

[1] C.G. 39.1.341.
[2] Minnesota State Historical Society, *Donnelly Papers*, R. Delany to Donnelly, 11 Jul. 1868.

indefinite time to come will be, controlled by the foreign population and the criminal classes, by Tammany Hall, and by the
leaders of the Solid South'.[1] To its adherents therefore the real
strength of the Republican party rested upon the quality of the
people which it represented and the quality of the measures which
it endorsed. Its strength, said one of them, 'consists on its adherence to principle, and that embodiment of its principles,
equality of rights among men. . . . It was that for which it was
organized; and instead of being a source of weakness it is . . . a
source of strength and power.' The founding fathers of the party,
though not readily identifiable, were nevertheless revered, and an
orator of 1875 declared that 'all today admit that their aim and
purpose was noble, meritorious and majestic beyond precedent.
They sought liberty, enfranchisement, moral, mental and material
elevation of the colored half of the Southern population, and
consequent upon that the needed improvement of their white
counterparts. This purpose was inspired by conscience, conviction, a sense of duty and responsibility. . . . Who today, dares say
they were wrong?'[2] Partisan self-portraits need not be taken too
seriously, but it is worth noting that these assertions were not
mere extravagances intended to beguile the simple voter, but-
were confidently accepted by most of the Northern intelligentsia.
'The literary men of the country are with us by an immense
majority', wrote James G. Blaine, 'and they are a "great power".'[3]
Emerson, Whitman, Whittier, Lowell and Motley were all convinced Republicans; so were powerful editors such as Greeley,
Whitelaw Reid and Horace White; the faculties of the Northern
universities were Republican and so were the great majority of the
ministers of religion.[4] The Republicans claimed that their party

[1] G. F. Hoar, *Autobiography of Seventy Years*, I, 200.
[2] Address of J. F. Manning, of Worcester, Mass. at Frankfort, New York, 25 Oct. 1875.
[3] L.C. *Washburn Papers*, Blaine to Washburn, 24 Oct. 1868.
[4] The identification of the Northern intellectuals with the Republican party raises some
interesting speculations. The writers could see tangible evidence of their effect upon
public opinion, and the politicians were conscious of the contribution of the intellectuals
to the strength of the party. Not until the New Deal was any comparable intellectual
group led to identify itself with the aims and aspirations of a majority party. On the general
question of the intellectuals and American politics see Seymour Lipsett, *Political Man*
(New York and London, 1960) Ch. X. The alliance between the intellectuals and the early
Republican party was disrupted under Grant and never restored.

was the party of reform and of respectability; this was a combination of unique force, and it was all the stronger because they believed that the roots of the party were deeply spread in the decent instincts of the American people. 'It is the main security of our Republican party', declared a campaign pamphlet of 1872, 'that it rests not upon the shoulders of a few political leaders, but upon the self-thinking masses; it is the most encouraging feature of Republican progress that it has educated the people to a point where public men only become the mouthpieces of the popular will.'[1] The main point about the Republican party is not whether these claims were true or false but that they were made and believed; this made it a political instrument of enormous power.

The Republican party formed a spectrum of opinion and though it is customary to distinguish sharply between Radicals and moderates or conservatives it is not easy to discover the line which divides them. A man could be Radical in his view of what ought to be done about the Southern ruling class and conservative on the negro question; he could, like Senator Stewart of Nevada, believe in universal amnesty and universal suffrage, or he might believe that traitors should be hanged and suffrage left to the future; he could like John A. Bingham believe that once protection for civil rights had been written into the law the Southern States could be safely readmitted, or he might like Roscoe Conkling have no interest in civil rights provided that Southern leaders were excluded from public life. Within this spectrum there were continual variations of tone, and under the logic of events men came to accept ideas which they would previously have rejected and to reject some to which they had been attached. The most striking example of this shift is the attitude of ordinary Republicans towards negro suffrage. In 1866 Republican opposition prevented a commitment to adult male suffrage by 1876; in 1867 negro suffrage was accepted as an integral part of Reconstruction; in 1869 the party was solidly behind the Fifteenth Amendment which made it unconstitutional to deny the vote because of race, creed, or previous condition of servitude.

[1] The quotation comes from *The Republican Party*, a campaign pamphlet of 1872.

The politicians were not men apart from the people; they would fight on ground which was politically tenable, would keep the faithful united in time of stress, and attract the uncommitted when conditions were favourable. Then as now the American party system was a marvellously sensitive machine for registering the currents of opinion, and beneath the surface of congressional politics a continuous debate was in progress about the great issues of Reconstruction. In the newspapers, in correspondence with their constituents, and in reports from their local supporters the congressmen had ample means of discovering exactly what was going on at the grass roots, and they knew that they could ignore what was happening only at their peril. Garfield, in a letter to some critical constituents, put a case suspiciously like Burke's to the electors of Bristol: 'I believe a representative should get all the light on every matter of public importance that his position enables him to and then to speak and vote in such a manner as will, in his judgment, enhance the best interests of his constituents and the whole country. . . . But while he is in office his course should be guided by his own judgments, based upon the suggestions of his constituents and all other attainable information.'[1] The spirit was the spirit of Burke but the representative who faced biennial elections would find, in all probability, that his independent judgment happened to coincide with that which he judged would be most acceptable to his constituents.

A situation in which men are fairly well agreed upon their basic premises but vague and confused over immediate prospects is likely to favour the men who know what they want and where they intend to go. The function of Radicalism was to act as a catalyst which would precipitate Republican opinion around certain precise objectives. They 'made' policy in the sense that they said a little sooner than the majority what the majority would soon decide to be necessary and true; but they did not and could not create the climate of opinion in which their success was possible. The Radicals were not a party, they had no independent organizations, and what power they possessed depended upon

[1] Smith (ed.), *Life and Letters of James A. Garfield*, I, 382.

their influence within local Republican organizations. In some areas Radical ascendancy was a natural result of recent history, in others the Radicals had to fight for control, and in others they remained as critics of those whom they regarded as tainted with conservatism. Their arguments were always strong because they appealed both to the experience of the immediate past and to good American traditions; for the Radical had in him something of the old abolitionist, something of the Jeffersonian Democrat, and something of that educated and active middle class which was doing so much to change the world on both sides of the Atlantic. The sin of slavery, the immortality of the Declaration of Independence, and progress towards a brighter future were his rhetorical stand-bys, and in the post-war mood of America they were potent symbols.

Generalizations about Radicalism do not tell one who the Radicals were, and many historians, following some contemporaries, have fallen into the easy habit of calling 'radical' everyone whom they dislike. If it is necessary to show that the Radicals were conspirators forcing an unwelcome policy upon an unsuspecting nation they become a small vindictive minority, but if it is desired to discredit the Republican party the Radicals are swollen into a controlling majority. Gideon Welles's diary provides an example: until December 1865 he refers to the Radicals as a fanatical group which is unlikely to command much support in the party; but once Congress had met he discovered that more and more men responded to Radical arguments and the distinction between 'Radical' and 'Republican' is soon lost, and the Radical minority becomes the Radical Congress. Confusion about the nature of Radicalism is increased by the fact that so few people know the names of any Radicals other than Charles Sumner and Thaddeus Stevens; those who have read more deeply in the literature of Reconstruction may be able to add a few more names such as Ben Wade of Ohio, Henry Wilson, George Boutwell and Ben Butler all of Massachusetts, and William D. Kelley of Pennsylvania. The catalogue, with its emphasis upon Massachusetts and Pennsylvania tells something about the character of

F

Radicalism, but not everything: how many are aware, for instance, that Ignatius Donnelly, the later Populist leader, was an ardent and faithful Radical in the Thirty-ninth Congress? Opportunities of separating Radicals from moderates are rare but there is one vote in the second session which appears to have divided them. On 28 January 1867 eighty-eight moderate Republicans and Democrats voted for a resolution moved by John A. Bingham to refer the Reconstruction bill, proposed by Thaddeus Stevens, to the Joint Committee on Reconstruction. They were opposed unsuccessfully by sixty-five Radicals. The question had been long and hotly debated, there was no possibility that any member was in doubt about the issues raised, and it was understood as a straight fight between those who wished to reconstruct Southern society and those who would have left Reconstruction to the South subject to certain guarantees.[1] The vote is analysed in the accompanying Table and reveals an interesting picture of moderate and Radical Republican strength. New England, with no Democratic representatives, showed an almost equal balance between moderates and Radicals, but there was a significant difference between Maine, New Hampshire and Vermont on the one hand (seven Radicals to three moderates) and, on the other, Massachusetts, Connecticut and Rhode Island (seven moderates to four Radicals). New York showed a heavy preponderance of moderates — eleven to six — and if the Democrat vote is added there were seventeen to six against Radicalism. Pennsylvania and New Jersey showed a sharp polarization of opinion between Radicals and Democrats: the two States mustered only two moderate Republicans against twelve Radicals and eight Democrats. The same sharp divisions between the two extremes was shown in Maryland with no moderates, two Radicals and one Democrat. In the Midwestern border States the Republicans were moderate in Kentucky and Tennessee but Radical in Missouri. A most interesting result emerges from the 'old' Midwest — the States of Ohio, Indiana and Illinois admitted to the Union before 1820 —

---

[1] The circumstances of this vote are explained below pp. 181 ff. An analysis which depends upon a single division cannot be conclusive at every point, but its importance as a crucial vote was apparent at the time and warrants the conclusions which follow.

TABLE

The vote taken on 28 January 1867 on Mr Bingham's motion to refer Mr Stevens's Reconstruction Bill to the Joint Committee on Reconstruction.

	Aye		Nay	Not voting	
	Rep.	Dem.	Rep.	Rep.	Dem.
Massachusetts	4	—	3	2	—
Maine	1	—	3	—	—
New Hampshire	1	—	2	—	—
Vermont	1	—	2	—	—
Connecticut	2	—	1	1	—
Rhode Island	1	—	—	1	—
TOTAL New England	10		11	4	
New York	11	6	6	4	4
TOTAL New York	17		6	8	
Pennsylvania	2	6	10	4	2
New Jersey	—	2	2	—	1
TOTAL Pennsylvania and New Jersey	10		12	7	
Maryland	—	1	2	1	1
Delaware	—	1	—	—	—
West Virginia	2	—	—	—	1
TOTAL Atlantic border States	4		2	3	
Kentucky	4	3	—	1	—
Tennessee	5	—	1	2	—
Missouri	—	2	4	3	—
TOTAL Midwest border States	14		5	6	

| | Aye | | Nay | Not voting | |
	Rep.	Dem.	Rep.	Rep.	Dem.
Ohio	10	2	5	2	—
Indiana	4	1	2	2	—
Illinois	5	3	4	2	—

TOTAL 'Old' Midwest	25	11	6

| | Aye | | Nay | Not voting | |
	Rep.	Dem.	Rep.	Rep.	Dem.
Michigan	1	—	5	—	—
Iowa	—	—	5	1	—
Wisconsin	—	1	4	1	—
Minnesota	—	—	2	1	—
Kansas	—	—	—	—	1

TOTAL 'New' Midwest	2	16	4

| | Aye | | Nay | Not voting | |
	Rep.	Dem.	Rep.	Rep.	Dem.
California	1	—	2	—	—
Nevada	1	—	—	—	—
Oregon	—	—	—	—	1

TOTAL Far West	2	2	1

Notes: The vote 'aye' is given in the *Congressional Globe* as 88 but only 84 names are listed. The list of non-voters is also incomplete.

Of the 84 recorded affirmative votes 28 were cast by Democrats; of the 56 remaining members voting 'aye' three subsequently voted, on 2 March, to sustain Johnson's veto of the first Reconstruction bill and may therefore be classed as Administration Republicans. The tally of moderate Republicans on this vote therefore stands at 53.

Of the 39 non-voters, 28 were Republicans, and four of them subsequently voted to sustain Johnson's veto of the first Reconstruction act and one did not then vote. This leaves 23 regular Republicans. If they divided between moderates and Radicals in roughly the same proportion as the recorded vote they can be classed as 10 moderates to 13 Radicals; but this must be taken as the extreme upper limit of the estimate of Radical strength among the non-voters. The distinguishing characteristic of Radicalism was enthusiasm in this particular cause and it is unlikely that so many as 13 had found reason to be absent on that night; a low estimate would be five Radicals to 18 moderates.

The recorded vote, supplemented by these calculations, gives the moderate Republican strength as from 63 to 71, and the Radical strength as 70 to 78. There were also 7 Administration Republicans and 39 Democrats.

where the moderate Republicans were in a majority of nineteen against eleven, and with the Democrats the region cast twenty-five votes against Radicalism. In sharp contrast was the 'new' Midwest of States admitted in and after 1837 — Michigan, Iowa, Wisconsin, Minnesota and Kansas — where every Republican vote save one from Michigan was cast on the Radical side. Finally the two Radical votes from California strengthen the impression that Radicalism had a strong appeal in recently settled areas. From this analysis it appears that the two great Radical strongholds were in Pennsylvania and the 'new' Midwest. Other areas in which Radicalism showed strength were the more rural part of New England and in two former slave States, Maryland and Missouri. Taken together these areas contributed 39 of the 65 Radical votes. Outside the three States already mentioned Radicalism was in a minority, though the balance of forces in Massachusetts was fairly even. The areas of moderate predominance were first and foremost New York, then the 'old' Midwest, and the Midwest border States; together these regions provided no less than 46 of the 53 moderate Republican votes. If Pennsylvania is left out of account Radicalism appeared as the political programme of the more recently settled and rural areas; old settled areas, especially those with a number of developing towns and diversified economic activities, tended to be anti-Radical. Here perhaps is a hitherto unsuspected influence of the frontier upon American history.

Urban Radicalism was a significant factor in Philadelphia, which produced three Radical votes, and one vote each came from Baltimore, Chicago, St Louis and Cincinnati. Three moderate Republicans and one Democrat came from New York city, two from Boston, and one each from St Louis, Providence and Cincinnati with one Democrat from Philadelphia. Thus the big cities voted ten to seven against Radicalism; the margin was not great but may have some significance.

When attempts at separating moderates from Radicals have been made there must still remain elements of doubt. Both appealed to the same traditions and often employed the same slogans, and the line which divided them was often one of temperament and emphasis rather than of fundamental attitudes. James A. Garfield, who cast a vote against Radicalism on 28 January 1867 once described his position as trying to be a Radical without being a fool.[1] Spalding, another Ohio moderate, complained in 1866 that he had recently been styled the 'great radical of Ohio' but was now being attacked as 'somewhat conservative'.[2] William Pitt Fessenden, the most influential man in the Senate, might be defined as a Radical if one looked at his votes, but a moderate if one took into account his cautious and practical temperament and his later vote for the acquittal of Andrew Johnson in the impeachment trial. Somewhere in the middle of the Republican spectrum there was a distinction to be made between the men who hoped that Johnson's restoration plus 'guarantees' would suffice, and those who believed that the character of Southern society must be changed before the Union could be safe or the negro free; but the mildest 'guarantee' involved some trespass on State rights, so that there was a natural bridge between Republican moderation and Republican Radicalism which did not exist between the moderates and those who believed in the Constitution as it was.

It is tempting to represent the Radical Republicans as a Jacobin minority, riding the crest of a revolutionary wave, and winning their way because they knew where they were going and expressed in precise terms the assumptions which the moderate majority had implicitly accepted. The truth in this analysis is, however, qualified by the facts of American political life, and it is more accurate to say that the Radicals approached as near as was possible to the 'Jacobin' model within the American framework. The actions of any vigorous minority were circumscribed by the American political system; they could never hope to wield executive authority which is essential to 'Jacobin' success, and their chances of winning a congressional majority would depend upon skill, argument and accident rather than upon any coercive

[1] Mary L. Hinsdale (ed.), *Garfield-Hinsdale Letters: Correspondence between James A. Garfield and Burke A. Hinsdale* (Ann Arbor, 1949), p. 396, letter of 1 Jan. 1867.
[2] C.G. 39.2.290.

instrument in their own hands. They might hope to capture the
central machinery of the party, but this was so weak, and its
powers so amorphous, that little could be done with it alone, and
real successes in American politics are to be won in presidential
elections and in the struggles for power within the separate States.
The Radicals had a glimmer of hope that they would do the first
when Ben Wade stood next in succession to the impeached
Johnson, but their hold upon individual States was always
insecure and the more they talked negro suffrage the less secure
were they likely to be. Like other American political groupings
the Radicals were alliances which depended upon circumstances,
and this limited the rate at which they could advance and the
cohesion which they could preserve; but unlike most other
American political groupings their cement was not interest but a
number of propositions about equality, rights, and national
power. G. W. Julian, old abolitionist, ardent Radical and active
Indiana politician, described the driving power behind Radicalism
in these words: 'Radicalism squarely met the issue tendered by the
Conservatives. That slavery caused the war and was necessarily
involved in its fortunes it accepted as a simple truism. Its theory
was that the rebellion *was* slavery, in arms against the nation, and
that to strike it was to strike treason, and to spare it was to espouse
the cause of the rebels. In the very beginning of the conflict
Radicalism comprehended the situation and the duty. . . . It
understood the conflict as not simply a struggle to save the
Union, but a grand and final battle for the rights of man, now and
hereafter; and it believed that God would never smile upon our
endeavours till we accepted it as such.'[1] For Radicals the task of
Reconstruction was to set the seal of law upon their victory for
the rights of man, and men who had accepted the idea that the
war should produce a better nation found it difficult to resist their
arguments.

Charles Sumner and Thaddeus Stevens, who have been always
associated together as the leaders of Radicalism, possessed vastly
different temperaments and exercised a very different kind of

[1] C.G. 39.1.3208–9.

influence. In March 1865 the *World* observed that 'when Mr Sumner makes an elaborate speech in the Senate, we have usually found, in the end, that the dominating idea of the speaker becomes a rule of policy for the Republican party. Oftentimes, the sentiments are, at first, unacceptable to the faithful members of that organization, and among those who flatter themselves with the idea that they can be members of a radical party, and yet conservative at heart, there is opposition, decided and outspoken; but all this antagonism to Massachusetts ideas, is, in due time, compelled to succumb under the whip of party drill'.[1] This is a fair description of Sumner's relationship to his party but completely inaccurate in its reference to the 'whip of party drill'. Sumner wielded no whips, and in the strict sense of party management he led no one. As the *World* remarked, his ideas always aroused antagonism within his party, and the correspondence of Republican politicians is filled with scathing references to Sumner's wild impracticability. As a later eulogist observed, 'he did not possess the peculiar ability of constructing politics in detail, of taking account of existing circumstances, and advantage of opportunities'.[2] No one, indeed, could give a stronger appearance of wrecking a policy by saying the right thing at the wrong time in the wrong way; yet it is equally true that almost everything for which he fought eventually came to pass and sometimes through the agency of the 'conservatives' who had condemned him most freely. It was this relation to the currents of opinion in his time, rather than any contriving of his own, which placed him 'foremost among the propelling, driving forces which pushed on the great work with undaunted courage, untiring effort, irresistible energy, and religious devotion'.[3] What weakened Sumner as a politician and made him so irritating as a man was his consciousness of this transcendental role: he *was* the personification of a moral idea and

[1] *World*, 7 Mar. 1865.
[2] Schurz, *Eulogy*, 51. George Boutwell recalled how he had visited Sumner and found him trying to draft a form of words for the proposed Fourteenth Amendment. 'He read seventeen drafts of a proposition not one of which was entirely satisfactory to himself, and not one of which would have been accepted by Congress or the country' (*Reminiscences of Sixty Years in Public Affairs* (New York, 1902), p. 42).
[3] Schurz, *Eulogy*, 52.

this made him infallible. No one could argue with Sumner because his conversation consisted of a monologue, and usually of a rehearsed monologue.[1] What was often described as his vanity deserves a name which gives a better indication of its power; what characterized Sumner was not self-satisfaction but an intense satisfaction with the things in which he believed. His vanity was the vanity of a prophet convinced that he did not speak with the tongues of men. The great moral and public figure had long ago swallowed the human being as his disastrous marriage demonstrated. He had indeed lost the facility for communicating with other men save at the level of oratory, and he had come to live in a world of his own making in which the forces of evil could always be easily identified and the course of rectitude discovered with equal ease.

Yet Sumner was a humane and intelligent man. He always professed that his hatred of the South was directed against a system and not against individuals. When it was proposed in January 1865 to retaliate against Southern prisoners for wrongs done to Northern prisoners in Southern camps Sumner protested that it could be for no one's good 'that our country should do an unworthy thing'; the rebellion, he said, was nothing but the 'barbarism of slavery' armed, and 'plainly it is our duty to overcome it; not to imitate it. And here I stand'.[2] He always opposed punishment for individual Confederate leaders for their part in the rebellion. In later years he was able to demonstrate that he had always favoured reconciliation. In November 1861 he had defended emancipation because it was the only road to harmony, for 'only through such reconciliation, under the sanction of freedom,

---

[1] Senator Fessenden disliked Sumner very much. *World* for 12 Mar., in its congressional report, recorded the following conversation which did not find its way into the *Congressional Globe*. Sumner was attempting to make a speech after a motion had been made to go into executive session, and was called to order by Fessenden.

Mr Sumner: I understand the rules of the Senate.

Mr Fessenden: Oh! yes; you understand everything, but some of the rest of us have rights as well as you.

Mr Sumner said he believed that he was in order, in stating, on a question of going into Executive Session, why the Senate should remain in open session.

Mr Fessenden: Oh, yes; you are always in order!

[2] C.G. 38.2.474, 28 Jan. 1865.

can you remove all occasions of conflict hereafter'.[1] In May 1862
he had unsuccessfully proposed that civil war victories should not
be preserved as battle honours on regimental flags because this
would keep alive animosity after the war. In the same month he
declared that 'people talk flippantly of the gallows as the certain
doom of rebels. This is a mistake. For weal or woe, the gallows is
out of the question. It is not possible as a punishment for this
rebellion. . . . In this work it is needless to say there is no place
for any sentiment of hate or any suggestion of vengeance'.[2] He
was transparently honest and 'there was in him not the faintest
shadow of dissimulation, disguise, or trickery'.[3] He would always
say what he thought, and this was a handicap as a politician; but
in Congress the quality of indiscretion was modified by his
reluctance to speak at all except in a formal and prepared oration.
His method was to propose something in the form of a bill or
resolution, without any elaboration of detail, and to proceed
directly to the discussion of principle; as a measure cannot become
law without drafting in detail Sumner, for all his voluminous
speeches, left singularly little impression upon the statute book.
No great measure is associated with his name, and he played very
little part in the tedious business of discussion and amendment
by which a proposed bill was hacked into shape in Congress.[4]

Yet for the moment no one could ignore Sumner's influence.
His tall commanding figure, the intensity of his moral convictions
and his long identification with the anti-slavery cause made him a
heroic figure. If at close quarters he seemed to be obsessed with
his own righteousness, incapable of understanding others, and
oblivious to practical difficulties, to the world at large he appeared
as a prophet with honour in his own country. Everything which
he had foretold had come to pass, and when he spoke of the future

---

[1] These points were selected by Sumner himself for a speech intended to be delivered at
Faneuil Hall, Boston, 2 Sep. 1872. *Works*, XV.

[2] From his own notes of a speech to be delivered at Faneuil Hall, 3 Sep. 1872; *Works*,
XV, referring to a speech on 19 May 1862.

[3] Schurz, *Eulogy*, 62.

[4] Boutwell said that after twenty-three years in the Senate 'the only mark that he left upon
the Statutes is an amendment to the law relating to naturalization by which Mongolians are
excluded from citizenship. The object of his amendment was to save negroes from the exclusive features of the Statute which was designed to apply only to Chinese (*Sixty Years*, 98)'.

no one could afford to ignore what he said. Sumner has been mis-
interpreted as a leader of party; in fact he was less than this as a
politician and far more as a national figure. He was the spokesman
of a movement which had transcended politics.

Thaddeus Stevens had a career and a character such as men in
an age conscious of psychoanalysis would hardly wish to expose.
He idolized his mother and talked about her frequently even in
later life, but of his father he said, 'I know little about him in
respect to the quality of his mind, but he had the reputation of
being able to throw down any man in Caledonia county'.[1] He
himself was of powerful physique but a club-foot had cut him off
from the world of men who threw each other down. He never
married and numerous stories circulated about his sexual irregu-
larities which he never attempted to deny but which his friends
believed to be largely untrue; for many years he had a mulatto
housekeeper who was believed to be his mistress but it is possible
that her main duty in life was simply to look after the old man.
He was abstemious and a non-smoker, but he had a passion for
gambling. He loved flattery and as he grew older his desire for
praise became a mania even while he avowed a cynical belief in
the untruthfulness of men. He always responded to charitable
appeals, sometimes without much inquiry about the credentials
of the appellant; he compensated for this generosity after he had
given by finding fault with the object or with the person who had
asked. He liked to appear rich but in his private life he seemed to
care little about money. In debate he was probably one of the most
formidable men who have appeared on the American scene. In
contrast to the florid oratory of the day his speeches were brief,
often brutally clear, and left nothing unsaid. He rarely introduced
an appeal to sentiment, but could be very effective when he
did so. He had an excellent memory, and he was at his best

[1] Much of the material for this character sketch is drawn from an elaborate assessment
of him which is found in the Stevens Papers, Library of Congress, Vol. 16. It is very
perceptive and may have been written by E. A. McPherson, who knew him well and who
was collecting material for his life. The best biography is Fawn M. Brodie, *Thaddeus
Stevens: Scourge of the South* (New York, 1959). R. N. Current, *Old Thad Stevens*
(Madison, 1942) is useful for its material but is too unsympathetic to explain Stevens as an
individual. Ralph Korngold, *Thaddeus Stevens*, (New York, 1955) is, by contrast, too sympathetic, but his chapters on Reconstruction are useful.

when brought suddenly into argument and forced to use his powers of repartee. Strong men quailed before the lash of his tongue as before whips and scorpions, but it should be remembered that the effect of sarcasm depends upon isolating the victim from the crowd; the power of Stevens's language was derived in part from his facility for saying sharply what other men felt. After his death a candid friend wrote, 'We have denied to Mr Stevens pre-eminence in intellect, culture and eloquence. It remains to show wherein his great strength lay. His parliamentary qualifications, his tact, his wonderful readiness of repartee, his ferocity of invective, his acknowledged vigor of intellect, will not wholly account for his position as, during reconstruction, if not during the war, the most influential character in American politics. The secret of his strength, we imagine, is to be found in that source to which mere politicians so seldom look — his high, all-embracing devotion to a noble idea.'[1]

As an opponent of slavery and as an advocate of equality the record of Stevens was impeccable; he had led a battle for negro suffrage in Pennsylvania as early as 1826, he had fought for the establishment of free common schools, and in Congress he had shown as unyielding an opposition to compromise as Calhoun himself. When he claimed that his whole life had been inspired by the Declaration of Independence no one accused him of hypocrisy, and when he appeared to yield a point no one believed that he had for one moment relaxed his ultimate purpose. With this ultimate inflexibility Stevens combined great flexibility in manoeuvre; he would make a move but if it became apparent that it could not carry he was ready to desist and approach from another direction. He made no secret of the fact that he regarded

[1] L. Cortissoz, *Whitelaw Reid*, 134. Representative Cake of Pennsylvania described how Stevens had pressed him to change his vote against an appropriation for a College in the District of Columbia, and later said to him, 'Young man, let me implore you in all your after life never to oppose any measure for the education of the people. Follow this advice and you will never regret it' (C.G. 40.3.140). Kelley said that his notorious scheme for the confiscation of rebel estates was not intended as a punishment; 'He was incapable of a vindictive act. He regarded the system of land monopoly, which had prevailed in the South, as the essential support of slavery, and he would abolish it. . . . He knew that a landed aristocracy and a landless class are alike dangerous in a republic, and by a single act of justice he would abolish both.'

the Fourteenth Amendment, when it had finally emerged from ordeal by Congress, as a defective measure but he pressed for its adoption because he had been convinced that it was the best that could be obtained. He was prepared to shelve negro suffrage, and to drop a favourite plan for the confiscation of rebel estates when opinion was against him: by contrast Sumner would never let go or let up once he had become convinced, and nor, for that matter, would Andrew Johnson. Because Stevens was himself sure of his own inner consistency, and because others gave him credit for it, he was able to play the game of politics with men as they were and not as they ought to be.

Yet with all his power in Congress and in the Republican party it would be wrong to over-estimate what Stevens could do. He had only a small, though devoted, personal following; he commanded no patronage; he could compel no man to do what he did not wish to do. His power depended upon his personality not upon his position. What the rank and file congressman feared most was the ability which Stevens possessed of saying the biting thing which would find its way into the newspapers at home and which might be remembered by their constituents when their own more worthy services were forgotten. Stevens could damage a congressman in his party organization in his State, but only because he appealed to ideas which belonged to the common stock of Northern opinion. The true secret of his power lay in the conviction with which he was able to tell the Northern people that 'Having crushed into atoms the ephemeral empire, whose cornerstone was slavery, they will establish a united and enduring nation on the solid foundation of universal freedom. Such a nation possessing the most fertile soil and every variety of climate, will soon abound with untold riches, and will swarm with millions of just, intelligent and brave freemen, who will bid defiance to all the despots of the earth'.[1] On the one hand was this

---

[1] Speech at Lancaster, Pennsylvania, 22 Jan. 1864. Georges Clemenceau was the Washington correspondent of the Paris *Temps*, and left a good sketch of Stevens's power. In *American Reconstruction, 1865–1870*, ed. F. Baldensperger, trans. Margaret MacVeagh, (New York, 1928) he wrote that the Radicals 'will forever have the glorious distinction of having led to a successful conclusion the far-reaching revolution through which the

promise of the future and on the other a return to past frustration which was promised by conservatism; this was the contrast which Stevens exploited with such skill, but it was not one manufactured by him but planted by the war in Northern minds.

Though Sumner and Stevens are often the only names heard in text-book accounts of Reconstruction they stood amid a remarkable group of self-made politicians.[1] Amongst them one of the most forceful was Senator Ben Wade, who had been born in 1800 of an old but poor family on a small Massachusetts farm and received little formal education. In 1821 Wade moved to Ohio and followed various occupations before beginning the study of law in 1825; with a rapidity which might be the envy of lawyers in more settled societies he was called to the bar in 1827 or 1828 and joined the firm of Joshua Giddings at the very fountainhead of political abolitionism. He became a State senator, then a judge, and in 1851 was sent to the United States Senate where he was soon recognized as an anti-slavery leader. During the war he was chairman of the key Committee on the Conduct of the War. Wade was vigorous, impulsive and likeable; men deprecated his rough methods of speech and distrusted his judgment but never questioned his sincerity and integrity. In 1864 Gideon Welles, though thinking that 'the old man was a little acrimonious towards the President', found Wade 'very pleasant and affable'. In 1868, when much water had flowed under the Reconstruction bridge Welles lamented that 'Wade has become

country has just passed' (p. 97, 10 Aug. 1867). Of Stevens he wrote 'Devoted heart and soul to the service of one ideal, the immediate abolition of slavery, he threw his whole self with no reserve and no personal afterthoughts into the cause he had chosen. . . . It must be admitted that Mr Stevens stands out as a man of only one idea, but that does not matter a whit, since he had the glory of defending that idea when it was trodden in the dust, and the joy of contributing largely to its triumph. That should be enough accomplishment for one man, when the cause to which he has devoted his life and his soul is that of justice' (p. 226).

[1] Most of the information which follows is drawn from the *Dictionary of American Biography* and the *Biographical Directory of the American Congress* supplemented where indicated in the footnotes. A great deal of work remains to be done on congressional biography, and the character of Republicanism, and of Radicalism in particular, will not be fully understood until biography has been firmly placed in its social setting. What follows is therefore tentative, speculative and based on incomplete evidence; but as I read through the secondary sources I began to form a strong and coherent impression of Radical leadership and it seemed worthwhile to convey this impression in the same way.

demoralized, and is not the plain, single-minded, honest, un-ambitious man he was a few years since'.[1]

Senator Henry Wilson of Massachusetts had been born as Jeremiah Colbath in 1812 on a very poor New England farm. At the age of twenty he changed his name to Henry Wilson, and established himself as a shoemaker at Natick in Massachusetts; here he built up a considerable business and the 'cobbler of Natick' was actually a successful employer of some hundred men. His happy relations with his work-people foreshadowed the future career of one who was to prove himself the canniest vote-getter in all New England and to rise to the highest positions without ever losing touch with the simple voters of his State. Throughout his adolescence he had been an omnivorous reader, and in spite of his lack of education became a widely informed man. He entered State politics as a Whig Free Soiler and was for a time editor of the anti-slavery *Boston Republican*. For a short period, which he was always to regret, he joined the Know-Nothings but withdrew in protest against their intolerance and refusal to adopt anti-slavery views. It was nevertheless a largely Know-Nothing vote which secured him, in 1855, election to the Senate of the United States, but once there he proved a natural recruit for the Repub-licans and played a much more effective part than Sumner in establishing the new party in Massachusetts. During the war he was a vigorous and efficient chairman of the Military Affairs Committee. The respect and even affection with which Wilson was regarded in his State was indisputable, and more than any other man he reflected the opinions of the rural and small town New Englanders. He would travel from one end of Massachusetts to the other, calling at farms, stores, workshops and private houses; always affable, always observant, and always distilling the opinions and prejudices which he encountered. When diffi-cult matters were under discussion he might, for a period, appear anxious, uncertain and indecisive but 'at length when the time came, and he had got ready, the easterly cloud seemed suddenly to have been charged with an electric fire and a swift and resistless

[1] Beale (ed.), *Diary of Gideon Welles*, II, 198; III, 362.

bolt flashed out, and the righteous judgment of Massachusetts came from his lips'.[1] Political effectiveness combined with moral certainty made Wilson a man of power, and a younger colleague believed that no man 'in the Senate in his time, not even Sumner, had more influence over his colleagues than he'.[2]

Senator Zachary Chandler of Michigan was a less attractive man than Wade or Wilson. Like them he was born in rural New England and had only a rudimentary education; unlike them the strain of idealism, if ever present, was so deeply buried in the art of a business-politician as to be invisible to most observers. Born in 1813 he moved twenty years later to Detroit, established a general store, and eventually became a very wealthy man with extensive interests in trade, banking and land speculation. He was a founder member of the Republican party and was elected to the Senate in 1856. He was a member of the Joint Committee on the Conduct of the War. As a result of the war he became aggressively anti-British, and in January 1866 he attempted unsuccessfully to persuade the Senate to adopt a resolution calling for non-intercourse with Great Britain in retaliation against her refusal to consider the *Alabama* claims. Chandler's power as a senator lay, however, in his chairmanship from 1861 to 1875 of the Committee on Commerce from which position he controlled the channels by which Federal money flowed into the expanding economy of the Middle-West. He used this position as a lever to cement his own political power in Michigan, and constituents could often be persuaded to instruct their delegates in the State legislature or at party conventions to support Chandler whatever their private opinions of the man.[3] He was one of the large number of politicians who earned the censure of Gideon Welles for excessive

---

[1] Hoar, *Autobiography of Seventy Years*, II, 217.   [2] Ibid.

[3] In 1875, when Chandler was fighting for re-election by the State legislature, he let it be known in the district of a hostile Republican that a bill for the improvement of the Paw Paw River 'should receive his tenderest care'. The representative then found himself under pressure from his electors and announced that he was changing his vote 'as he could in this way serve his constituents in a vital matter'. On the same occasion another representative announced that 'contrary to my convictions but in response to a petition signed by 412 of my constituents, and to the persistent demands of a lobby twice as large, I vote for Zachariah Chandler'. (W. C. Harris, *The Public Life of Zachariah Chandler*, 126 ff.) In spite of these efforts Chandler was defeated for re-election by a combination of Democrats and dissatisfied Republicans.

whisky drinking, but he has left no record of pleasant con-
viviality.[1] His unattractive character naturally appeals to those
who wish to discredit rather than to understand Radicalism, and
on occasions his name is even joined with those of Stevens and
Sumner as an author of the Reconstruction policy; but he did not
speak on Reconstruction questions and it is impossible to detect
his hand in the formulation of policy. The more interesting
question is why a man such as Chandler should have been a
Radical, and the answer lies partly in former Southern obstruction to the expansive economic aims of the new Midwest and
partly in the popularity of Radicalism with his Michigan constituents.

Two other Senators, J. H. Howard of Michigan and Timothy
Howe of Wisconsin, played a prominent part in Reconstruction
debates on the Radical side. Howard was born in Vermont in 1805
and moved to Michigan in 1833; he was first a Whig, then an
original member of the Republican party, and became a senator
in 1862. He was a man of some culture with a good knowledge of
law and literature, and had translated Marie Anne le Normand's
Historical and Secret Memoirs of the Empress Josephine into
English. Howe was born in Maine, the son of a doctor, was
educated at the Maine Wesleyan Seminary, studied law, and moved
to Wisconsin in 1845. He became a conservative Whig in politics
and incurred the displeasure of the local anti-slavery men by
insisting that the State ought to honour her obligations under the
Fugitive Slave Law. He was, however, elected to the Senate in
1861 as a Unionist, and under the impact of war his opinions
rapidly became more radical; by the time of the Reconstruction
controversy he was a supporter of negro suffrage and showed a
good grasp of the constitutional implications of Radicalism. He
was a hard money man, and after Reconstruction his career ran
on orthodox Republican lines to the Postmaster-Generalship
under President Arthur.

---

[1] Gideon Welles said that 'Chandler is steeped and steamed in whiskey, coarse, vulgar
and reckless' (Beale (ed.), *Diary of Gideon Welles*, II, 633). In Feb. 1867 he attributed
Chandler's opposition to anger 'because he cannot dictate all the Michigan appointments'.
Ibid., III, 53.

Two of the most influential Republican senators who usually voted with the Radicals but showed a conservative strain which led them to vote for Johnson's acquittal in the impeachment trial, were W. P. Fessenden of Maine and J. W. Grimes of Iowa. Of Fessenden it will be necessary to say something at greater length hereafter, but Grimes may be mentioned here. He was born in New Hampshire, but not like some of his colleagues in the depths of rural poverty; he attended Dartmouth College though without staying long enough to take a degree, studied law, and moved to Iowa in 1836. He was a member of the first Territorial legislature and in 1854 became Whig governor of the State, making a distinguished record in a tenure which saw a revision of the Constitution, the removal of the State capital from Iowa City to the commercial centre at Des Moines, the permanent establishment of a State university, the creation of a free system of public education and of State institutions for the deaf and dumb, the blind and the insane, and the enactment of prohibition laws. He joined the Republicans in 1856 and was largely responsible for placing his State firmly in the ranks of the new party. He joined the Senate in 1859 and became chairman of the Committee on Naval Affairs, in which position he saw much of Gideon Welles who thought that he had 'very respectable talents but of a suspicious jealous nature, inclining to be misanthropic'.[1] He had an intense dislike of Sumner and Stevens, and though he spoke little on Reconstruction matters he worked closely with Fessenden in trying to steer policy along lines which would incorporate the main points of Radical policy without the excesses of Radical zeal. In common with a good many other Western Republicans he became increasingly critical of the high tariff policy.[2]

In the House one of the most articulate and attractive of the Radicals was William D. Kelley of Philadelphia. He was an

---

[1] Beale (ed.), *Diary of Gideon Welles*, II, 447.

[2] C.G. 39.2.696, 24 Jan. 1867. Grimes asked what the tariff policy meant and answered, 'It means that two or three large manufacturing interests in the country, not satisfied with the enormous profits they have realized during the last six years, are determined at whatever hazard to put more money in their pockets; and to this end they have persuaded some and coerced other manufacturing interests to unite with them in a great combination demand for what they call protection to American labor, but what some others call robbery of the American laborer and agriculturalist'.

admirer and faithful lieutenant of Thaddeus Stevens but expressed his Radicalism with a warmth and human sympathy which was often lacking in the older man. He was born in 1814. His father had been a leading jeweller in Philadelphia but failed in 1812 and died in the year of his son's birth, so that William D. Kelley's early years were passed in poverty. He was apprenticed to the family craft and became an accomplished gold and silversmith, but while learning this trade he was also studying law and was admitted to the bar in 1841. In 1847, as a Democrat, he was appointed to a State judgeship and was continued in office when, as a result of constitutional changes in 1851, the post became elective; for the rest of his life he was usually known as Judge Kelley. He joined the Republican party in the first year of its formation, won election to Congress in 1860, and was subsequently re-elected fourteen times for the same Philadelphia constituency; at the time of his death in 1890 he had a longer continuous service as a representative than any other man live or dead.[1] Enthusiasm was the keynote of Kelley's political character and, more than any other man, his speeches carry a sense of the buoyancy and idealism of early Republicanism. Welles thought that he had determination, and zeal but not profound or correct ideas; he thought him 'sincere and a better man than many others, but yet not always safe or sound'.[2] This was high praise from Welles for a man who was a fervent opponent of Johnson's Reconstruction policy, an earnest advocate of negro suffrage, an ardent protectionist, and, to top his other heresies, a convinced and eloquent greenbacker. In later years Kelley was to distinguish himself mainly as a protectionist and the nickname 'Pig Iron Kelley', which has passed into the text-books, conveys the impression of a hard and self-interested man; in fact his protectionism, like his other enthusiasms, sprang from a somewhat naïve idealism. He had no personal interests in iron and steel, and for him the appeal of the high tariff lay in the protection which it provided for labour and the small entrepreneur. His honesty

[1] This point was made several times in the eulogies on Kelley when his death was announced. *Congressional Record*, 51st Congress, 1st Session, 2276 ff.
[2] Beale (ed.), *Diary of Gideon Welles*, II, 413.

was transparent even when wrong-headed, and the mists of free-trade moralism should not obscure either his integrity or the broad emotional appeal of the protectionism which he preached.

By all accounts George S. Boutwell was not, like Kelley, an attractive man. His reputation was that of a cold and calculating person without human sympathy; he was consistent in his support of extreme Radicalism and particularly of negro suffrage, but never succeeded in conveying to others any sense of generous enthusiasm. In a pattern which is becoming familiar in this review of Radical leaders he was born in a poor New England family and had a rudimentary education supplemented by self-education. He began work at the age of thirteen, and in 1837, at the age of seventeen, moved to Groton, Massachusetts, and obtained employment as a clerk in a general store. He began to write political articles, became active in the local Democratic party, and from 1842 to 1850 represented Groton in the State Assembly. In 1850 he played a leading part in the alliance between Democrats and Free Soilers which sent Sumner to the Senate and made himself Governor. He was re-elected in 1852 and by 1855 was active in the Republican party. For a short period in 1862–3 he was an efficient Commissioner of the Inland Revenue and then entered Congress. He was probably one of the best 'men of business' in the Republican party, with an extensive though pedestrian knowledge of finance, but he was also one of the most active opponents of Johnson and a leading spirit in the impeachment. In 1869 Grant made him Secretary of the Treasury where he distinguished himself by a successful programme of debt reduction, which he regarded as a great moral objective, and by his hostility to civil service reform. In all, Boutwell seems to have been representative of that type of New Englander which would later produce its most distinguished son in Calvin Coolidge. Yet it is fair to Boutwell that he began his political career as the spokesman of one unpopular cause and ended it as the leader of another; for the last seven years of his life he was President of the Anti-Imperialist League formed to resist the annexation of the Phillipines.

Elihu B. Washburn did not vote on 28 January 1867 when the

Radicals stood up to be counted, and the abstention may have been deliberate; he did not play any part in the Reconstruction debates though he was a member of the Joint Committee on Reconstruction and his correspondence in the Library of Congress shows that he maintained a close interest in happenings in the South. Though not important in the formulation of policy he nevertheless occupied a key position in the Republican party for it so happened that his constituency, Galena in Illinois, was the home town of General Grant and Washburn had been the general's sponsor in the early days of the war and more recently his closest link with political life. Washburn's comparatively inactive role in Reconstruction probably arose from his reluctance to entangle the Grant candidature for the Presidency too closely with any one wing of the party, but on most occasions he followed the Radical line and was probably instrumental in leading the General gently away from Johnson and towards Radicalism. Washburn was born in Maine in 1816; his parents owned a small country store and he and his very able brothers were left to make their own ways in the world. From farmwork and teaching he got to the Harvard Law School in 1839, and in the following year moved to Galena which was then a pioneer lead-mining town. He became prominent in the Whig party as an ardent Clay man, and in 1844 nominated his leader at the Baltimore Convention. He entered Congress in 1853 and became a Republican. His great interest in politics was in government economy, and his persistent scrutiny of expenditure inevitably earned him the nickname of watch-dog of the Treasury. He was also an active opponent of the railroad corporations in the Midwest, and had a long-standing feud with the Illinois Central. He was to close his political career in an unexpected blaze of excitement as Minister to France during the Franco-Prussian War.

Two Western lawyers who played an active part in Reconstruction policy were James F. Wilson of Iowa and George H. Williams of Oregon. Wilson was born at Newark in Ohio and moved to Iowa in 1852 when twenty-four years old. He was largely self-educated but became a prominent and well-informed lawyer. He entered the House of Representatives in 1861 and, sharing in the rapid promotion enjoyed by many young Republicans, became chairman of the Judiciary Committee. In this position he had a key part to play in framing the Thirteenth Amendment and in helping to draft other important Reconstruction measures. His speeches show him to have been a thoughtful man with a good perception of the wider issues involved in the controversy. Williams was born in 1820 at New Lebanon in New York and became a lawyer; he moved to Iowa in 1844 and in 1852 was appointed Chief Justice of Oregon Territory where he remained to take a leading part in the affairs of the new State. In 1860 he was a Douglas Democrat, but was elected to the Senate as a Unionist-Republican in 1864. He was soon in good standing with the Republican leadership and was appointed to the Joint Committee on Reconstruction; he had an important and formative role in making the Reconstruction acts, but his work seems to have been that of a draftsman and interpreter of Radical policy rather than that of an initiator. He became Grant's Attorney-General in 1871 but in 1875 the Senate refused to accept his nomination as Chief Justice of the Supreme Court. At the end of his long life (he died in 1910) he was a supporter of the 'Oregon system' of democratic reform fathered by William U'Ren, and thus moved a full circle from Western Democracy, through Radical Republicanism, to Progressive Republicanism.

One Radical leader, and one of the most resilient figures in American politics, was outside Congress (though about to be elected in 1866). Benjamin Franklin Butler made more considerable enemies than most men, but retained, throughout his long and erratic career, the support of poor voters in the industrial areas of Massachusetts.[1] He was born in 1818, studied law and was called to the bar in 1840. He became a notoriously successful criminal defence lawyer and a terror not to the evil-doer but to the honest but confused witness. He entered politics as a Democrat, was

[1] There is an interesting but very hostile account of Butler in Hoar, *Autobiography of Seventy Years*, II, 330 ff. There was a standing feud between Butler and the Hoar family; cf. Benjamin F. Butler, *Butler's Book* (Boston, 1892), 925–6.

elected to the lower House of the Massachusetts Assembly in 1853 and to the State Senate in 1859, depending largely upon the support of labour and Roman Catholics. He played a leading part at the ill-fated Charleston Democratic Convention in 1860, and again at the Baltimore Convention, and finally came out for Breckinridge. At this stage he was a nationalist of the Jacksonian school and on Lincoln's call to arms he immediately took a Massachusetts militia regiment, which he had previously formed, to Washington. During the war, in which he became a Major-General with even fewer military qualifications than most Federal officers, his career was startling. His fame or notoriety rested upon three things: to solve the embarrassing problem, for Federal commanders, of what to do with slaves escaped from Confederate masters he ordered that they should be treated in his Command as 'contraband property'; as military Governor of New Orleans he achieved a reputation for brutal efficiency and left a name forever odious to Southern ears by ordering that Southern ladies who insulted Federal soldiers should be treated as common prostitutes; and as commander of an amphibious operation against Fort Fisher he committed an inexplicable error of judgment which led to the withdrawal of his force against the advice of his naval colleague and in direct contravention of orders given him by Grant. Throughout his war service he was followed by rumours of corrupt dealings, bribe taking and even plain theft; in assessing these unproven accusations it is fair to remember that wherever Butler went he made enemies who wanted nothing better than to ruin his reputation. The disgrace of Fort Fisher would have ruined most men, but in public life Butler was never defeated and he remained a powerful man among the New England working class. Hardly was he saved from the possibility of a Court Martial than he was pushing himself as a candidate for cabinet office, and had actually enlisted the support of Ben Wade in this project.[1] He was chosen for Congress in the election of

---

[1] L.C. *Butler Papers*, Butler to Wade, 1 Mar. 1865. 'There is a possibility that in the commotion, the Radicals may get a member of the Cabinet if they will accept me as such.' He did not want 'an open movement evoking opposition' but a quiet one. His efforts were increased after Lincoln's death.

1866, and was soon to the fore as an enemy of the President; he opened the case for the prosecution in the impeachment trial, but he also devoted a good deal of his energy to fighting against a return to the gold standard. He was to end his extraordinary career as the Greenback-Labor candidate for President in 1884.

Was Butler a scoundrel or an able and much maligned man who encountered one major misfortune? His support for the Union was early and consistent; once converted to the idea of negro equality he never repudiated it; his advocacy of the greenbacks eventually made him a political outlaw; and none of the slanders against him were ever substantiated. Was he an opportunist who ruined his chances by taking the wrong opportunities at the wrong time, or was there a bedrock of conviction? Whatever the answers to these questions Butler strikes a discordant note in the Radical orchestra; he was a popular demagogue in touch with the new stirrings of industrial democracy.

In contrast to Butler one can cite another restless man, a member of the Thirty-ninth Congress and a perennial reformer whose life touched upon almost every political crusade which agitated the nineteenth century. George Washington Julian was born in Indiana in 1817; his father was a man of modest means but of some local influence who died in 1823. Julian was brought up by his widowed mother and received only a rudimentary education; but in an age when the legal profession was open to talents he was able to gain sufficient training to be called to the bar in 1840. By 1845 he was in the State legislature as a Whig, but abolitionist convictions led him into the Free Soil party in 1848 and as their representative in Congress he was an opponent of the 1850 compromise. He was the vice-presidential candidate of the Free Soil party in 1852 and, as might have been expected, was an early and active member of the Republican party. He did not get back to Congress until 1860 but he was given a place on the Committee on the Conduct of the War and made chairman of the Committee on Public Lands; in the latter position he had considerable influence upon the making of the Homestead Act of 1862 and had ever after a close interest in and knowledge of

Western land problems. During Reconstruction he made some important speeches and had a special position as a spokesman of the old Midwestern abolitionists. He did much to make negro suffrage acceptable to his section. Besides his firm advocacy of racial equality he was an equally consistent spokesman for the rarer cause of equality between the sexes. He became a Liberal Republican in 1872, supported Tilden in 1876, and poured out a great number of articles on reform topics. Grover Cleveland made him Surveyor-General of New Mexico where his reforming instinct and his knowledge of land problems enabled him to root out many frauds. As a Radical Republican and as a Cleveland Democrat he was at the centre of an established political movement, but most of his life was passed as a critic and outsider. He was the type of man who is unlikely and unfitted to direct the affairs of state, but without whom the health of any political society is likely to be the poorer.

This survey of Radical leadership is instructive. Wade, the oldest of them, was sixty-five at the close of the war, and the youngest, James F. Wilson, was thirty seven; all the others were between forty-five and fifty-three. Most of them were qualified to cast their first votes for presidential electors in 1840; the great issues during their politically formative years were the depression of 1837–43, the frustration of the Whigs by Tyler's strict construction, abolitionist petitions and the gag rule, Texas, the Mexican war and the Wilmot proviso. The impact of these events must be seen upon a typical life history: rural New England, early poverty, handicaps overcome by self-education and migration, the law or occasionally business as the key to success, early involvement in State politics as Whigs or Free Soil Democrats, and an enthusiastic welcome for Republicanism. Most of them had been intimately concerned with the fortunes of fast growing communities in which the rural flavour was still strong, but which depended for their growth upon the resources and skills of a developed capitalist society. Expansion, growth, mobility, equal opportunities, and moral certainty were the pivots upon which their personalities turned; personal and public experience led them to the point at which that older, stratified and socially assured society — personified by the Southern gentleman, the poor white, and the oppressed black — was utterly repudiated. The Radical experience and the Radical conclusion was not the possession of a few fanatics in Congress but of millions of Americans of this generation; Radicalism was not an aberration but a broad stream which gathered up most themes of American history; therein lay the power of Radicalism and the explanation of its impact upon the post-war crisis. Nor does Radicalism stand alone in the Western world for the same blend of business acumen, practical politics, moral conviction, humanitarian feeling and hostility to privilege was found on both sides of the Atlantic; it was no accident that Sumner was a friend of John Bright or that a young French reporter called Georges Clemenceau admired Thaddeus Stevens.

· IV ·

First Congressional Reconstruction

The first session of the Thirty-ninth Congress, meeting from December 1865 to July 1866, was one of the most important in American history. Its work was summed up in the Fourteenth Amendment which effected a fundamental alteration in the character of the Constitution and which could have been enacted at no other time. In the course of its debates a number of other proposals were discussed which were to effect Southern society, sectional attitudes and racial relations in the United States. Decisions were taken in the course of a developing political crisis which imposed upon the American system of government the most severe test which it has ever endured, and raised inconvenient questions (which have since been left un-answered) about the capacity of American government to deal with a great national problem. There are several ways in which the history of this momentous session have been and could be studied: what is here proposed is to examine the evolution of policy as the result of a number of initiatives, originating from different parts of the political spectrum, each leaving its imprint upon the political situation, but none achieving its ultimate objective. Caught in a vortex between these powerfully directed political thrusts — between desire for a speedy restoration of the Union, loyalty to party, sectional prejudices, and obligations arising from the war, between the demands of a political crisis and the wishes of his constituents—the ordinary man in Congress had to make his own decisions. The surprising thing is that in the end so many of them made the same decision.

The first initiative came from the President with his policy of restoration. The second was the Radical initiative engineered by

Thaddeus Stevens, but with a concurrent but separate movement launched by Charles Sumner and aimed at immediate universal suffrage. The third was that of Senator Lyman Trumbull with bills for the extension of the Freedmen's Bureau and for protecting civil rights. The fourth and last initiative was that of the Committee on Reconstruction, in which the key figures were William Pitt Fessenden and John A. Bingham. When the anger of debate died down no one had got exactly what they wanted. The President had failed to convince Congress that the Southern States should be readmitted without more conditions than he had imposed upon them. The Radicals were far from the reconstruction of Southern society which they desired. Charles Sumner was not within sight of negro suffrage. Lyman Trumbull had failed to convince the President that his solution, embodying the minimum guarantees for civil rights, could be grafted upon the policy of restoration. The moderate Republicans who had written the Fourteenth Amendment had failed to obtain from Congress an explicit commitment to re-admit the Southern States if they ratified it.

When Congress met, President Johnson occupied a position of great potential strength. Though criticisms were levelled against the governments which he had set in operation in the Southern States, no one could deny that these States were now controlled by men who had undertaken to be loyal to the United States, who had abolished slavery, annulled secession and repudiated the Confederate debt, or that the great desire of the majority of Southerners was to resume their rights and obligations as States in the Union. If such a result had been forecast a year before it would have been regarded as a wild and foolishly optimistic dream. Very few Republicans regarded the prospect of a breach between President and Congress as anything but a political calamity, for even at the lowest level of party calculation they knew what had happened to other congressional parties which had separated from their executive leader and divided amongst themselves. Nor did they see why 'guarantees' should not be added to the President's plan. They were not satisfied that restoration, so far as it had gone, provided sufficient protection to negroes and Southern Unionists against local discrimination or sufficient protection to the Union against its avowed enemies. Yet negro suffrage as a counter-weight to disloyalty was unacceptable to the bulk of the party; nor were they attracted by the Radical proposition that the Southern States must be kept in tutelage for a long period until the fabric of their society had been changed. Indeed the prospects for a Johnson policy with modifications were bright; men sought assiduously for hints that the President would move with them, and Johnson's annual message, in which he asked Congress to admit the Southern States and so set the seal upon 'restoration', was very well received. However, nearly all Republicans were agreed that the ultimate responsibility for Reconstruction must lie with Congress and not with the President, and that therefore Congress must be given time to deliberate and inquire before committing itself. Many admitted that the President had behaved with propriety in taking action under the war power, and there was no ready assent to the Radical theory of executive encroachment; but it was now the duty of Congress to make the final decisions. At the outset most Republicans did not think of themselves as opposed to the President but neither did they accept the notion that the rebel States had resumed their rights with surrender, and if they regarded them as States in the Union they did not infer that the national government ought to be inhibited by pre-war theories of State rights. It was the tragedy of Johnson that he came to tie his restoration policy to such theories, and ended by sacrificing the policy itself upon the altar of constitutional dogmatism.

A major hindrance to the momentum of the President's initiative was that he became mesmerized by the Radical initiative launched as Congress met. There is evidence of discussion amongst Radical leaders in the days preceding the meeting of Congress but none that they had decided upon a clear-cut and far-reaching plan. It would be easy to persuade Republicans that no Southern member should be admitted until approved by Congress, but the Radicals saw great dangers in the piecemeal discussion in Congress of individuals and separate States; special cases might well demand special treatment and they were very conscious of the claims of Tennessee, the President's own State, which had sent to Congress a delegation of unimpeachable loyalty. The admission of Tennessee might set a precedent for the admission of 'loyal' Senators and Representatives from other States and this would preclude the more far-reaching proposals which the Radicals hoped to advance. For this reason the Radicals fixed as their immediate objective some procedure which would tie the hands of Congress for the time being and which would ensure that the problem of Reconstruction was discussed as a whole. They were therefore enthusiastically behind a proposal to set up a Joint Committee of Fifteen — six Senators and nine Representatives — to which all matters affecting the admission of States were to be referred, and which was to report before any action could be taken by Congress. A committee of seven reported this proposal to a caucus of Republican members on 2 December, but at first opinion seemed to favour a motion from the Ohio delegation which would have left each House to make its own arrangements; then 'Stevens angry, resisted, threatened to leave the caucus. Finally carried his point as stated, viz, a Joint Committee of fifteen'.[1]

The House adopted the caucus resolution as soon as it met, but the Senate was less precipitate and finally accepted the committee proposal after modifying the provision that no action should be taken until the committee had reported and after throwing out a provision that matters affecting reconstruction should be referred to it without debate. Even with these qualifications the passage of the resolutions setting up the committee were recognized as an important step and has been usually interpreted as a Radical triumph. The Radicals had won a tactical victory but there is no need to exaggerate what they had done: they had formalized and provided the procedural structure for a widely felt determination that Congress must be allowed freedom to act.

[1] Charles R. Williams (ed.), *Diary and Letters of Rutherford B. Hayes*, 5 vols. (Columbus, 1922–6), III, 7–8.

Even the *New York Times*, edited by Representative Henry Raymond, who was a political protegé of Seward and was to become a principal defender of the administration in the House, defended the appointment of the committee because 'the main question involved can then be discussed and decided upon its intrinsic merits, without being complicated or embarrassed by questions of regularity of the elections or returns in the case of individual members. Without any such provisions as this, the question would be debated upon the presentation of each new certificate, and we should have a perpetually recurring wrangle instead of a decorous and formal discussion'.[1] The criticism that the committee was a constitutional innovation which broke down the separation between the two Houses was easily answered: an unprecedented situation required procedural innovation and when the committee had presented its report each House could act upon it as it saw fit.[2] The case against the committee, which apparently convinced and profoundly disturbed President Johnson, and which has been repeated by many subsequent historians, was that it was intended to come under Radical control and did in fact do so. It would have been better for his own understanding of the situation if Johnson had taken at its face value the representation made to him, on behalf of the committee, that they 'desired to avoid all possible collision or misconstruction between the Executive and Congress in regard to the relative positions of Congress and the President. . . . and that they thought mutual respect would seem to require mutual forbearance on the part of the Executive and of Congress'.[3] It is true that this expression of goodwill was accompanied by a request that no action affecting Reconstruction should be taken by the President while the subject was under consideration by the

[1] Quoted from the *New York Times*, 5 Dec. 1865 in B. B. Kendrick, *Journal of the Joint Committee of Fifteen on Reconstruction* (New York, 1914), 151.

[2] Beale (ed.), *Diary of Gideon Welles*, II, 396. 12 Dec. 1865. 'Most members have said their principal object was to have the two houses in perfect accord and of one mind. I have declared this an indirect attempt to defeat [or evade] the Constitution which intended separate action. Hence the two branches. This proposed committee, I maintain is revolutionary and calculated to promote if not designed to create alienation and sectional parties.'

[3] Kendrick, *Journal of the Joint Committee of Fifteen on Reconstruction*, 40-1 (minute of the Committee for 9 Jan. 1866).

committee, but this was, after all, asking the President to exercise the same self-restraint as Congress. There was indeed nothing in the first success of the Radical initiative which the President need have regarded as more than a tactical set-back. A President who expects a Congress to act immediately upon his political initiative is expecting too much; it was his unfortunate misunderstanding of the true nature of the Joint Committee, and his obsession with the notion of Radical conspiracy, which caused him to discard the strongest card in his hand which was the evident anxiety of so many Republicans to co-operate with him.

The Radical initiative was not intended to halt with the appointment of the committee. They certainly hoped to use it as the means whereby Congress would be committed to certain propositions about the future of the Union. In the House Stevens threw out a number of propositions which would set on foot the social and political revolution which he desired. It was first necessary to establish the necessity for constitutional amendments; before the Southern States were re-admitted, the Constitution must 'have been so amended as to make it what its framers intended; and so as to secure perpetual ascendancy to the party of the Union; and so as to render our republican government firm and stable for ever'. The amendment dear to Stevens's heart was one declaring that all laws, national and State, should apply equally to all persons, thus establishing unequivocally not only equality under the law but also equal privileges provided by law.[1] Short of this sweeping change the immediate problem of the place of the South in the Union was to be met by basing the apportionment of congressional seats upon voters and not upon population, by imposing an export tax on cotton as the only means by which the South could be made to pay its fair share of expenses, by repudiating the Confederate debt and guaranteeing the national debt, and by declaring that no State should be allowed to participate in making amendments until it had been admitted to the Union by Congress. During the period of tutelage for the Southern States they could enjoy Territorial status, and Congress

[1] C.G. 39.1.74 and C.G. 39.1.

could use its power to provide the economic basis for negro freedom by the confiscation of the estates of Confederate leaders and by their division among the freedmen under a Southern Homestead law. Stevens did not press for immediate negro suffrage because he believed that this must be preceded by economic security and educational progress, but he did assert that the door must be left open. 'This is not "a white man's Government" ... ,' he said, 'To say so is political blasphemy, for it violates the fundamental principles of our gospel of liberty. This is man's government; the Government of all men alike; not that all men will have equal power within it. Accidental circumstances, natural and acquired endowment and ability, will vary their fortunes. But equal right to all the privileges of the Government is innate in every mortal being, no matter what the shape or color of the tabernacle it inhabits.'[1]

It is perfectly clear what Stevens was doing. He was trying to press Congress towards the goal which he had announced in a widely reported speech to his constituents. 'Heretofore,' he had said, 'Southern society has had more the features of aristocracy than of democracy; the Southern States have been despotisms. Is it possible that any practical equality of rights can exist where a few thousand men monopolize the whole landed property. . . . How can republican institutions, free churches, free social intercourse exist in a mingled community of nabobs and serfs, of owners of twenty-thousand-acre manors, with lordly palaces, and the occupants of narrow huts inhabited by low white trash? If the South is ever to be made a safe republic let her land be cultivated by the toil of its owners, or the free labor of intelligent citizens. This must be done even though it drive the nobility into exile. If they go, all the better. It is easier and more beneficial to exile seventy thousand proud, bloated and defiant rebels than to expatriate four million laborers, native to the soil and loyal to the government.'[2] Stevens intended to launch a political movement to revolutionize Southern society, and he has often been credited with such

[1] C.G. 39.1.74.
[2] Speech at Lancaster 6 Sep. 1865. Cf. Brodie, *Thaddeus Stevens*, 231–2.

H

an aim; what has been less noticed is his lack of immediate success.

Stevens was too old a hand to allow matters to be pressed to the vote when he saw that they would fail, and it is in the silence of Congress rather than in its actions that one must see the evidence for his failure. The proposal to alter the basis of Southern apportionment received serious consideration, but this was not a suggestion which was peculiar to Stevens or originated by him. His proposals for complete legal equality and confiscation were both damned by the lack of enthusiasm shown in Congress; the first was to re-emerge in an attenuated form in the first clause of the Fourteenth Amendment but the second was doomed for ever. Congress also refused to commit itself to any proposition about the status of the rebel States, and took little notice of the argument, upon which Stevens would continue to insist without avail, that they should play no part in the ratification of amendments. So far as Stevens was concerned the Radical initiative was losing momentum, and all his ascendancy in the House had failed to win support for his projected revolution; it is possible that he realized that a movement which has ceased to move is in danger of death and switched to a vigorous attack upon the President's policy where he was more likely to win support. Stevens was a political opportunist who was always ready to take the bird in hand, but what success he achieved was less the result of his own flexibility than of Andrew Johnson's inflexibility.

While Stevens tried to promote his policy in the House, Sumner was attempting a somewhat different initiative in the Senate. For him the main objective, and the panacea for the Southern problem, was negro suffrage, and he hoped to make a wide suffrage the condition for restoration. As soon as Congress met he proposed five conditions for re-admission: the complete re-establishment of loyalty, equal rights and enfranchisement for all, the repudiation of the rebel debt, the organization of an educational system without racial discrimination, and the choice for Congress of citizens of constant and undoubted loyalty. He followed this with four proposals for the reconstruction of Southern society: constitutional conventions to be elected by those who had taken no part in the rebellion, no recognition by Congress of any convention which excluded negroes or Union soldiers, no State law or constitution to be 'set up as an impediment to national power', and no State to be recognized as republican 'where large masses of citizens who have been always loyal to the United States are excluded from the electoral franchise'.[1] The plan would be similar in operation to the Wade-Davis Bill, with the additional provision that the constitutional duty of Congress to guarantee republican government should be interpreted to prevent recognition of any State which did not enfranchise at least a majority of their negro population. The weakness in his case, apart from the difficulty of converting a Northern majority to the idea of universal suffrage, was that loyalty defined solely by past record would leave the Southern States without effective governments while loyalty based upon a declaration of future intentions did not differ from what Johnson had already done. Sumner tried to meet this by associating the idea of loyalty with acceptance of the plan for negro suffrage; the North should adopt his definition of republican government and it was to this new concept that Southern allegiance must be given. Like Stevens, Sumner failed to rouse enthusiasm for his version of Reconstruction policy; he was thwarted by the failure of several Northern States to grant negro suffrage within their own borders, by a genuine reluctance to give power in the South to men who had just emerged from slavery, and by the general hope that a little tinkering would make the Johnson governments work as the North wished them to work. A symptom of Sumner's failure was the refusal of the inner group of Republican Senators to give him the place on the Joint Committee which he very much wanted.[2]

---

[1] C.G. 39.1, 4 Dec. 1865.

[2] Fessenden wrote of his appointment as chairman of the committee that 'Mr Sumner was very anxious for the place, but, standing as he does before the country, and committed to the most ultra views, even his friends declined to support him, and almost to a man fixed on me' (Quoted by Kendrick, op. cit., 175 from Francis Fessenden, *Life and Public Services of William Pitt Fessenden* (Boston, 1907) and by Charles A. Jellison, *Fessenden of Maine*, (Syracuse, 1962) p. 201 from Fessenden family papers). Sumner was senior as a senator to Fessenden and if placed on the committee must therefore have been given precedence; the feeling that he could not be chairman meant therefore that he could not be included in the committee.

Sumner was the prophet of the Fifteenth Amendment, but much water would have to flow under Republican bridges before agreement to either universal or impartial suffrage could be secured.

Having failed to gather momentum for their proposals the Radicals were handicapped by their own creation of the Joint Committee. Though the Senate had refused to refer matters to the committee without debate its existence provided a convenient way by which moderates could shelve untimely proposals. It was a curious paradox that while Johnson became more and more convinced that the committee was the instrument of the Radical conspiracy, its chairman, Fessenden, was trying to organize it as a means by which the energies of Radicals could be set in safe channels and the schemes of the wild men prevented from obstructing the road to early Reconstruction. There were, however, two points at which the Radicals in Congress could still attack with some hope of success: these were the problems of suffrage in the Territories of the United States and in the District of Columbia. Here the power of Congress was constitutionally unassailable, and men who were not prepared to say that negroes could never vote, and who felt that the experiment of negro suffrage must begin somewhere, were ready to see it begin where the question was untrammelled by the rights of States. This meant that there was still the occasion for a good deal of discussion of suffrage on questions which lay outside the terms of reference of the Joint Committee. This may have preserved the illusion of a far-reaching Radical plot to force negro suffrage upon the South, and through negro votes to control the nation.

As the Radical drive came to a standstill the initiative was taken up by a very different kind of man. Senator Lyman Trumbull occupied a somewhat isolated position in the Republican party. He was not a popular man but he had been a close associate of Lincoln both in the national government and in the State of Illinois. Some reproached him for having considered himself a little superior to Lincoln, but he had as good a claim as any to be his political legatee.[1] He was regarded in the Senate as a sound constitutional lawyer who had combined firm opposition to slavery with considerable caution on Reconstruction problems. He was chairman of the Senate Judiciary Committee and as such had sponsored the Thirteenth Amendment. Trumbull's approach was based upon two assumptions. The first was that the Southern States would soon be re-admitted to the Union in the form which Johnson had given to them; the second was that the Thirteenth Amendment had given to Congress the power and the duty to protect the civil rights of every citizen in the United States. He intended to graft this national duty upon the restoration policy, but he was not a convert to the Radical design of overthrowing the Southern ruling class. He believed that the President would approve his objectives and had several conversations with Johnson on the question. The means proposed were two. The first was an extension of the Freedmen's Bureau in time and power so that it could assume the immediate task of protecting the negroes against local violence or deprivation of rights. The second, a Civil Rights Bill, looked forward to the time when the military force in the South would be withdrawn and provided a permanent machinery for the protection of civil rights. Unlike the Radicals Trumbull had proposed something which was likely to draw Republicans together rather than to divide them, and the passage of his measures through Congress was an easy triumph. He had, however, reckoned without the mind of Andrew Johnson, and on 19 February the President returned the Freedmen's Bureau Bill with an elaborate veto message.

The first two-thirds of this veto message were concerned with detailed criticism of the bill; some of these were valid if one assumed that everyone, including the President himself who was given considerable discretionary power in the bill, was going to

---

[1] Cf. Beale (ed.), *Diary of Gideon Welles*, II, 322. 'The late President well understood and rightly appreciated the character and abilities of Trumbull, and would not quarrel with him, though he knew and felt him to be ungenerous and exacting. They had been pretty intimate though of opposing parties in Illinois until circumstances and events brought them to act together.... When L. was taken up and made President, Trumbull always acted as though he thought himself a more fit and proper man than Lincoln, whom he had crowded aside in the Senatorial contest.'

act in the worst possible way. The difficulty was that the bill ought to have been seen in conjunction with the Civil Rights Bill which was not yet through Congress. Trumbull in answering this part of the veto message did not conceal his annoyance, but argued powerfully and reasonably; if he did not convince at every point he made short work of the notion that the object of the bill was to set up a permanent military despotism. It was, however, the last part of the veto message which had climacteric effects upon the relationship between President and Congress. Johnson drew attention to the fact that eleven States were unrepresented, and then went on to argue against the propriety of legislating for them in their absence; he did not go quite so far as to say that such legislation was unconstitutional, but he did make the exclusion of States which he believed to have been restored to their rights a ground for his veto. Johnson was, of course, fully aware that the 'guarantees' which Congress was trying to find would require some amendments to the Constitution and knew that the restoration of Southern votes to Congress would deprive any such amendment of the necessary two-thirds. Johnson implied in the veto that what he had done was complete and required no further discussion; he claimed the right to say that the conditions which he had imposed on the South were the only conditions which should be imposed; he ignored the problem of negro status and left this by implication to be determined by the white majorities in the Southern States. It was his apparent denial of the right of Congress to draw up the terms for Reconstruction, and his refusal to consider the national aspect of the negro problem which united the Republican party against him. The bill failed by one vote to obtain in the Senate the necessary two-thirds to override the veto; in the House it was re-passed with ease. Moderates voted with Radicals and Johnson had succeeded in giving unity to the Republican party at the very moment when it was threatened with division.

*   *   *   *

The steps by which Johnson arrived at his decision to veto the Freedmen's Bureau Bill in the way in which he did can be inferred

from the diary of Gideon Welles. Of all members of the Cabinet
Welles was the most closely identified with the President's point
of view, and if he did not sow ideas in Johnson's mind he certainly
gave him repeated assurance that he was right.[1] It was unfortunate
that Welles, who was a New England man, was so conditioned
that he gave Johnson a uniformly incorrect picture of Northern
opinion. It was also unfortunate that his principal source of information about Republican policy was Charles Sumner, who
paid weekly visits to his department on official business and talked
freely about Reconstruction problems. Sumner was whole-
hearted in his opposition to the President's policy and prone to
exaggerate the support for his own point of view.[2] He thus
provided ample evidence for Welles's version of the Radical
conspiracy. As the crisis developed Welles came to regard everyone who did not share his strict State rights theories as a Radical
and as this included most Republicans he found daily confirmation for the view that the party was bound hand and foot by
Radical intrigue. He never sought for a less superficial explanation
of the growing support for policies which he deplored. Welles
was probably responsible for putting the idea of impeachment
into the President's mind and he did nothing to correct the
absurd idea that an assassination plot was brewing. At the outset
of Congress he told the President that the Joint Committee was
'revolutionary, a blow at our government system, and there had
been evident preconcert to bring it about'.[3] On 18 December he
told him 'that I was confirmed in the conviction that there was a
deep and extensive intrigue going on against him'.[4] On 13 February Welles found the President in an agitated frame of mind;

[1] John H. and Lawanda Cox, who have studied the various hands at work in the
composition of Johnson's Freedmen's Bureau and Civil Rights vetoes ('Andrew Johnson
and his Ghost Writers,' *Mississippi Valley Historical Journal*, XLVIII (Dec. 1961),
460 ff.) conclude that Welles was an influential adviser.

[2] Cf. Beale (ed.), *Diary of Gideon Welles*, II, 393, 397, 414–5. Sumner told him that three
of the Cabinet were with Congress, and that one of them had urged him to bring in a bill
'which should control the action of the President and wipe out his policy. It has got to be
done. Half of the Cabinet as well as an overwhelming majority of the two houses of
Congress are for it, and the President must change his whole course. If he did not do it,
Congress would'. Welles was disturbed and commented, 'Sumner is truthful and therefore his statement is reliable'.

[3] Beale (ed.), *Diary of Gideon Welles*, II, 387.   [4] Ibid., 398.

the Freedmen's Bureau Bill was now through Congress and the President spoke of 'the extraordinary intrigue which he understood was going on in Congress, having nothing short of a subversion or change in structure of the government in view. The unmistakable design of Thad Stevens and his associates was to take government into their own hands . . . and to get rid of him by declaring Tennessee out of the Union. A sort of French Directory was to be established by these spirits in Congress, the Constitution was to be remodelled by them, etc.'.[1] Welles did not object to these fantastic views which probably coincided with his own.

The difficulty was, as the Radical George Boutwell pointed out in a letter to Ben Butler, that 'the President does not know our people — that is he is not upon such terms with the Republicans . . . as justifies a full and free discussion of the topics and questions which threaten to wreck the party'.[2] There was plenty of opportunity for consultation with Northern men. Among the Republican leaders he saw Garfield, Trumbull and Grimes; others were ready and willing for an informal talk if the President desired it, but it was not until nearly the end of January that he arranged a meeting with Fessenden who was the weightiest man in the Senate. Whatever was gained by this interview was immediately lost by the publication, in a New York newspaper, of the account of an interview with a 'distinguished Senator' in which the President spoke against suffrage in the District and against amending the Constitution; the 'distinguished Senator' was in fact Dixon of Connecticut, a supporter of the President of no distinction or influence whatever, but it was characteristic of Johnson that he did nothing to correct the possible confusion or to explain to Fessenden why his own discussion had gone so differently. In his old days as a Senator, Johnson had always been a lonely figure; relying upon his power in Tennessee and standing outside the main Southern and Northern groups and probably despising the manipulators who tried to arrange the business of Congress. As President he certainly failed to understand the

[1] Ibid., 432.   [2] L.C. *Butler Papers*, Boutwell to Butler, 9 Dec. 1865.

importance of establishing contact with men in the party which had elected him. Shut up in the White House, taking little or no exercise, working with extraordinary and commendable industry, cut off from those who wished to work with him and seeing only those who agreed with him or had favours to ask, he came to live in a world which had less and less contact with political reality.

The picture drawn by Johnson and Welles of conspiracy and accumulating enmity was largely one of their own making. Privately and publicly leading Republicans professed their hope that the President would not break with them. Early in the session James A. Garfield, who had just had a conversation with the President in which he gave him 'the views of earnest men North as I understand them,' wrote to a friend that 'Sumner and Boutwell and some more of that class are full of alarm — less, however, than when they came. Some foolish men among us are all the while bristling for a fight and seem to be anxious to make a rupture with Johnson. I think we should assume that he is with us, treat him kindly, without suspicion, and go on in a firm calmly considered course, leaving him to make the breach if any is made'.[1] At the same time Boutwell, one of the 'foolish' men and a determined Radical wrote to Ben Butler suggesting that he should see the President who 'apprehends or is made to believe in the existence of a feeling of hostility to him, which is of the imagination altogether'. Boutwell admitted that some thought or feared that the President was already determined to abandon the party. 'This notion', he went on, 'is equally erroneous. The existence of these errors may prove however as injurious as the facts themselves.'[2] And while good Republicans found themselves ignored they were distressed to hear that he had been seeing Southerners and Democrats on terms of apparent intimacy.[3] In Congress

---

[1] *Garfield-Hinsdale Letters*, 76. 11 Dec. 1865.
[2] L.C. *Butler Papers*, Boutwell to Butler, 9 Dec. 1865.
[3] General Richard Taylor, C.S.A., son of President Taylor, visited Washington in 1866 to petition for the release of Jefferson Davis (Taylor, *Destruction and Reconstruction*, 321). The President deferred consideration of his request but summoned him on several occasions 'to talk about Southern affairs' (p. 326). 'At his instance I had many interviews with him and consulted influential men from different parts of the country.' There was nothing improper in seeking information from Southern men, but Johnson does not seem to have been at the same pains to inquire about feelings in the North. James Harlan, a member of

Fessenden, Trumbull and John Sherman all made clear their earnest wish for a *rapprochement* with the President; none of them liked Stevens, and Fessenden was not on speaking terms with Sumner; they knew what must be done to satisfy Northern opinion but they did not want to be hurried into foolish measures. The President was their obvious ally; but the proffered alliance was consistently ignored.

Another presidential misconception, which was also fostered by Welles, was that the Radical 'conspiracy' if challenged would break, and that once broken a great reserve of support for the President would be uncovered. Welles indeed believed that presidential patronage should have been used against the Radicals as early as the autumn of 1865 when their criticisms were first made public.[1] On 30 January Welles was urging him to make a 'public enunciation of his purpose, and at a proper time, and as early as convenient or as there was an opportunity, to show by some distinct and emphatic act his intention to maintain and carry into effect his administrative policy'. 'On this', he added, 'we concurred.'[2] Welles believed that a break-up of the Republican party was approaching and seems to have believed in some alliance between administration Republicans and moderate Democrats; what he never seems to have contemplated was the unfortunate fact that the administration Republicans would be a corporal's guard, or that the President's 'public enunciation of his purpose' in the veto message would unite against him all but this small fragment of the party.

On 22 February, Washington's birthday and two days after the veto, a crowd of admirers went to cheer the President at the White House. Confronted with the unexpected spectacle of a friendly and enthusiastic crowd Johnson felt that he was meeting the real people of the United States, who would stand by him against the Radical plotters, and emotion brought forth a torrent

the Cabinet, tried to reassure fellow Republicans; he wrote, 'I do not fear the result of Copperhead flattery on Johnson. He is as firm as rock, and as infallibly right on all the main points involved in the great struggle as the most ardent could desire' (L.C. *Washburn Papers*, Harlan to Washburn, 12 Jun. 1865). Harlan resigned from the Cabinet in July 1866.

[1] Beale (ed.), *Diary of Gideon Welles*, II, 587.　　　[2] Ibid II, 421.

of words. The old stump orator was once more on the attack, belabouring his enemies, and contrasting their evil designs with his own record and rectitude. When he had finished he had branded Stevens, Sumner and Wendell Phillips as disunionists who were as treasonable as Jefferson Davis and the other great secessionists, and had painted in lurid colours their intentions. 'I make use of a very strong expression when I say that I have no doubt the intention was to incite assassination and so to get out of the way the obstacle from place and power. . . . Are they not satisfied with the blood which has been shed? Does not the murder of Lincoln appease the vengeance and wrath of the opponents of this government? Are they still unslaked? Do they still want more blood?' Whatever they threatened he would stand by the Constitution which said that no State should be deprived of its representation and he would oppose all who were trying to subvert it by amendment. And 'somehow or other the people will find out and understand who is for and who is against them. . . . I believe that they will not desert me.'[1] The speech stunned Northern opinion. The uninformed saw the spectacle of a President playing the demagogue and branding with infamous accusations men who might not always command universal admiration but who had given much to preserve the Union and destroy slavery. The informed saw more and less: they saw a window opened into a world of fantasy in which the President had come to live and to them this world was incomprehensible.

Even after the veto and the speech hope for an understanding with the President lingered on. Interest focused on the second and more important of Trumbull's two bills. The bill first declared that all persons born in the United States, excepting Indians not taxed and subjects of foreign powers, were citizens of the United States. It then defined the rights of citizens as equality in courts of law and 'full and equal benefit of all laws and proceedings for the security of persons and property'. This clause invalidated the discriminatory provisions of the black codes, but it said nothing about suffrage and, perhaps more curiously, nothing about jury

[1] McKitrick, op. cit., 294.

service. These things were regarded by Trumbull as privileges which were at the discretion of State legislatures and not as inalienable rights.[1] In fact Trumbull had attempted to clothe the promise of the Declaration of Independence in legal garb; he had not gone an inch beyond what he believed necessary to sustain the rights to life and liberty and had left the pursuit of happiness to look after itself. This was the Republican commitment to protect the status of the freedmen stripped to its bare essentials. Nevertheless even so guarded a definition of right required power to sustain it, and the bill went on to make it an offence exclusively cognizable in the Federal courts for any person to deprive another of these rights. Thus civil rights were placed on the same footing as laws affecting interstate commerce or the obligation of contracts. But the provision of legal remedy was not sufficient if men were too intimidated to avail themselves of it, and there followed a provision that Federal district attorneys, together with marshalls and commissioners appointed by the courts, were empowered to prevent breaches of the law, and these officials with officers and agents of the Freedmen's Bureau and other officials appointed by the President were 'authorised and required' to institute prosecutions. The President was also required to order Federal officials to take action in districts where breaches of the law had taken place or were expected, and in the last resort he could use troops. Appeals on questions of law, but not of fact, could lie to the Supreme Court.

There was no doubt that the bill made serious inroads upon the rights of States as previously defined, though the enforcement machinery resembled that of the Fugitive Slave Act. The innovation was justified by Trumbull as a necessary consequence of the Thirteenth Amendment, and by others as the use of a power which had always been latent in the Constitution though suppressed by the false arguments of the Slave power. But for most Republicans the decisive argument was the necessity for protection; for them the choice was not between leaving the status of the negro to be defined by State or by national power, but between

---

[1] Beale (ed.), *Diary of Gideon Welles*, II, 489–90.

continuing military protection or replacing it with civil machinery.

There were the strongly expressed hopes that Johnson would sign the bill and that if he did a new chapter could be opened in the relations between President and Congress.[1] This was not to be and on 27 March Johnson vetoed the bill with another long message, and again it was the arguments used which were so offensive to men who had been trying seriously to grapple with the problem of Reconstruction in what they believed to be a moderate and unavoidable manner.[2] It was, said Johnson, improper to legislate upon negro citizenship while the Southern States were unrepresented. The bill attempted to enact equality of rights 'in every State of the Union over the vast field of State jurisdiction covered by these enumerated rights', and 'hitherto every subject embraced in the enumeration of rights contained in this bill has been considered as exclusively belonging to the States. They all relate to the internal police and economy of the respective States. They are matters in which each State concern the domestic condition of its people, varying in each according to its own peculiar circumstances and the safety and well-being of its own citizens'. The use of the Federal courts was unconstitutional 'for the Constitution guarantees nothing with certainty if it does not insure to the several States the right of making and executing laws in regard to all matters arising within their jurisdiction, subject only to the restriction that in cases of conflict with the Constitution and constitutional laws of the United States the latter should be held to be the supreme law of the land'. Johnson ignored Trumbull's argument that the Thirteenth Amendment, in making slavery unconstitutional, had made the equalization of right a national responsibility. It followed as a matter of course that Johnson then objected to all the proposed machinery for enforcement, and he ended with a general indictment of the bill as 'another step, or rather stride, toward centralization and the concentration of all legislative powers in the National Government. The tendency of the bill must be to resuscitate the spirit of

---

[1] Williams (ed.), *Diary and Letters of Rutherford B. Hayes*, III, 19.
[2] Richardson (ed.), *Messages and Papers*, VI, 405 ff.

rebellion and to arrest the progress of those influences which are more closely drawing around the States the bonds of union and peace'. The unasked question in the veto message was whether 'the bonds of union and peace' could ever be drawn more closely while the Northern obligation to the negro remained unhonoured. By his veto Johnson formally refused to recognize that this obligation could be met within the Constitution, informally he had already declared against amendments which might convey the power to meet it, and explicitly he demanded the re-admission to Congress of the Southern States which would make amendment impossible.

This time the solidarity of Republicans was to be expected. The bill was easily re-passed in the House; in the Senate it scraped through by a bare two-thirds. The intensity of feeling was betrayed by the means, not very creditable to those concerned, by which a Democratic senator was unseated to secure the necessary two-thirds majority.[1] But young Ignatius Donnelly, then an

---

[1] John P. Stockton of New Jersey. His predecessor's term expired on 4 Mar. 1865. Under the laws of New Jersey a senator was elected by a joint meeting of the two houses and a majority in both houses was required to convene such a meeting. There was a Democratic majority in the State Senate, but an even balance of parties in the lower house. The Republicans hoped to stall off a vote convening the joint session until the fall elections had improved their position; this they were unable to do but hoped to profit from Stockton's unpopularity in his own party. He was the son of Commodore Stockton and was heavily backed by money from his father's Camden and Amboy Railroad. They therefore voted with some Democrats that election in the joint session must be by a majority and not by a plurality. Democratic leaders who had supported this to bring their own dissidents into line now found that a minority of Democrats would vote against Stockton under any circumstances, and in the joint session they pushed through a vote rescinding the requirement for a majority and allowing a plurality; with this change of rules Stockton was elected. The Republicans had been out-manoeuvred and their protest to the United States Senate was turned down by the Judiciary Committee. But in late March, with another presidential veto looming on the horizon, it became vital to the Republicans to secure a two-thirds majority in both Houses and the flaw in Stockton's title provided the opportunity. A number of Republicans, including Trumbull, voted to sustain Stockton's election, but after the Senate tied on a first vote Stockton was unseated on a second by 23–20. Two Democratic senators were ill and unable to attend; a Republican (Morrill) broke a pair with one of these in order to vote against Stockton; one Republican (Foot) was dying and absent, another (Morgan) was absent at the first vote and voted for Stockton at the second. When Morrill broke his pair Stockton cast his own vote for himself, but this was then disallowed. Morrill argued that a pair did not extend to cases of this kind in which the Senate was acting primarily in a judicial capacity. On the second and final vote three Republicans who had voted on the first for Stockton, switched their votes.

Cf. McKitrick, op. cit., 319–23. Welles wrote, 'I apprehend that I can never think so well of some of the gentlemen who have been conspicuous in this proceeding. . . . I am passing no judgment on his election, for I know not the exact facts, but the indecent, unfair, arbitrary conduct of the few master-spirits is most reprehensible' (Beale (ed.), *Diary of Gideon Welles*, II, 465).

obscure Republican congressman, commented in his diary, that
'there is scarcely anything more magnificent in history than the
final action upon the Civil Rights Bill, when it was passed over
the President's veto, by the vote of every Union man elected from
a Northern State'.[1] Donnelly was wrong in claiming every Union
man, but the sentiment expresses the importance of the occasion
and the exultation of the Republican party. Never before had
Congress over-ridden a President on a major political issue, and
there was special gratification in feeling that this had not been
done to carry some matter of material interest, such as a tariff, but
in the cause of disinterested justice. The cool dissection of later
historians may have explained and denigrated their motives, but
it is only in these terms that Republican sentiment can be understood. 'I am convinced', wrote Donnelly of the Thirty-ninth
Congress, 'that a purer, more patient, and at the same time abler
and more patriotic body of men never convened in any age or
country.... Assembling almost in the hour of triumph, no
clamor for revenge escaped them; no cry for blood or confiscation
was heard; all they asked were those measures which were
essential to the future of the nation. With all this moderation they
exhibited a heroic determination to do right, which neither the
threats nor the blandishments of Executive power could shake for
one instance. They were indeed worthy representatives of that
quarter of a million of heroic men whose dust sanctifies the
southern land.'[2] Donnelly's picture may have as little relation with
reality as that of Johnson's 22 February speech, but the mood
must be understood if one is to understand Congress and Reconstruction.

Despite the triumphant passage of the Civil Rights Act the
initiative launched by Lyman Trumbull had failed. He had hoped
to provide a superstructure of law which could be placed upon the
foundations of Johnson's Reconstruction; instead he had precipitated a crisis and brought about a breach between President and
party which was unlikely to be healed. Moreover events had

[1] Minnesota State Historical Society, *Donnelly Papers*. This and the following passage
were left unchanged in the 1892 revision of the diary (see above p. 64, n. 1).
[2] Ibid.

pushed the moderate men appreciably nearer to the Radicals, and it could be anticipated that if moderation failed, the case for drastic action would become more and more plausible. On the one hand was a President, intimate with men whom all Republicans distrusted, and apparently reviving in all its former dogmatism the State rights theory which many believed to have been the cause of the war; on the other hand stood the Radicals still urging that the only way to reconstruct was to reconstruct Southern society. If the moderate or bewildered Republican was asked to choose between the two there was little doubt in which direction he would move. Oddly enough Gideon Welles, who so persistently misunderstood the political situation, found himself in a situation which aptly illustrated the moderate dilemma. In his own State of Connecticut a moderate Democrat, English, who supported the President's policy was contesting the governorship with General Hawley who inclined to the Radicals. What advice should Welles give to his Connecticut friends? He found that the President would be gratified if English won, yet commented that he did not 'comprehend the whole circumstances', and noted that 'most of his friends are supporting Hawley and some of his bitterest opponents are supporting English'.[1] He summed up the difficulty in his diary in this way: 'General Hawley's sympathies and feelings are with the Radicals. . . . English, on the other hand, is wholly with the President, and totally, earnestly opposed to the Congressional policy. The election of English would secure a friend to the President, but English and those who support him opposed his [the President's] election and most of them opposed the war. Hawley, while not in full accord with the President on present questions, and I am afraid not on the rights of States, supported his election, and was an earnest soldier from the beginning of the war.' Even though suspecting that Hawley 'would plunge into centralism, for thither go almost all Radicals, including his old Abolition associates',[2] Welles could not bring himself to support

---

[1] Beale (ed.), *Diary of Gideon Welles*, II, 456. And see also ibid., 458–9 for an account of an interview with Hawley.

[2] Ibid., 462. Johnson sent the following telegram to a supporter in Connecticut: 'In reference to the Election in Connecticut and elsewhere. . . . I am for the candidate who is

a Democrat. The dilemma was one which confronted Republicans in all parts of the country, and most of them decided, with enthusiasm or with reluctance according to their temperament and conviction, to stick by their party.

*   *   *   *

The civil rights veto delivered the death blow to another policy which had been initiated in Congress by Senator Stewart of Nevada. Stewart had had an adventurous life; born in New York he had moved to Ohio and then to San Francisco in the flush days of 1850. He had taught elementary mathematics as a young man, spent a short time at Yale, taken up mining in California and then turned to law, becoming Attorney-General of California at the age of twenty-seven and then moving to Nevada where he was concerned with the development of the Comstock Lode. In 1863 he had come to Congress as one of the first senators from Nevada. Stewart thus represented the new type of far-western politician: a man who had amassed wealth and influence through enterprise and an eye for opportunities, who could combine economic ruthlessness with a strong strain of somewhat naïve idealism, and who had stood apart from the bitterness of sectional controversy. His proposal was calculated to win support from all those who did not feel themselves irretrievably committed to any constitutional or political dogmatism, and who wished to combine speedy Reconstruction with the minimum of constitutional change and guarantees for the future. What he proposed was universal suffrage as the condition of universal amnesty. Actually what he proposed was not universal but impartial suffrage, for the Southern States could impose what qualifications they wished for suffrage provided that they did not discriminate on grounds of race, creed or colour, and those qualified to vote in 1860 could not be disenfranchised by any newly imposed test. In other words

for the general policy, and the specific measures promulgated by my Administration in my regular message, veto message, speech on 22nd of February, and the veto message sent in this day 27 March 1866. There can be no mistake about this. I presume it is known or can be ascertained, what candidates favor or oppose my policy or measures as promulgated to the country.' A copy of this telegram is in L.C. *Butler Papers*, where it may have formed part of the impeachment dossier.

I

the Southern States would have been free to impose a literacy test without sacrificing the votes of illiterate whites. When a State had made such a suffrage law, provided equal civil rights for all and repudiated war debts it could be admitted to Congress and a general amnesty for all would follow. Stewart's resolutions specifically denied the intention to give Congress any control over suffrage. Considerable support was promised from very different quarters; the plan provided a satisfactory status for the negro without the assumption of new national power, left the Southern people with considerable freedom of choice and gave them an opportunity to wipe out the past at a comparatively low cost. At the same time many Northerners had doubts about giving Southerners a free hand, which would allow a future Southern legislature, armed with a general amnesty, to alter the laws enacted to obtain it. But these objections would disappear if Stewart's proposal was coupled with a Civil Rights Act, giving the national government at least a reserve of power with which to protect rights. Johnson's dogmatic return to State rights theory opened men's eyes to the dangers of universal amnesty and weakened support for Stewart. A more cogent reason for the failure of his plan was that after the civil rights veto no measure of Reconstruction could be carried save by a majority of two-thirds in both Houses; every Republican vote would be necessary and this had the effect of raising the stock of the Radicals. Moderates found themselves in the position of men who, having agreed that certain things must be done, now found it impossible to do them without concessions to men who wanted more, and Stewart's attempt to walk in the middle of the road came to nothing.

In all these discussions upon the formulation of policy there remains one question which has not been asked. What were the opinions, and what was the influence, of William Henry Seward, Secretary of State, sometime standard-bearer of the Republican party, and still a powerful figure in his own State of New York if not in the nation at large? Here if anywhere was the man equipped by experience and position to act as an intermediary between the

President and the Republican party. It is true that Seward had earned the lasting displeasure of the Radicals, and that some of them attributed Johnson's defection to him, but there was still much common ground between the Secretary and the moderate Republicans whose actions were going to decide the course of events. Moreover Seward knew and understood every pulse which moved among Republicans; he shared their aspirations, he could think their thoughts, and he could judge what were practicable Republican politics. He was also a likeable man who could remain on good terms even with those whom he opposed, and he had shown a genius for compromise and negotiation; but these very qualities made him avoid a fight whenever possible. It is possible that Seward would have handled Reconstruction a great deal better than Johnson, but his own differences with the President never came to the point at which he was prepared to insist or to resign. He was growing old, he had been seriously wounded when Lincoln was murdered, and he had always preferred to wait upon events or to guide them by personal diplomacy rather than by overt action.

The researches of John H. and Lawanda Cox have shown exactly what part Seward played in the preparation of the veto messages and where he differed from the President.[1] The Freedmen's Bureau veto contained much that was taken directly from a draft prepared by Seward, but his objections rested upon an argument that the existing Freedman's Bureau Act was still in force and provided adequate powers for the protection of the negroes. He included a statement, which Johnson omitted from his message, that 'Freedmen who were emancipated by the nation as a means of suppressing the civil war are entitled to national

---

[1] John H. and Lawanda Cox, 'Andrew Johnson and his Ghost Writers', *Mississippi Valley Historical Review*, XLVIII (Dec. 1961), 460 ff. This study shows that Johnson also received drafts of the veto messages from Welles, Senators Doolittle and Cowan, an unidentified writer, and, for the second veto, Henry Stanbery. The largest portions of both vetoes were taken from Seward's drafts but, as shown below, these were the least important parts of the messages. Welles emerges as the most influential adviser, and Henry Stanbery (who was not yet in the government but had come to Washington to present the government case in *ex parte Milligan*) played an important but subordinate part in drafting the civil rights veto. Johnson wrote nothing himself but some important parts of the veto messages appear in none of the drafts and were probably dictated by him.

protection until the country shall have resumed its normal and habitual condition of peace', and he suggested that the President should support an extension of the existing Act if it should become necessary. Seward had no hand in the final passages of the veto message in which Johnson maintained that congressional legislation for the South was unconstitutional so long as the Southern States were unrepresented, or in his claim that 'Each member of Congress is chosen from a single district or State; the President is chosen by the people of all the States. As eleven States are not at this time represented in either branch of Congress, it would seem to be his duty, on all proper occasions, to present their just claims to Congress'. These passages, which constituted the real challenge to Congress, were Johnson's own distinctive contribution. Seward's draft, with its concentration upon detail and its avoidance of any major constitutional problem, would have been admirably designed to drive a wedge between the moderate and Radical Republicans; Johnson's message made their co-operation inevitable.

In the civil rights veto message the President again borrowed extensively from a draft prepared by Seward, but the differences between the two men were even more marked. Seward approved the objectives of the bill, and concentrated his criticism upon the enforcement procedure; he derived congressional power to protect civil rights from the privileges and immunities clause and he believed that the declaration of negro citizenship would be approved by the courts even though Congress had no express power to make it. Johnson on the other hand upheld the practice of racial discrimination as practised by the States, objected to negro citizenship, and branded the bill as operating 'in favor of the colored and against the white race'. He rejected a significant sentence from Seward's draft which said that Congress ought 'to provide by legislation proper measures, when necessary, to secure to citizens of the United States anywhere, the rights which the Constitution guarantees'. In a final appeal to the President Seward said, 'If you can find a way to intimate that you are not opposed to the policy of the bill but only to its detailed provisions, it will be a great improvement and make support of the veto easier to our friends in Congress,' but this advice was reflected only in one equivocal passage which was inconsistent with the rest of the message.[1]

If the veto messages had been delivered as Seward drafted them the course of Reconstruction history might have been different. What Seward intended to say to Congress was 'you may legislate to protect the rights of the negroes, but in doing so you must have due regard to constitutional precedent, Southern susceptibilities, and the details of administration'. This was the line which Seward's spokesman, Henry J. Raymond, tried to follow in Congress, but it was one which Johnson's vetoes made impossible to maintain. Seward might have separated the Republicans who wanted a limited but honourable settlement from the Radicals who wanted a reconstruction of Southern society; Johnson made Radical leadership the only alternative to congressional surrender. Yet though Seward was a wiser he was also a weaker man than Johnson; he preferred to conciliate Johnson whom he knew to be wrong rather than the moderate Republicans who were men after his own heart. His decision to remain in the Cabinet and to give support to the President can be praised for its recognition of loyalty to the administration of which he was a member, or condemned because loyalty was less important than policy. It would be wrong in a historian to judge too harshly of a man whose mind must have been sorely troubled by conflicting claims upon his conscience. It was not an easy time for any man who wished to steer between extremes.

*   *   *   *

[1] John and Lawanda Cox, op. cit., believe that the presumed additions made by Johnson to the various drafts indicate a definite attempt to appeal to racial prejudice. It is probable that this was not deliberate but an unconscious reflection of his own racial attitude. His supporters sometimes saw the issue clearly as is shown by the following story. On 18 Apr. 1866 he addressed a Convention of Soldiers and Sailors in Washington and in the course of some remarks upon presidential powers he asked rhetorically, 'What is the veto power? What does the veto mean?' A voice from the crowd shouted in reply, 'It is keeping the nigger down'. This incident was reported in the Washington *Daily Morning Chronicle* in a cutting which was sent by Sir Frederick Bruce, the British minister, with a despatch to the Foreign Secretary (F.O. 5.1064). The newspaper commented that 'There is something in this brief response which might furnish Mr Johnson with wholesome food for reflection, as showing how his "policy" is understood by those who hailed it with most delight'.

While the policies launched from the White House and in Congress were brought to a halt decisions which were vital for the future were being taken by the Committee of Fifteen. Yet Johnson's picture of 'an irresponsible central directory' rigged and run by Thaddeus Stevens was wide of the mark. The final recommendation of the committee showed the influence of moderate Republicans as well as of the Radicals, and were made after a long process of argument, bad temper, and compromise. The committee approached its task as a deliberative not as a dictatorial body, and criticism of its delays were more frequent than those of its precipitation. Much subsequent criticism of the committee has been based upon the assumption that it ought to have acted as a committee of inquiry; it is blamed for its partial selection of evidence and for its failure to give an impartial hearing to Johnson policy. The committee was not, however, appointed to carry out the task of a British Royal Commission, and its function was closer to that of a British Cabinet. The main lines of the policy were determined before the committee began its work; the brief had been presented by Republican opinion, and the committee's task was to produce the evidence and present the case in detail. A distinction must however be made between presenting the case for 'guarantees' and that for drastic changes in Southern government and society; the committee was intended to show that not enough had been done but it was not expected to launch a revolution.

The report of the committee when finally presented said little or nothing which was not being said before the meeting of Congress. It was not intended to be a new statement of the problem but a re-statement, backed by inquiry and discussion, of the Republican version. Of the negroes it said that 'it was impossible to abandon them, without securing them their rights as free men and citizens. The whole civilized world would have cried out against such base ingratitude, and the bare idea is offensive to all right-thinking men. Hence it became important to inquire what could be done to secure their rights, civil and political'.[1] On the

[1] *Report of the Joint Committee*, xiii.

question of Southern loyalty it said that 'the burden of proof rests upon the late insurgents who are seeking restoration to the rights and privileges which they willingly abandoned, and not upon the people of the United States who have never undertaken, directly or indirectly, to deprive them thereof. It should appear affirmatively that they are prepared to abandon their hostility to the government, and to live in peace and amity with the people of the loyal States, extending to all classes of citizens equal rights and privileges, and conforming to a republican idea of liberty and equality'.[1] On the President's policy the report recognized his wide powers as commander-in-chief, and gave him credit for what had been done in bringing order to the South, but it asserted that 'it was not for him to decide upon the nature and effect of any system of government which the people of these States might see fit to adopt. This power is lodged by the Constitution in the Congress of the United States, that branch of the goverment in which is vested the authority to fix the political relations of the States to the Union, whose duty it is to guarantee to each State a republican form of government, and to protect each and all of them against foreign and domestic violence and against each other'.[2] On the President's policy of restoration and pardon, the report observed that 'the feeling of kindness and conciliation manifested by the Executive, and very generally indicated through the northern press, had the effect to render whole communities forgetful of the crime they had committed, defiant towards the federal government and regardless of their duties as citizens'.[3]

In collecting its material and examining witnesses the committee intended to supply the evidence to substantiate these propositions. The evidence was in no way falsified, but as practising lawyers the members of the committee knew how to use friendly witnesses and to extract damaging admissions from hostile ones. One member of the committee, George Boutwell, was particularly proud of the way in which he handled Alexander Stephens, former Vice-President of the Confederacy and led him to a voluntary exposition of his continued belief in a State rights

[1] Ibid., xv–xvi.   [2] Ibid., vii–ix.   [3] Ibid.

theory which was certain to be offensive to Northern readers.[1] A great deal of evidence was collected about the refusal to treat the negroes as free men, entitled to fair wages and a choice of employment. Evidence of prejudice, violence, and, in a few cases, of terrorism on the part of Southern whites was produced. Nor was it difficult to show that former Confederates were preferred by the people, and that Southern Unionists were being driven out of public life. Thus in examining Southern whites the committee intended to demonstrate that they adhered to the principles of rebellion despite the formal act of surrender.

The committee found the evidence which it expected to find; Johnson could perhaps have produced as good a case producing evidence of racial harmony and Southern acceptance of the situation, but he had not done so.[2] Under the circumstances it was not likely that the committee would produce anything but a partisan case, and there was nothing abnormal in its behaviour. The conventions of party government assume that each party has a policy which it will support with evidence and argument, and implement when it has power. The plea for 'impartiality' usually implies partiality for the Democrats and the Southern whites. The committee was a predominantly Republican body, appointed to make the Republican case, and to suggest legislation which the Republican party might enact. There could be no 'impartial' reconciliation between the immediate admission of the Southern States without further conditions and admission after the provision of new guarantees. One could not ignore the existence of two policies, or pretend that the one which could command the most votes, or best exploit the machinery of the Constitution, would win; one could however argue about the nature and purpose of the additional guarantees, and these arguments were the major pre-occupation of the committee from January to April 1866.

As usually happens on a committee of this size some half-dozen men played an effective part. These were William Pitt Fessenden, the chairman, Thaddeus Stevens, John A. Bingham, George

[1] Boutwell, *Sixty Years*, II, 67.
[2] Johnson refused to furnish the Committee with evidence in his possession about conditions in the South (*Report of the Joint Committee*, ix).

Boutwell, and Roscoe Conkling with the addition, as a negative influence, of Reverdy Johnson. Fessenden was not a great man or a dominant personality, but he was the kind of experienced and shrewd man of affairs, with an integrity which men respected, who have often commanded more prestige in the Senate than men with more striking talents. Slightly built, with an anxious appearance and straggling grey whiskers, he could easily be overlooked in a crowd. He was not an orator of the classic American type, but he won attention through the solidity of his information, the cogency of his argument, and his obvious desire to discover what was practical without loss of principle. In December 1865 he was in bad health, inclined to be short-tempered, and on bad terms with some of his fellow senators including Charles Sumner; but no man was more likely to pick up the various threads of Republican thought and weave them into a presentable garment. In opinion he inclined to the Radicals, by temperament to conservatism, and this fitted him well for the task of discovering the consensus of Republican opinion. 'We are embarrassed', he wrote, 'by men of extreme opinions who think all ways except their own are necessarily bad ways, and by others who cannot wait till the proper time through fear that their own names may not be sufficiently known in connection with the work to be done.' But he thought that the committee contained 'a large majority of thorough men who were resolved that ample security should attend any restoration of the insurgent states, come what will, while they desire if possible, to avoid a division between Congress and the Executive, which can only result in unmixed evil'.[1] By mid-January he was conscious

[1] Fessenden, *Life of W. P. Fessenden*, II, 18. Quoted Kendrick, *Journal of the Joint Committee on Reconstruction*, 175. Despite my appreciation of Fessenden's quality I am unable to go so far as Kendrick who calls him 'one of the three or four ablest and most farsighted statesmen of his time' (op. cit., 181–2). Fessenden was politically experienced, he was a shrewd man of business, and he mingled wisdom with idealism in just proportions, but he lacked the personality which would have marked him down as a real leader. Nor can I agree with Kendrick that he was 'typical of the conservative Republican senators'. In the first session of the Thirty-ninth Congress he was always closer to the Radicals, though modifying their eagerness with native caution. In the second session he began to retreat from Radicalism and this culminated in his vote for acquittal at the impeachment of President Johnson. He voted against the Tenure of Office Act but supported all the other Reconstruction measures. Charles A. Jellison, *Fessenden of Maine*, (Syracuse 1962) provides a useful survey of Fessenden's career; on Fessenden's chairmanship of the Joint Committee it does not add to the account given by Kendrick op. cit.

that 'the work of maintaining the peace between the President and those who wish to quarrel with him, aided as they are by those who wish him to quarrel with us, is a most difficult undertaking. The fools are not all dead'.[1] He was particularly pleased that Charles Sumner had not been given the place on the committee which he so much desired.

The aims and tactics of Thaddeus Stevens in the committee are clear. He was completely sincere in his advocacy of racial equality and in his belief that for this, and for the future harmony of the Union, a drastic reform of Southern society was necessary; but he had already failed to muster support for his policy in Congress. In the committee however he might gain some essential points without closing the door upon more sweeping changes. He advanced what he regarded as sound principles wherever he saw an opening, but fought to avoid commitment to a plan of Reconstruction which fell short of his desires. When arguing for points which were in his programme he was an old man in a hurry, but when arguing about the procedure by which the Southern States should be restored to the Union he was evasive and obstructive; but he had also a strong sense of what was politically possible and was not the man to lose what he regarded as a move in the right direction because it did not pass every test. The immediate steps which he regarded as essential were the adjustment of Southern apportionment in Congress, and the exclusion from public life and influence of as many 'rebels' as possible. These points were means to an end and not the end itself, and whenever he saw a chance to advance the cause of equality he took it.

The same could not be said of Roscoe Conkling, the flamboyant, ambitious and arrogant representative from New York. Conkling was interested in power and in the effect of power upon his own career. It is difficult to attribute to him any higher principle, and the fame which he was to earn during the Grant era as the most notorious of spoilsmen was not misplaced. It is doubtful whether Conkling thought much about the South, but he thought a great deal about Washington. His primary concern

[1] Kendrick, op. cit., 175.

was for the future of the Republican party, and for his own future within it. He was therefore an advocate for severe terms, for political disabilities imposed upon as many as possible, and for a lengthy process of Reconstruction. Conkling could see no reason to accelerate the return of the Southerners to Congress, and when they did come back he hoped that they would not be represented by the same type of monumental Southern gentlemen who had dominated Congress before the war. On the other hand Conkling voted consistently against the proposal to give national protection to civil rights, though in later years he was responsible for the theory that the Fourteenth Amendment intended to give to corporations the equal protection of the laws.

It is less easy to assess the character and motives of George Boutwell of Massachusetts. He was not popular in the Republican party, and his reputation was that of a cold and calculating Radical without the human sympathy which redeemed Stevens even when most exasperating.[1] Boutwell was, however, a man of some ability, and there is no reason to doubt his sincerity. His speeches in Congress were lucid expositions of the extreme Radical case, and in the committee he made repeated efforts to advance the cause of negro suffrage. Like Sumner he represented the Radicalism of Massachusetts which could see no reason to delay justice on grounds of expediency and which believed that negro suffrage would automatically achieve the objectives of Reconstruction.

In sharp contrast to the three Radicals was John A. Bingham of Ohio. Bingham had a consistent anti-slavery record, and was deeply concerned with the problem of civil rights, but he was to emerge both in the committee and in Congress as champion of the moderate Republicans who wished to reconstruct as painlessly as possible. He believed that the one essential was a recognition of national responsibility for civil rights. He believed that Reconstruction offered the opportunity for introducing a beneficial

---

[1] Horace White wrote to E. B. Washburn in Oct. 1868 that Boutwell was 'one of those silent conscientious fanatics who are more dangerous to a party than a score of irrepressible "critters" like Wade, Chandler and Butler'. He had, said White, 'a maggot in his head' (L.C. *Washburn Papers*, 18 Oct. 1865).

reform of general application: the guarantee of the rights of all individuals against the power of government. He was not at this stage a thorough-going supporter of negro suffrage but he was prepared to accept it if useful for his main policy. His position was similar to that of Lyman Trumbull, but he voted to sustain Johnson's veto of Trumbull's Civil Rights Bill because he believed that the Constitution did not permit this measure without amendment. A further objection to Trumbull's measure was its exclusive concern with the negro in the South; he wanted a measure which would be truly national in scope. If this could be obtained he was not particularly interested in other 'guarantees' against the resurgence of Southern power. He supported the proposal to reduce Southern apportionment if the negroes were not enfranchised, but he was against the disenfranchisement of Southern whites, and accepted their disqualification from office only when it became clear that the party would not be content with less. He believed that Reconstruction policy must come to terms with the leaders of the South, and he wished to make it as easy as possible for them to co-operate with the North on the new basis of equal right.

Reverdy Johnson was an old Southern Whig and now the only Democrat in Congress who could command some respect from Republicans. As an eminent lawyer and a former cabinet minister he spoke with the voice of experience, and he managed to remain on good terms with most of his political opponents. Unlike the majority of Democrats in Congress he did not believe in the biological inferiority of negroes, and he had voted for the Thirteenth Amendment.[1] Apart from this his political ideas were those of an orthodox supporter of State rights, but he knew that majority opinion in the North was likely to insist upon some constitutional change. In the committee his efforts were therefore aimed to make the changes as inoffensive to the South as possible, and, though he could not support the Fourteenth Amendment, he did not regard it as unreasonable. He hoped that the Southern

---

[1] C.G. 39.1.373. "I believe that they are capable of as much and as high civilization as the white race. I have seen as much native talent exhibited in the black race as I have seen exhibited in the white race."

States would see fit to accept it, and later, when they had failed to do so, he was to vote for the Reconstruction Acts. In the committee his main aims were therefore to promote opportunities for second thoughts, to oppose the extreme Radicals, and to help the moderates without endorsing their constitutional doctrines.

The remaining Republican members of the committee did not contribute a great deal to its deliberations. George H. Williams was a lawyer whose reputation at the time probably exceeded his real abilities. He inclined to the Radical side, but on some votes he was found with the moderates. His main contribution to the work of the committee was that of a legal draftsman. J. W. Grimes of Iowa was a man who said little but commanded considerable influence as a man of judgment and integrity. He was a close friend of Fessenden, and usually voted with him. Southern Unionists were represented by Henry T. Blow of Missouri, who had played an important part in securing his state for the Union; he was thought to hold Radical opinions, but in the discussions and votes he usually supported Bingham. Jacob M. Howard, Justin S. Morrill and Elihu B. Washburn were men of some note in the party, and regularly attended the committee meetings but do not appear to have taken the initiative on any important occasion. Howard could be classed as a Radical; Morrill and Washburn belonged to the centre of the party, much concerned over the condition of the South, in favour of 'guarantees', but anxious for a workable solution.

The weakest Republican in the committee was Ira Harris of New York, who had little influence in Congress and was losing it in his own State; politically he was a moderate and his one positive contribution — a proposal to disenfranchise all 'rebels' until July 1870 — was an attempt to meet Radical views with a drastic measure of short duration. The two remaining members of the committee were Democrats of little consequence. Henry Grider was an innocuous Kentucky Whig of the Clay school who had joined the Democrats, Andrew Jackson Rogers of New Jersey was a violent negro-phobe whose speeches in Congress did much harm to the cause of white supremacy which he intended to serve.

A notable omission from the committee was that of a Republican who supported Johnson's policy, but apart from this it represented as wide a sweep of congressional opinion as could have been obtained. In reckoning his majority of 'sound men', Fessenden would probably have counted upon Grimes, Harris, Morrill, Bingham, Washburn, Blow and perhaps Williams. Among those who wished to quarrel with the President he would have placed Stevens, Boutwell, Conkling and probably Howard. With the three Democratic members it would thus be possible to vote down anything which he thought too Radical. On the other hand Radical proposals which seemed practical might well attract Morrill and would certainly attract Williams and Washburn, (making a 'radical' vote of seven) against three Democrats and three conservative Republicans (Bingham, Blow and Harris). In such a division the vote of Fessenden and his friend Grimes would decide the question, and on several occasions Fessenden's own vote was of crucial importance. As well as the balance of opinion in the committee it was necessary to consider the balance of power in Congress, where a two-thirds majority in both Houses would be necessary to carry an amendment. This meant that any considerable group of Republicans would be able to veto a proposal which they disliked so much that they would prefer to risk the failure of a whole policy rather than support it. In the Senate a comparatively small defection would defeat an amendment.

The need to meet all shades of Republican opinion soon became apparent.[1] The committee Republicans, with Johnson, were soon able to agree that the law of apportionment must be changed, but when the means were discussed they were soon in difficulties. The simple and straightforward solution was to base apportionment on legal voters, but the New Englanders immediately made it clear that they would not accept this. Compared with the Western States New England had a small proportion of adult males, and would lose representation if the legal voters

[1] The following account of the proceedings of the committee are taken from Kendrick, op. cit., and will be found under the appropriate dates in the *Journal* which he reprints, pp. 37–129.

scheme were adopted instead of keeping population as the basis. It therefore became necessary to abandon the legal voters suggestion and to find some way of excluding unenfranchised negroes from the count. Fessenden and Howard would have preferred to by-pass this difficulty, by insisting upon impartial suffrage in all States; but the other Republicans rejected this either because they disliked negro suffrage or because (like Stevens) they did not wish to have negro suffrage while the Southern gentry retained their dominant position. Accordingly the committee accepted, and reported to Congress, a proposal that when any citizen of the United States was denied the elective franchise on grounds of race, creed or colour, all members of that race should be excluded from the basis of representation. Again the delicate balance of opinion in the Republican party was demonstrated, for Sumner launched an impassioned attack in the Senate upon the proposed amendment. Sumner was angry because he had not been appointed to the committee, was prepared to look with a critical eye upon its recommendations, and objected to the proposal because it would recognize (though penalizing) racial discrimination. After delivering three speeches of great length, erudition and virulence Sumner persuaded two moderate and four Radical senators to vote with him and the Democrats in opposition, and on 9 March the Committee on Reconstruction was back to starting-point on the vexed question of apportionment.

Meanwhile the committee had been grappling with two other leading questions: civil rights and Tennessee. On 12 January Bingham began his fight for nationalizing civil rights with a proposed amendment that 'Congress shall have power to make all laws necessary and proper to secure to all persons in every state within this Union equal protection in their rights of life, liberty and property'. At the same time Stevens proposed his favourite amendment that 'all laws, state or national, shall operate impartially and equally on all persons without regard to race or color'. Both were referred to a strong sub-committee of Fessenden, Stevens, Howard, Conkling and Bingham. Nothing more was heard of the Stevens version, but the Bingham version emerged with the addition of 'political rights and privileges' to the civil rights of life, liberty and property. This was on 20 January, but the apportionment clause took precedence, and when the Bingham clause was discussed it was referred again to a new sub-committee after Howard and Boutwell had failed to insert a stricter definition of political rights. On 27 January the sub-committee reported the amendment with one alteration in wording but none in substance. After further discussion on detail, Stevens moved to report the proposed amendment to Congress, but the committee divided 5 to 5, with 5 absent or not voting (Harris, Conkling and Boutwell voting against with two Democrats). On 3 February another attempt was made by Bingham with a version which omitted political rights, and on 10 February four of the non-voters of 27 January joined those in favour. In the House of Representatives Bingham took charge of the measure, but it soon became apparent that it could not receive the necessary two-thirds. Many Republicans showed themselves hostile to the proposal as too great an encroachment upon the power of the States, and the Democrats were solidly opposed. Debate was deferred and the civil rights amendment, in this form, was not heard of again. Once again the committee was back to the starting-point.

When the majority of the committee had agreed upon the Bingham amendment the way was clear for a consideration of the admission of Tennessee. Many Republicans hoped that this Southern State could be considered separately from the others. It had always had a large Unionist element; it had been firmly reconstructed on a loyalist basis by Andrew Johnson when military governor. The State had disenfranchised rebels, its new Constitution disqualified them from office for five years, and its senators and representatives elect were men with unassailable Unionist records. From the Radical point of view the only flaw was a failure to provide negro suffrage. It was also the President's own State and many hoped that its early admission would help to unite him with the Republican party, while an unfavourable decision would condemn his work as military governor. Stevens was, however, firmly opposed to letting any rebel State back into

Congress without spelling out conditions. To do so might create a precedent, and the whole position which the Radicals were trying to build up might be undermined if Congress began to treat each State as a special case.

On 17 February Bingham proposed an enabling bill which simply declared that Tennessee, having presented a Constitution which was Republican in form, should be admitted to Congress. At first this seemed to go well, but then Williams proposed to refer the matter to a select committee. This was carried by 8 to 7, with Fessenden in the majority, and his doubts about the Bingham plan were shown by his choice of Williams, Conkling and Boutwell for the select committee. When they reported back it was with a substitute which recommended admission on certain fundamental conditions. The State was never to assume or pay any debt contracted in aid of the rebellion, and to accept responsibility for its share of the debt of the United States. It must maintain forever in its Constitution the provision disavowing secession. It should preserve in its Constitution the provision excluding from the elective franchise and from public offices, for not less than five years, all who had supported the rebellion. These conditions were to be ratified by a majority of qualified electors. Bingham immediately moved to strike out the disenfranchising and disqualifying clause, and Boutwell moved to add a further condition that the State should make no distinction in the franchise on grounds of race or colour.

On the very morning that this discussion on Tennessee was held, Johnson was placing his veto of the Freedmen's Bureau Bill before the Cabinet; by the evening of the same day the veto had been sent to Congress.[1] When the committee reassembled on

---

[1] Beale (ed.), *Diary of Gideon Welles*, II, 434–5. The argument of H. K. Beale (*The Critical Year* (New York, 1930), 81–3) that Johnson decided to veto the bill because he had heard that the committee had refused to recommend the admission of Tennessee is untenable. The proceedings of the committee were secret and even if Johnson had heard privately about the argument on Tennessee on 17 Feb. he could not have known anything about the report of the select committee proposing conditions for the State's admission, nor, in view of the close voting on the Tennessee question, could anyone anticipate how the select committee's report would be received. On 19 Feb. the Cabinet met at 10 a.m. to consider the veto message and the committee at 10.30 a.m. to consider the report of the select committee.

the following day it did so therefore against a background of gathering tension. Boutwell's suffrage clause was turned down by 5 to 6, with Fessenden, Grimes and Blow not voting; and Bingham then moved his original proposal as a substitute. At this stage Stevens suddenly intervened to say that 'his opinion as to the expediency and propriety of this action . . . had been materially changed since yesterday. The first duty of the committee was to declare the power of Congress over this subject of reconstruction'. He therefore proposed to postpone all other business and to submit to Congress a resolution that 'in order to close agitation upon a question which seems likely to disturb the action of the government, as well as to quiet the uncertainty which is agitating the mind of the people of the eleven states which have been declared to be in insurrection, no senator or representative shall be admitted into either branch of Congress for any of the said states until Congress shall have declared such state entitled to representation'. This was carried by 10 to 4 (Bingham and Blow voting against with two Democrats). On a further vote to report the agreed resolution to Congress all the Republicans voted in favour. It was subsequently passed by large majorities in both Houses of Congress being read and accepted as a direct rebuttal of the argument in Johnson's veto message that the 'right of Congress to judge, each House for itself, "of elections, returns and qualifications of its own members . . ." cannot be construed as including the right to shut out in time of peace any State from the representation to which it is entitled by the Constitution'. Incidentally the veto had enabled Stevens to shelve the question of Tennessee at the moment when the unqualified admission advocated by Bingham stood a good chance of acceptance, and when the principle of disqualification and disenfranchisement was likely to come under heavy fire. Johnson had therefore enabled Stevens to win a tactical victory in the committee; but at the sacrifice of any positive fruits to show for the committee's labours. By early March the civil rights amendment was virtually lost in the House, the apportionment amendment was lost in the Senate, and the admission of Tennessee had been deferred. In the files of the committee was a growing volume of evidence about the South, but two months' work had produced no positive measure save the declaratory resolution.

It would be wrong, however, to attribute the stalemate which had developed entirely to the veto. This provided a shock for Republican opinion which Stevens was able to exploit, and it brought to light a fundamental difference of opinion between the President and the majority of the party, but it was not responsible for the difficulties of the committee. These difficulties arose out of the political situation, and of the tussle between moderates and Radicals. An important though not conclusive point had been gained by the Radicals on 17 February when Fessenden showed his doubts about Bingham's plan for the admission of Tennessee by voting for reference to a new select committee, and by his choice of three Radicals for that committee. Evidently he wanted an opportunity to consider stiffer proposals. Fessenden was not the man to vote on such an important question without a careful consideration of the consequences and his action was the symptom of a shift in moderate opinion towards Radicalism. The union of moderates and Radicals against Johnson was already in the making before the veto and it is interesting to speculate upon the forces which were promoting it.

One possible answer is to be found in the nature of the evidence which the sub-committees on the various States were producing. The vital assumption for moderates was that if certain basic safeguards could be written into the Constitution, the Southern whites could be safely left to manage their own affairs; but witness after witness was bringing evidence of hostility to Southern Unionists, of discrimination and violence against negroes, and of the incapability or unwillingness of Southern courts to provide impartial justice between the races. The Southerners professed, in what was becoming a favourite phrase, that they had 'accepted the situation', but clearly they did not understand the situation in the same way as the Northern majority. It might therefore be necessary to improve their understanding by further safeguards such as the Radicals demanded. Moderates might have had a stronger case if they had been sure of the President, for much would depend upon the use which he made of the military force at his disposal in the Southern States. The evidence on the effects of his pardoning policy had already disposed committee members against him, and, though the extent of his opposition to the congressional majority was not apparent until the veto and the 22 February speech, there was already a good deal of doubt about his intentions. There may also have been rumours that military commanders, who were trying to use their authority to protect negroes, were not *personae gratae* at the White House.

Against this background of disquiet and doubt, a second and personal incident was important. This was Fessenden's interview with the President on 28 January. It has often been surmised that the two men simply failed to communicate with each other, but it is equally plausible to suppose that they came to understand each other only too well. On the date of the interview Fessenden knew that the committee's proposal for tying apportionment to negro suffrage would shortly be before Congress, and as an honest man he could hardly have concealed this from the President in what was intended to be a full and exploratory discussion. On the day before the committee had divided five to five on the notion to report Bingham's civil rights clause to Congress, and though this meant that it was temporarily set back, three or four of the five absentees would certainly vote in favour if the motion were reconsidered. Fessenden knew therefore that some version of the civil rights amendment would probably be presented to Congress and again he could hardly have concealed this from the President. One can imagine how Johnson received the news that it was intended to alter the law of apportionment in a way which brought pressure upon the States to grant negro suffrage and that Congress would also seek power by amendment to protect civil rights in the States. This was the 'centralism' which he believed would destroy the American system of government. It is also possible that Johnson found confirmation, in his talk with Fessenden, for his belief that Stevens controlled the committee. It would have been natural for Fessenden to stress the weight of opinion behind the two proposed amendments, and Johnson, aware of Stevens's proposal in Congress for the equal application of all laws upon all citizens, may well have concluded that the Radicals had taken control. These hypotheses make the veto of the Freedmen's Bureau Bill more intelligible. He saw an urgent need for presenting the argument against excessive use of national power, for rallying opinion behind an early restoration of the Southern State to Congress (which would block amendments to the Constitution), and, as an interim measure, for detaching from Radical leadership sufficient numbers of moderate Republicans. At the time of the interview Tennessee had not yet been discussed in the committee, and Johnson may not have realized that Bingham, the prime mover behind the civil rights amendment, was also the spokesman for the immediate admission of that State. Thus it is unlikely that Fessenden's interview did anything to correct the President's erroneous understanding of moderate Republican opinion.

On Fessenden's side it is equally plausible to suppose that he understood from the interview the depth of the President's hostility to 'centralism'. If he did not do so at the time, the publication of the interview given by the President to Dixon must have caused him to think over carefully what had been said. The President was now on record as opposing amendment of the Constitution, and as describing the agitation for negro suffrage in Washington as 'ill-timed, uncalled for, and calculated to do much harm'.[1] Johnson must have known that the whole direction of the committee's effort was based upon the assumption that amendment was necessary, and, though he was not at liberty to reveal any knowledge of the apportionment proposed, his reference to suffrage in the District of Columbia showed plainly his dislike of any measure which would force negro enfranchisement upon whites who did not want it. His conversation with Dixon must therefore have seemed a calculated and uncom-

---

[1] A bill granting negro suffrage in the District of Columbia had been debated in Congress but had not reached a final vote.

promising rejection of the case which Fessenden had tried to put before him. If this interpretation is correct, Fessenden's attitude towards the admission of Tennessee can be readily explained. Supposing that the President intended to use his influence against the two proposed amendments, they were likely to fail. If this happened it would be necessary to use the existing power of Congress to impose additional 'guarantees' as an insurance against Southern abuse of 'home rule'. Bingham's plan for the admission of Tennessee might create a bad precedent, and it would be wise first to explore the possibility of further guarantees. Hence Fessenden's vote for the motion to refer Bingham's plan to a new committee.

Fessenden was not, however, prepared to throw all his influence on to the Radical side; he was seeking a compromise solution which would satisfy both Bingham and Stevens. On 3 March, with the attitude of the President known to all, he brought forward a new version of the Tennessee plan which Bingham agreed to accept. This declared that Tennessee *had* complied with certain necessary conditions, asserted that the people were therefore 'in a condition to exercise the functions of a state within their Union; and can only exercise the same by the consent of the law-making power of the United States'. Having inferred the right to impose conditions and preserved the paramount authority of Congress, the moderate desire for immediate admission could be satisfied, and the Radical machinery of fundamental conditions ratified by the State was dropped. Though this form was agreed on 3 March, the Radicals had made clear their opposition to it, and had perhaps intimated that they would carry the fight on to the floor of Congress. Accordingly on 5 March Bingham, who appeared to have won his fight, re-opened the argument. He himself proposed an additional clause that the admission of Tennessee was to be agreed 'upon the express condition that the people of Tennessee will maintain and enforce in good faith their existing constitution and laws excluding those who have been engaged in rebellion against the United States from the exercise of the elective franchise for the respective periods of time therein provided for, and shall also exclude for a like period of time the same persons from eligibility to office'. Stevens immediately pressed an additional clause that this new condition must be ratified by the legislature or by the people of Tennessee before the act could take effect. The new amendments were accepted, and also a proposition by Conkling adding to the 'express conditions' the repudiation of the rebel war debt and the refusal of compensation for freed slaves. On Stevens's additional clause Fessenden and Grimes voted in favour while Bingham and Harris voted against with the Democrats. If Fessenden had voted the other way the motion would have been tied, and lost if Grimes had followed Fessenden, as he usually did. Thus the recommendation for the admission of Tennessee was finally agreed and presented to Congress. The Radicals had not got everything which they wanted, but they had come very near to it; in producing this result their own strength in Congress, the breach with the President, and the decisions of Fessenden had played decisive parts.

*　　*　　*　　*

The Reconstruction Committee had yet to find a general policy which it would recommend to Congress. On 16 April it heard Senator Stewart explain at length his plan for universal amnesty and universal suffrage, but proceeded no further with it. Stevens must have been searching his mind for a plan which was positive enough to satisfy those who wanted early action, flexible enough to allow the ferment of social and political revolution to work in the South, and sufficiently precise on the question of negro suffrage to win the support of Sumner and his friends in the Senate. Outside aid came unexpectedly in the form of a visit from Robert Dale Owen, son of the famous English socialist pioneer who was now settled in Indiana. Owen came with a fully articulated plan of Reconstruction, which was, as Stevens told him, much better than anything hitherto discussed in the committee.[1] The distinctive feature of Owen's plan was that it threw all the pro-

[1] Owen's account of his interview with Stevens was given in the *Atlantic Monthly*, Jun. 1875. It is summarized with ample quotations in Kendrick, op. cit., 296–302.

posed changes into one amendment, instead of tackling each
subject separately, and made this composite amendment play an
integral part in the process of Reconstruction. The first section
forbade discrimination by the States in civil rights on grounds of
race, creed or colour, or previous condition of servitude. The
second proposed that no discrimination in suffrage should be
made after 4 July 1876. The third that until 1876 no class of persons, any of whom were deprived of suffrage, should be counted
in the basis of representation. The usual provision for the repudiation of rebel debt and of compensation for emancipated slaves
followed. Finally the proposed amendment copied the Thirteenth
Amendment by giving power to Congress to enforce its provisions
by appropriate legislation. The accompanying plan of Reconstruction made the amendment the pivot upon which it turned;
when it had become law, and when it had been ratified by any
State lately in insurrection, and when that State had modified its
constitution and laws in conformity with it, such a State should
be admitted to Congress. But until 1876 no former officer of the
Confederate forces, and no member of the Congress or Cabinet
in 1860 who supported the rebellion, should be eligible for
election to Congress.

The Owen plan had considerable merits. It met the immediate
requirement for the protection of civil rights and the theoretical
commitment to negro suffrage. By fixing the date of complete
enfranchisement a decade ahead, it gave Southern society time to
adapt itself to new conditions, but it also prevented the Southerners from gaining increased representation until the negroes had
the vote. It kept former Confederate leaders out of Congress until
their influence could be off-set by negro suffrage, but the disqualification proposed would not disrupt State governments. At
the same time the plan was open to objections from both sides of
the Republican fence. Bingham thought that the civil rights clause
was imprecise, and that the nationalizing of rights ought not to be
confined to negroes. Stevens was probably disturbed at the prospect
of the Southern leaders enfranchising the negroes immediately,
and riding to power on the shoulders of a docile negro electorate.

He had also pointed out to Owen that reduced apportionment would leave each State with two senators who could do as much or more harm than any number of secessionist Representatives. The suffrage proposal was vulnerable for when, by accident or design it leaked out, the Republican congressional delegations from New York, Illinois and Indiana decided in separate caucuses that a definite commitment to negro suffrage would damage their chances in the next election (which would be of such vital importance to the Republican party). Radicals welcomed the introduction of 'political disabilities' as a part of general Reconstruction policy, but in their eyes the proposal was inadequate because it would leave the Southern gentry in control of their States. In the light of these objections it is not surprising that the plan was modified in almost every particular before it emerged from the committee. Owen's plan provided a new impetus at a time when the committee was almost at a standstill; it provided a working draft for what ultimately became the Fourteenth Amendment, but when presented to Congress its component parts were suggestions which had engaged the attention of the committee before Owen's intervention.

The first casualty was the suffrage clause, which Stevens proposed to replace by the original proposal reducing the count for apportionment by the whole number of any race against which discrimination was made because of race, colour and previous condition of servitude in the suffrage. Williams then introduced a solution which had probably been prepared in advance by the 'sound men' on the committee. When any male citizens were denied the suffrage the basis of representation should 'be reduced in proportion which the number of such male citizens shall bear to the whole number of male citizens'. The deletion of any reference to race or colour in the new version may have been made to meet the objections of Sumner, while proportionate reduction of representation, rather than leaving all negroes out of the count when any discrimination was made, appealed to those who hoped that the Southerners would be encouraged to experiment with negro suffrage subject to a literacy or property test.

The committee next turned to political disabilities. A motion by Boutwell to exclude a large part of the Southern ruling class from Federal office forever was rejected by the narrow margin of 8 to 6. Harris then moved that all persons who had voluntarily supported the rebellion should be disenfranchised in Federal elections until 4 July 1870 (that is only for the elections of 1866 and 1868). This was first rejected by 8 to 7, but after discussion this vote was reconsidered and the proposal accepted by 8 to 5. Fessenden and Grimes had changed their votes and once more the ability of the chairman to decide the crucial points, which split Radicals from moderates, was demonstrated.

Earlier in the discussions Bingham had succeeded in expanding the wording of the civil rights clause, but in doing so had made a significant departure from the wording of his original civil rights amendment. The amendment which had been lost in the House of Representatives had given Congress power to make all laws necessary and proper 'to secure to the citizens of each state all privileges and immunities of citizens in the several states; and to all persons in the several states equal protection in the rights of life, liberty and property'. The new version said that no State should make laws 'which shall abridge the privileges or immunities of citizens of the United States; nor shall any state deprive any person of life, liberty or property without due process of law; nor deny to any person within its jurisdiction the equal protection of the laws'. The first version had made Congress the judge of what was necessary and proper to secure equal civil rights; the second allowed the States to use their discretion in the first instance. Remedy against State action which infringed the amendment could be heard in the courts of the United States, but it would be incumbent upon the judges to decide what was meant by the amendment and whether it had been observed. It was true that Owen's original section giving Congress power to enforce the amendment to appropriate legislation remained; but the new form of amendment made it likely that Congress would act only when it was apparent that the States had failed in their duties. In effect the initiative was transferred from the national government to the

States, and the way was open for evasion of the spirit if not of the letter of the amendment.

Next the committee accepted Owen's plan for re-admission of the States to the Union when the amendment had become law and had been ratified by the States concerned. Fessenden, however, preserved the discretionary power of Congress by securing an alteration of the obligatory 'shall be admitted' to 'may be admitted into Congress'. Finally the committee agreed to propose a bill excluding forever from national office various classes of Confederate leaders. Thus on 28 April after three months' work, but largely as the result of decisions taken in the last week, the Committee on Reconstruction had devised a policy for presentation to Congress. The policy had still to run the gauntlet of debate in Congress.

In the House Stevens permitted no delay; using the previous question, and indignantly repelling any attempt to discuss the disenfranchisement clause he secured a quick vote on the amendment. It passed by six more affirmative and four fewer negative notes than had been given on the re-passage of the Civil Rights Bill. A notable vote in favour was that of Henry Raymond, whose *New York Times* was the principal Republican newspaper supporting the President. In the Senate matters could not be hurried. Much to the relief of the party leaders Sumner made no opposition to the suffrage clause. A useful addition to the civil rights section was made by a declaration that all persons born in the United States, and subject to their jurisdiction, were citizens of the United States, thus writing into the Constitution a formal reversal of the Dred Scott decision. The main controversy arose over the political disabilities. There was general agreement among Republicans that the resurgent power of Confederate leaders must be checked, but a widespread dislike of the principle of disenfranchisement. In some States this would mean a virtual return to the ten-per-cent plan, which the Radicals had denounced as minority government. After much discussion the Senate adopted the new principle of disqualifying from both State and national office all those who had once, as office-holders, sworn an oath of allegiance to the United States and subsequently supported the rebellion. The disabilities could be removed only by a two-thirds vote of both Houses of Congress. This final decision was made in a prolonged caucus of Republican senators. In the words of the Democratic senator, Thomas Hendricks, 'For three days the Senate chamber was silent but the discussions were transferred to another room in the capitol, with closed doors and darkened windows, where party leaders might safely contend for a political and party policy.' Not even the Press had been able to learn what passed.[1] One can, however, imagine the tussle between Radicals who wanted to destroy forever the power of the Southern 'aristocracy' by imposing sweeping disqualification and conservatives who wished to conciliate this same 'aristocracy' with acceptable terms. It is, however, reasonable, in the light of all contemporary discussion, to suppose that the majority wanted a plan which would work, and the least plausible explanation is that the political disabilities were inserted by the Radicals with the express intention of securing the amendment's rejection in the South. Moderates may have taken comfort in the substitution of temporary for permanent disqualification, as in the committee's proposal, of which nothing more was heard.

With the Senate amendments the Fourteenth Amendment finally passed both Houses of Congress, and during the remaining weeks of the session some of the loose ends of Reconstruction were tidied up. Tennessee immediately ratified the new amendment and was admitted with an enabling act reciting the conditions which had been fulfilled; Johnson signed the bill though with a written protest against the idea that conditions could be demanded. A new Freedman's Bureau Act was passed over the veto. Partly in consequence of their own divisions, and partly as a result of Johnson's opposition, the Republicans failed to pass a bill for negro suffrage in the District of Columbia, and failed to admit Nebraska and Colorado to the Union as States. A more significant omission was that of a general Reconstruction Act, either in the form proposed by the committee or in any other. In the debates it was clear that Stevens was anxious to avoid any commitment

[1] C.G.39.1.2939

which would bind Congress to admit the Southern States under specified conditions, and equally clear that Bingham and his friends wanted a precise specification of the terms of Reconstruction. Either as a genuine alternative or as a diversionary tactic, Stevens introduced the first formal proposal to reconstruct the Southern States as distinct from reconstructing the Union: conventions were to be called and elected on a colour-blind suffrage, but all who had taken the oath of allegiance to the Confederacy were deprived of citizenship and would have to go through the process of naturalization in order to re-acquire it; these conventions were to make Constitutions which would enact complete equality in civil and political rights, and the States would forfeit representation if these provisions were ever abrogated; when these conditions had been complied with the States would be re-admitted to Congress. Meanwhile the original restoration bill proposed by the committee came under heavy attack from old abolitionists because it did not make negro suffrage mandatory. It became clear that the Radicals in the House would obstruct the passage of any Reconstruction act which was not drastic and that the moderates would resist any bill which delayed early restoration of the Union or attempted to alter the fabric of Southern society. Caught between these two fires the restoration bill died in the House and the Senate took no action upon it. Men were left free to assume either that, following the precedent of Tennessee, a State which ratified the amendment, would be admitted to Congress, or that the amendment was only a first step towards Reconstruction and that further consideration could begin when it had been ratified. From this misunderstanding were to spring many consequences. A further point remained uncertain, perhaps by accident, but more probably by deliberate evasion of a question which would throw wide the chasm between Radicals and moderates. Stevens had insisted that the Southern States should play no part in amending the Constitution, and for him their acceptance of the amendment would mean no more than their submission to the authority of Congress. Moderates on the other hand believed that though deprived of representation the Southern States were not 'conquered provinces', had not forfeited all their rights in the Union, and must play their part in the fundamental task of constitutional change. The Stevens view had not won much support, though it was logically neater than the idea of States as partly in and partly out of the Union. The Radicals had no wish to bring the question to a decision in the present mood of Congress, while the moderates, believing that they were on the verge of a practicable plan, did not wish to challenge the Radicals once more. Though Democratic senators insisted that Southerners would reject the amendment however it was proposed to them, Republicans (with the necessity of a two-thirds vote always in their minds) preferred to evade the question of whether such rejection would or would not mean the loss of the amendment. In a sense the lack of decision was a point for the moderates. It left submission to the States to the discretion of the Secretary of State, and everyone knew that Seward, regarding the Southern States as full and legal States, would send the amendment to their legislatures for ratification. But Radicals were left free to argue that avoidance of decision implied a tacit acceptance by Congress of their case.

Reactions to congressional policy varied from outright condemnation to qualified approval. Few could muster great enthusiasm, but Republicans defended what had been done as the best which could be obtained in the face of divided opinions and presidential obstruction. There was some dismay at the failure to pass a Reconstruction act. Anticipating this omission the editor of the Chicago *Tribune* wrote privately in July that the people would be 'chagrined and astonished to find out that the Amendment *means nothing*, that no conditions of reconstruction have been devised or proposed officially, that in short it is the intention of Congress to exclude the South permanently or for so long as the Republicans have control of Congress. . . . We must have some perfected plan else our party will surely suffer defeat. We can't stand on nothing. We can't defend a scheme or a policy of exclusion or a mere do nothing policy'.[1] A good many Mid-

---

[1] L.C. *Washburn Papers*, White to Washburn, Jul. 1866.

western Republicans were to solve this dilemma by telling their constituents that ratification of the amendment by the Southern States was the condition for re-admission. On the other hand Stevens made no secret of his belief that much remained to be done. In September he was telling Pennsylvanians that Congress deserved censure for its omissions. 'While it was impossible, obstructed as we were, by the President and the Copperheads, to make this a Republic of "liberty and equality," we might have approached it more nearly than we did. We might have treated the rebel States as what they are, in fact, conquered provinces, and, through enabling acts, we could have fixed the qualifications for voters so that every loyal man could participate in the formation of their organic laws. We should thus, with entire certainty, have secured the government to loyal Union men, have formed, in every one of those States, constitutions giving equal privileges to all, and which would have curbed the rising spirit of rebellion which is now rampant in every one of those States.' He believed that Congress ought to have extracted an indemnity from the Confederates by tax and confiscation, but it had not even reversed the President's pardons which illegally restored property despite the Act of Forfeiture of 1862. 'I admit', he said, 'that Congress became demogogical in the last hot days, when all manhood was melted out of everybody.' He probably meant by this the sensitivity of congressmen to the unpopularity of negro suffrage and their fear of the 'unanswerable arguments' against negro equality which would 'ring in every low bar room and be printed in every blackguard sheet throughout a land whose fundamental maxim is "all men are created equal" '.[1]

On the other hand, in moderate Republican ranks, there was a general feeling that Congress, without achieving a striking success, had steered between extremes to reach a respectable conclusion. Raymond believed that by its modifications of the Fourteenth Amendment 'the Union majority in the Senate have taken an important step towards the vindication of their party from the disgrace and the weakness inflicted upon it by Mr Stevens'

[1] L.C. *Stevens Papers*, speech at Bedford, Pennsylvania, 4 Sep. 1866.

intemperate malignity'.[1] The New York *Herald* thought that it was really Johnson's own policy, and there was a widely expressed hope that, whatever he had said in the past, the President would now recognize what had been done as a platform upon which he could join with the party once more.[2] However, Johnson soon made it clear that he remained the most important critic of congressional policy. He made clear his opposition to any change in the Constitution while States were unrepresented in Congress, and to all conditions for restoration in the form of amendments. He repeated his belief that the law entitled the Southern States to representation unconditionally. On 22 June with the amendment completed in Congress, he sent a message disassociating himself from it and asserting that 'a proper appreciation of the letter and spirit of the Constitution, as well as the interests of national order, harmony, and union, and a due deference for an enlightened public judgment, may at this time well suggest a doubt whether any amendment to the Constitution ought to be proposed by Congress and pressed upon the legislature of the several States for final decision until after the admission of such loyal Senators and Representatives of the now unrepresented States as have been, or may hereafter be, chosen in conformity with the Constitution and laws of the United States'.[3] Johnson was not going to press the Southern States to ratify, and his open opposition, with some vocal support from his Northern supporters, encouraged the hope that the Republican party would be weakened and perhaps overthrown in the autumn elections. Presented with a choice between acquiescence in a congressional policy which they disliked and putting their faith in a President who spoke their own language there was little doubt which Southerners would choose. They remained unaware of the fact that Andrew Johnson, who had never possessed much understanding of the Northerner people, was losing even that which he had had. As his popularity increased in the South, his chance of winning approval in the North receded.

---

[1] C.G. 39.1.2502. For Raymond's attitude see also McKitrick, op. cit., 358.
[2] McKitrick, op. cit., 356.   [3] C.G. 39.1.3349.

The weakness of the policy determined by Congress was that it hovered between the two concepts of the war. There was considerable force in Thaddeus Stevens's argument that the Southern States ought to have been treated as 'conquered provinces' because it corresponded to the facts of a situation in which Northern power had effective control over the defeated South; there was equal force in his suggestion that they ought to be treated as Territories, enjoying local self-government at the discretion of Congress, and entitled to re-admission as States when their condition was such that they could be brought in good faith to accept the Constitution as amended by the Northern majority. The political weakness of Stevens's case was that this logical analysis of the relationship of the Southern States to the Union was recognized as the preface to a revolution in Southern society. This raised alarms and drove more moderate or less clear-headed Republicans back from the idea of a dictated peace, as the consequence of unconditional surrender, to the idea of a negotiated settlement, They clung to the idea that the Southern States must be treated as States, though out of their proper political relationship to the Union. The Southern States were to be asked but not compelled to accept the terms proposed. The onus of decision was passed to the Southern States at a moment when they still were able to defy Congress but hardly capable of taking a statesmanlike view of the future. In retrospect it can be asserted with some confidence that it would have paid the Southern States to have ratified the amendment. They had nothing to lose which they were not already certain to lose. The objectionable disqualification clause disenfranchised no one and there was good prospect of persuading a sufficient number of Republicans to join with the Democrats in the near future to secure the necessary two-thirds to remove the political disabilities. Even though disqualified, the former leaders of the South would retain their influence and Southern representatives in Congress were more likely to be their friends than their enemies. The Southern States were therefore in a good position to do more quickly what they eventually did under the far more stringent Reconstruction Acts of 1867. But

L

the summer of 1866 was hardly a time at which Southerners could take a cool and far-sighted view or to reckon correctly the price which would have to be paid for reconciliation with the Northern majority. One is driven to the conclusion that the Southern States would have been better off, and that future sectional and racial relations would have been better, if they had been told that they must take it and could not leave it.

A further weakness lay in the refusal of Congress to take a clear and unequivocal line on the racial question. If racial equality — equal rights and impartial suffrage — had been presented to the South as a clear condition for Reconstruction, much later trouble might have been avoided. Few Southerners would ever admit the principle of social integration, or of the capacity of the negro for advancement, but a majority were already well on the road toward the acceptance of legal equality. Forced to accept it they might well have adjusted themselves to the new situation; forced to choose, it was inevitable that they would choose a system of discrimination based on a belief in the biological inferiority of the black race. Their rejection of the Fourteenth Amendment takes its place in the long series of defence mechanisms created by the South to resist the logic of the proposition that men are created equal, and it was an error on the part of Congress to allow them the opportunity. It was an error because in the existing climate of opinion in the North, the racial question would not lie down. 'In this Republic', Stevens told his constituents, 'the same laws must and shall apply to every mortal, American, Irishman, African, German or Turk. It is written by the finger of the Almighty law-giver, "Ye shall have one manner of laws, as well as for the stranger as for one of your own country; for I am the Lord your God".... This doctrine may be popular or unpopular, I shall stand by it until I am relieved of the unprofitable labours of earth. Being the foundation of our Republic, I have full faith in its ultimate triumph.'[1] Away in Midwestern Indiana, where Republicans were locked in a grim struggle with copperhead Democrats, the old abolitionist G. W. Julian found to his

[1] L.C. *Stevens Papers*, speech at Bedford, Pennsylvania, 4 Sep. 1866.

delight that the question of negro suffrage could not be ignored, that it came to the fore whatever steps might be taken to keep it out of discussion.[1] The powerful ferment of the old abolitionist creed had worked its way deep into the fabric of Northern society, and its simple logic was increasingly difficult to resist.

Thus the congressional moderates, the men who wished to combine speedy Reconstruction with satisfaction of what they believed to be the just demands of the North, had landed themselves and Congress in a peculiarly difficult position. They had stated their terms but left enough unsaid to arouse suspicions of their real intentions. Caught between the dogmatism of Johnson and the extremism of Stevens they had tried to reach a solution which would satisfy everyone, including if possible the President, and the result was an impossible situation. The Fourteenth Amendment was to have far-reaching effects — it was to be the touchstone and perhaps the redeeming feature of congressional Reconstruction — but the manner in which it was presented to the Southern States was a cruel error.

If Congress can be blamed for doing too little, it can also be blamed for doing too much. The idea of political retribution for the Southern leaders was nourished by the hope that they would be repudiated by the Southern people. Had this been true the history of Reconstruction would have been very different; but it was untrue, and the continued belief that it could be made true imparted to Republican policy an unreality which was as dangerous as that which inspired Andrew Johnson.[2] Yet the exclusion of the 'rebel' leaders from public life was not foisted upon Congress by a few malign and vindictive men; in some form or other it was a policy common to most Republicans. The tragedy of Reconstruction is not that it was planned by bad men, but by

---

[1] Julian, *Political Recollections*, 263.

[2] There is an interesting comparison to be made between the treatment of the South in 1865 and of Germany in 1945. In both situations the victors (or a majority of them) decided that their future security depended upon a reformation of the political society of the defeated. In 1945 the Germans themselves were prepared to repudiate the men who had led them in the war and, in large measure, to reject their own immediate past; there were also men ready and able to supply leadership once the Nazis had been displaced. In the South there was no repudiation or rejection, and no satisfactory group to take over leadership from the old ruling class.

honourable men with a high sense of the responsibility which rested upon them.

It would be unjust to blame Congress too much for its acts and omissions. Whatever was to happen to Northern opinion during the next twelve months, Congress had faithfully mirrored both its certainties and its doubts during the troubled months since December. The foregoing account has demonstrated how often important decisions seemed to be the result of chance, of personal idiosyncrasy, of shifting votes by two or three men in the Committee of Fifteen, and of subtle changes in the balance of power in Congress; yet at the end of it Congress had not done much more than to implement decisions already reached by the majority of Northern opinion in December. The motive force behind policy had its origin deep in the Northern society; decision-making in Congress had given it legislative form, but the politicians had been significant only when their ideas echoed those of substantial groups among the Northern people. Thus the first attempt at Reconstruction by Congress is a fascinating study of the interplay between political opinion and political leadership; its faults and its weaknesses were not those of a revolutionary minority but those of a democratic society stirred with idealism, bitterness and bewilderment.

· V ·

Second Congressional Reconstruction

When Republican congressmen reassembled in December 1866, for the second session of the Thirty-ninth Congress, anger, bewilderment and confidence struggled for possession of their minds. Their anger was directed against the President and the South, bewilderment sprang from failure to produce a policy for Reconstruction, and confidence fed upon the results of the congressional elections. The President showed no sign of seeking an accommodation with Congress; the leaders of the South seemed willing neither to recognize the authority of Congress nor to do of their own free will what was required of them, and the Republican electoral victory in the North had been overwhelming. Congressmen, who might have wavered before the election, were now re-assured by the evidence of popular approval and could throw upon their constituents the responsibility for decision; yet in the South the ruling groups seemed equally assured of their ability to make a settlement on their own terms, and they too were fortified by the support of their own people. Johnson has been blamed for encouraging Southern resistance, but his actions were a symptom rather than a cause of the common interests which were drawing all white Southerners together. Johnson's opinions and actions were significant because they provided an excuse for Southern action, and because he alone represented Southern interests in the national government. An accident of political history had ensured that the chief opponent of the policy of the national government was its head; and this was a situation unlikely to clarify men's ideas or promote a satisfactory solution in the crisis of Reconstruction.

The results of the election were impressive. Maine had started in September with a Republican majority of 27,000; Lincoln had carried the State by just over 21,000 in 1864. In New York, where the influence of Seward and Thurlow Weed might have been expected to combine with that of the most powerful Democratic organization in the country, the Republicans secured a majority of 14,000; the margin was small enough in a big State but double that of Lincoln two years before. The big Midwestern States rolled in huge Republican majorities: 43,000 in Ohio, 60,000 in Illinois, 30,000 in Michigan, 40,000 in Iowa. The Republicans just scraped home in Connecticut — where the Democrats were numerous and better organized than in any other New England State — and in New Jersey which Lincoln had lost in 1864. Special significance was attached to the majority of 14,000 in Indiana — home of the most vigorous copperhead movement during the war and recently the scene of a serious Republican split over negro suffrage — and of 25,000 in Wisconsin where one of the senators, James Doolittle, was the leading Johnson Republican. Except in Vermont, Massachusetts and California more votes had been polled than in any presidential election, and the more votes cast the larger proportionately had been the Republican majority. In 1860 Lincoln had carried seventeen States and the war had been fought to establish his and their right to rule; in 1866 the Republicans carried twenty States and it was hard to deny that such a majority had a right to determine the future of the nation. Even if every Southern State had voted and returned a solid Democratic representation, the Republicans would still have had a substantial majority. It would not, however, have been large enough to amend the Constitution or override a veto. The dilemma was therefore just what it had always been: must the majority of the people voluntarily divest themselves of the power which would secure the gains of the war? In December 1865 it had been possible that their representatives would agree to do so if 'guarantees' could be provided; after the election of 1866 the idea of 'guarantees' dropped into the background and was succeeded by the notion that the nation could not be safe without drastic modifications of Southern society.

The Republican success in 1866 was explained in various ways. Naturally the Republicans claimed it as a massive and spontaneous popular endorsement of their policy; the Democrats hinted at corruption (but not too loudly, for the Democratic Tammany organization was all too vulnerable to this charge), lamented the prostitution and mercenary character of the Press, and generally accused 'the Radicals' of having misled the people and exploited their prejudices. There is no need to take these accusations too seriously — though some historians have done so — for they form the common currency of American political vituperation. They are never wholly untrue and seldom explain very much except the willingness of the critic to believe that the American people can be bullied, bribed, deceived and easily persuaded to act irresponsibly. The election of 1866 can be explained without searching for causes among malpractices which are the normal accompaniments of political activity; one should rather concentrate upon what was abnormal in producing so striking a political victory.

The problem can be tackled at two levels by asking what had stimulated the interests of the people and what had stimulated the activity of the politicians? The two cannot be truly separated, for the people rely upon the politicians to explain what is afoot, and the politicians and people are both influenced by the same mysterious currents of opinion and by the same calculations of interest. The politicians may fail when the people are apathetic, while strongly held popular opinions may be frustrated unless there are politicians willing to organize and present them. For convenience the problem of opinion and the problem of organization can be considered apart, but both are component parts of one political system.

An unusual feature of the election of 1866 was the clarity and frequency with which the matters at stake were put before the people. For over a year the problems of Reconstruction had been discussed in the Press, at political meetings, and in private correspondence. It is possible to maintain the people were misinformed but not that they were uninformed. 'False issues have

prevailed. Nowhere have the real political questions been discussed,' wrote Gideon Welles; but he had a fixed idea that the
Democrats and administration Republicans ought to fight on a
narrow front 'against changes of the Constitution with only a
broken Congress, and States excluded'.[1] In fact this point had
already been settled for the majority before the election campaign
began, and the argument was not over the right to amend but over
the terms of the amendment and its bearing upon Reconstruction.
There were a good many ready to question the propriety of some
features of the Fourteenth Amendment, but far fewer to deny
that the Northern majority, having won the war, had the right to
determine the terms of settlement.

A favourite whipping boy for those who deprecated Republican victory was the Press. It is true that the majority of the
Northern Press favoured the Republicans, but the Democrats
had also their Press which was neither tame nor negligible. The
New York *World* circulated widely outside the city, and there
were well-established Democratic newspapers in most large
communities and in many small ones. These Democratic newspapers were as clear and uninhibited in their comments as the
Republican Press. Republican newspapers reflected the various
colours in the party spectrum, and could not hope to imitate the
uniformity of Democratic criticism. Accusations against the
Press came largely from Johnson Republicans who had expected
a larger share of the party journals, and adopted the President's
explanation of a 'mercenary and subsidized press' to explain their
disappointment. Even if the accusation were true it does not
explain how a 'mercenary' Press could distort an election result.[2]
Newspapers may tell their readers what to think; but people
usually buy the paper which tells them to think as they want.
Money may keep alive a newspaper which is propagating unpopular opinions and it may increase the effectiveness of a newspaper which is running with the popular tide; but in neither case

---

[1] Beale (ed.), *Diary of Gideon Welles*, II, 531, 534, 539, 574, 617.
[2] McKitrick, op. cit., 439 ff. 'Newspapers in critical times can enjoy relatively little
margin for the luxury of deviant opinions but must accommodate themselves to the
majority views of the public and function as reflectors of these views.'

is money having more than a marginal effect upon politics, and circulation figures tell the real story. A striking example of the fate which awaits a newspaper which is backing a loser was that of the *New York Times* which backed Johnson and lost readers, while its great rival, the *Tribune*, gained them. Finally the nerves of its editor could stand it no longer and he gave up his advocacy of the President's policy. The editor concerned was Henry J. Raymond, who had but recently promoted the pro-Johnson National Union Movement.[1]

The most effective contribution of the Republican Press was not in editorial dicta but in reporting conditions in the South. Here there was field for choice. According to one's inclinations, and without straying from the truth, it was possible to represent the Southerners as sadder but wiser men, anxious for harmony, reconciled to the loss of slavery, and resolved to give the negro a fair deal; or as vindictive obscurantists who had learned nothing, looked forward to a further attempt at secession or hoped to renew their former ascendancy in the nation, and determined to deny the negro his status as a citizen. Since scandals and outrages are easier to report and make better reading than unspectacular attempts to establish harmony, the Republican newspapers had an easy task. Much was going on in the South which was hard to deny or ignore, though it might be explained as the inevitable disease of a disordered and demoralized society. Thus the Democrats and the administration Republicans faced a dilemma in reporting Southern conditions: if they admitted the facts and attributed crime and violence to the aftermath of war, it was difficult to maintain that the Southern States were in a fit condition to govern themselves; if they denied the facts they sacrificed their reputation for veracity and involved themselves in recrimination over detail. Most supporters of Johnson's policy, from the

---

[1] McKitrick, op. cit., 420. It must have been at this time that Raymond told General Richard Taylor that 'it was useless to support the President, who was daily becoming more unpopular, and that the circulation and influence of his paper were rapidly diminishing in consequence of his adherence to "my policy" ' (Richard Taylor, *Destruction and Reconstruction*, 343). Taylor said that Leonard Jerome, a principal shareholder in the *Times* offered to bear all the losses, but to an editor the loss of subscribers, who may never return, is more important than financial insurance.

President himself downwards, chose to ignore Southern violence, while every issue of every Republican paper piled up evidence of its existence.

Of all Southern incidents the most striking and the most important was the riot or, as some would have it, the massacre of New Orleans in July 1866. The facts are involved and creditable to no one, but the outcome was that men (most of them coloured), whose provocation had not gone beyond words, were shot down by the police and assaulted by a white mob. Thirty-seven negroes and three white sympathizers were killed, against one killed and ten wounded among their assailants. It was impossible to explain this away, but no one was put on trial and the President, who had ample power as Commander-in-Chief and under the Freedmen's Bureau and Civil Rights Acts, to protect life, liberty and property, took no action. He even seems to have deliberately withheld from the Press a passage in General Sheridan's report which accused the police of conduct so 'unnecessary and atrocious as to compel one to say that it was murder'.[1] Johnson's inaction did not appear in a better light when it emerged that he had been ready to use military power to support the Southern officials in Louisiana if they had chosen to arrest negro and Unionist leaders. The doctrine of State rights apparently permitted the use of Federal forces to support action against the 'loyalists', black and white, but not to protect their lives.

Irritated by the increasing volume of accusation directed against him over New Orleans the President resorted to his favourite explanation. It was, he said, the Radicals in New Orleans and their friends and instigators in Congress who were responsible for the massacre. In a sense he was correct. There would have been no massacre if some men had not been ready to assemble in defence of what they believed to be their rights, and their willingness to do so was influenced by their belief in the good will of Congress. Yet even if the 'conspiracy' had been everything which Johnson believed it to be, it would be a poor country in which men could not protest against a régime which

[1] McKitrick, op. cit., 426–7.

they disliked or condemn policies of which they disapproved.

Louisiana had moreover a special significance. It was one of the two States which had organized under Lincoln's 'ten-per-cent' plan, containing an unusually large proportion of Southern Unionists, and a stable and well educated negro middle class. Yet almost every State and city official directly involved had been a Confederate elected by the white majority and pardoned by the President. For the Northern Republican the lesson of New Orleans was clear. In other Southern States the white Unionists and negroes might not be sufficiently strong to organize, as they had done in Louisiana, and could expect no better justice; and every day events in the South, fully reported in the Republican papers, demonstrated that New Orleans did not stand alone. Nor was all running smoothly within the Federal administrative and military machine. The President's passivity when confronted with the rights of States, could become active interference when confronted with military action aimed at the protection of negro rights. In this way he antagonized not only those who read about Southern outrages in their Republican newspapers, but also the men on the spot — the military commanders — who were attempting to grapple with a complex and delicate problem.[1]

The New Orleans riot, outrages against individuals in the South, and the President's failure to protect the negro with military power would not alone have caused the tide of public opinion to flow against him. Indeed, in normal circumstances, it might have been conceded that the President had a fairly good case. There are always difficulties in the use of military force to preserve civil order, and Federal troops in the South were not numerous enough to act effectively unless they had the co-operation of the local authorities. It was not easy to use the steam hammer of military power to crack the nut of local disturbance in a vast region of scattered population, and the best hope for civil

[1] For a discussion of Johnson's relations with the army officers see Harold M. Hyman, 'Johnson, Stanton, and Grant: a Reconsideration of the Army's role in the events leading to Impeachment', *American Historical Review*, LXVI (Oct. 1961), 85 ff.

order in the South was to allow responsible persons to devise their own means, within the traditional framework of the law, by which the social situation could be stabilized. Johnson was the last person to encourage Southern disorder, and he believed that the legal rights of freedmen ought to be respected. He probably knew that, under existing circumstances, it would be necessary to keep Federal troops in the South for some time to come, but he saw them as the ultimate sanction behind the authority of the United States, not as agents for the day to day work of police and justice. There was thus a good deal of practical common-sense behind his State rights view. The enforcement of law must depend upon the will of the local community, and in the past even the governments of States had been unable to maintain order and protect individuals in remote areas when local sentiment was aroused.

The Radical ideal of military protection for every freedman and Unionist was visionary, and practical difficulties reinforced theoretical objections to the use of military force as the instrument of domestic policy. On the other hand these practical difficulties did not necessarily dispose of the conviction that the rights of freedmen were a concern of the nation and that Southern Unionists had a claim upon the national government. Had Johnson been prepared to recognize the existence of this concern for right and of this obligation, and then faced the Northern people with a frank statement of the difficulties which were involved, he might have rendered valuable service as a mediator between North and South. He refused to recognize that the arguments, which had served the South in the past, were obsolete after secession, abolition and Northern victory, and this refusal made it impossible for him to establish sympathetic communication with the Northern public. The core of Northern feeling, which Johnson never touched, was the conviction that lives had not been sacrificed to restore the world of 1860. Deep currents of emotion ran in the Northern mind and the man who ignored them might preserve his integrity but could not win votes.

At the more superficial level of party organization Johnson helped to encompass his own defeat. His failure to discover the real frontier which divided the Radical from the moderate made it impossible for him to create the centre party for which he hoped. The idea of rallying upon the centre and leaving Southern and Northern extremists on either side was attractive, but by the summer of 1866 Johnson was no longer in the centre. The language employed by Johnson and his friends recognized the new centre of gravity in the party; in December a 'Radical' had been a man who wished to punish Southern leaders, overthrow the restored State governments and force negro suffrage upon the people; by July a Radical was anyone who thought that a constitutional amendment was necessary. Yet the true interpretation of the widening sphere of Radicalism was not the subjection of the party to a minority of extremists, but the discovery that the Fourteenth Amendment was a new point upon which moderate opinion could rally.

The impossibility of forming a coalition of the centre upon the Johnson position was shown by the history of the abortive National Union movement. Henry Raymond, who was one of its principal organizers and a leader of the Seward and Weed organization in New York, wanted to launch the movement by accepting the Fourteenth Amendment and fighting Radical opposition to the early admission of the Southern States. Gideon Welles, with his usual failure to understand a political situation, believed that the movement must begin with an unqualified repudiation of the amendment, and must campaign against ratification and for Southern representation as an existing right.[1] There can be little doubt that Johnson agreed with Welles, and Southerners who joined the new movement would not even consider the Raymond policy. Early rupture was avoided only by ignoring the amendment and concentrating solely upon the immediate and unconditional admission of the Southern States. Raymond's appraisal of the situation had been a realistic one, and its rejection meant that the National Union Movement won the support of no prominent Republican who had not already committed himself to Johnson. The movement did attract a large

[1] Beale (ed.), *Diary of Gideon Welles*, II, 531, 534, 539.

number of conservative Southerners and the appearance of reconciliation was hailed with enthusiasm by Johnson supporters. The weakness of this brand of reconciliation was that Southerners were meeting Northerners who had become politically insignificant and unable to explain Northern opinion to the South. Later events were to show that many wise heads in the South were prepared to concede much when brought face to face with Northern determination. The tragedy of the National Union Movement was that it did not bring Southerners into contact with men such as Bingham and Trumbull, who were near enough to the main stream of Republican thought to speak with confidence about its strength without giving the impression that everyone north of the Mason-Dixon Line was an ardent supporter of Sumner and Stevens. The Southerners met only those Northerners who had committed themselves to unqualified support of the State rights position or those like Raymond who had muzzled themselves against their better judgment.

The National Union Movement illustrated the classic difficulties of third party movements in America. It had to create its own organization, risk capture by one of the existing parties, or content itself with a minor role. Its chances of local success were increased at the decentralization of American parties, but its chances of national success were diminished by the need to capture or create organizations in so many different States. Developing only a superficial strength at the national level, and very little elsewhere, the movement failed to capture the Republican organization or to create its own in any State; and it retained influence at the time of the elections only by alliance with the Democratic party, which was proof in Republican eyes that its real purpose was the restoration of the secessionists to power. Association with the Democrats meant association with the copperheads, and Unionists in the movement wanted the Democrats to repudiate them as the price of alliance, but there was no reason why they should do so. In New York city and in the Midwest the Southern sympathizers, though suppressed during the war, remained an important source of Democratic strength; nor, despite Northern propaganda, had many of the copperheads played a less honourable part than the Southern Unionists whom Republicans extolled. The Democrats saw no reason why they should weaken their own organization by repudiating those for whom they had considerable sympathy even though they had regretted their wartime choice. Leading copperheads were prevented from attending the Philadelphia convention of the National Union Movement, but not without giving offence to a good many Democrats and arousing the suspicions of a great many more Republicans. A Republican politician in his State could not afford to carry the copperheads as well as Johnson, and the result was that most of them decided to carry neither. Once this decision was taken Republican politicians reacted to the threat of a rival claim upon the loyalties of Republican voters by closing their ranks and doubling their efforts. In many constituencies this meant a tacit acceptance of Radical leadership.

It has sometimes been believed that Johnson could have turned the tide by an adroit and masterful use of patronage. Gideon Welles believed that if the patronage had been used against the Radicals at an early stage the party would have been brought to heel. Johnson did make a large number of dismissals and new appointments in the summer and autumn of 1866, but this, it has been held, came too late. The implications of an argument which maintains that popular conviction could be changed in this way are interesting but misleading. Patronage plays an important part in party organization, but its part in the political symphony does not mean that it is conducting the orchestra. A party is a delicate mechanism and, if it is to function efficiently, all its parts must be working together. The role of patronage is to provide an incentive for the professionals, to furnish a reward for service, to provide a mark of public approbation, and to give the person administering the patronage an instrument by which he can encourage or discourage groups and factions within the party. Even this cautious statement requires modification for one must not see the President as an all-seeing eye, ready to promote or punish individuals at will, and patronage decisions are usually collective. The problem of an appointment has moved up and down the party structure, from the district to the State, from the State to the congressmen, from the congressmen to the Executive. In the Presidency the formal responsibility for making appointments meets the informal advice on how they should be made. There is no necessity for the President to act upon this advice, and he may receive conflicting recommendations through different channels, but he must receive information and advice from somewhere, and the party provides the recognized means of transmission. A recommendation made by a leading politician may reflect his own personal interest in an individual, but more often it is a request which has been assessed, filtered and transmitted through the party organization. The politicians engaged in this elaborate procedure do not regard themselves as playing a dirty game, but as taking the necessary steps to provide the country with public officials. Next to personal influence the surest way to a politician's favour was an assurance that a man was in good standing in his party. It is difficult to see how it could have been otherwise.

It was accepted that the patronage might be used to succour those factions in the party which the President favoured, but it was against the rules, as normally understood, to use patronage against the party itself. An attempt to disrupt the normal channels of recommendation and advice offended individuals and supplied grievances for hundreds of men all down the party ladder. These men were not free agents. Their position depended upon the party, upon their own reputation both in the party and in their community, and upon the success of the party with the voters. An attack upon their position, symbolized by a dismissal of a political friend, the rejection of their recommendations and by the appointment of men outside the party or alienated from it, was unlikely to lead to a wholesale revision of loyalties and declared opinions. It imposed a choice upon the party man — whether he should change course or continue as he was — but it would be more important for him to keep the good opinion of his neighbours, and of his party associates, than to oblige a remote executive authority. There was, after all, a well-developed pattern of party behaviour when a hostile President was in office, and its principal aim was to keep the party organization intact even at the cost of a lost election.

Things would have been different if the President had had a ready-made faction within the party which he could promote at the expense of those whom he believed to be his enemies. It might have been possible for him to isolate and weaken the Radical group; but in order to do so he had to build up their rivals in the party, not to attack the whole party by favouring men who were outside its regular organization. Johnson could have used patronage to build up a moderate faction against the Radicals, but he could not beat both moderates and Radicals because there was no other party group to which he could turn. And to forge an alliance with the moderates he had to agree to terms which they would accept and make acceptable to the voters. Here opinion was important. Patronage could not operate in an intellectual and emotional void; it could not by itself persuade men to do that which they had determined not to do, and in this situation it would be of little use to win individual politicians by Executive favour.

As the lines of conflict were drawn the weapon of patronage was likely to rebound upon its user. The acceptance of a Johnson appointment became an act of desertion, and there were even cases in which a man became suspect because he had not earned dismissal. In communities with sound Republican majorities the pressure of public disapproval might make it difficult to find any respectable appointee, and in marginal constituencies a deserter would inevitably be accused of selling out to the enemy. Party loyalty was a political virtue at all times, but feelings were heightened by the Republican party's acute sense of its historic missions; deserters betrayed not an organization but a cause.

Johnson's attempt to use patronage to break up the Republican party and to promote the National Union Movement — which existed neither as a separate organization nor as a faction — was therefore hopeless from the start. He could punish individuals, but, as bitterness against him grew, punishment would become a badge of honour in the party. And everyone had the strongest

M

possible reason for keeping the organization intact until 1868. Johnson's use of patronage did not crush opposition or bring a new movement to life, but stimulated the politicians to greater efforts and to reconciliation with each other. In the circumstances of 1866 this meant that moderates and Radicals worked together. However much they might dislike each other, they were bound together by bonds of mutual interest and associations which had already continued through several years of crisis.

If the use of patronage was ineffective it did have a nuisance value. The Republican politicians were conscious of having fought a good fight, and they expected their just rewards. At the top of the scale powerful senators could be alienated by what they regarded as improper disregard of their nominations as party leaders. The increasing bitterness shown towards the President by Lyman Trumbull and John Sherman seems to have been influenced by this sense of personal insult. At the bottom end of the scale a fourth class post-mastership might not be much in the sum of things, but it was important in the community which it served; if assigned to a man who was not of good standing in his party in his district it offended the sense of values of those in the community. Thus while the use of patronage could do little to deflect the current of opinion in the Republican party it did build up resentment and add to the picture of the President as a renegade and traitor.

The way in which the cards were stacked against Johnson was revealed during his unfortunate speaking tour in August and September. Americans of this period still demanded from their public men a solemnity which limited their opportunities for public speaking. A congressman led the campaign in his district, and occasionally a well-known political figure might deliver set pieces outside his own State. A distinction was also observed between the kind of speeches which a man might make to his constituents when asking for their votes, and what he might say as a national figure. To a President even campaign oratory was denied, and the candidate for national honours must stick to his record, confine himself to platitudes if he could not avoid speech, and pretend to ignore the fact that all over the country men were shouting his name with extravagant praise or unqualified condemnation. There was therefore something shocking in the very idea that a President should undertake a speaking tour as a part of an election campaign. The offence was slightly mitigated by the fact that Johnson was not fighting for his own election but for that of congressmen, but the depth of his personal involvement was obvious. Thus the speaking tour was an innovation at which many would look askance, and only resounding success could redeem it from impropriety. The purpose of the President was to bring into the open the latent popular sentiment which he still believed to be in his favour. He hoped that he could explain the issues in such a way that a popular response would sweep his enemies out of public life. The belief was pathetic and his handling of his audiences betrayed his lack of understanding of the Northern mind. His initial mistake lay in assuming that he was speaking to people who had been kept in ignorance by the politicians, and he seemed unaware of the concentrated discussion which had gone on for over a year in newspapers, public gatherings and private intercourse. In any large popular audience Johnson could expect to find much ignorance, but at the centre of every Northern audience were men who had made up their minds and who were surprisingly well-informed. In most Northern communities these men led opinion, and unless Johnson could shake them he had little hope of starting a movement in his favour. And what the well-informed hearer got was the repetition, with varying degrees of emotional emphasis, of arguments which he had already considered and rejected. There was another factor which Johnson did not anticipate. In his own State, among people whom he knew, Johnson had employed to perfection the art of enlisting the audience on his side against hecklers. It was a shock to him to find that the trick failed to work with these Northern audiences. Too often it was clear that the audience was with the heckler, and Johnson's repartees, which were meant to disarm, added strength to the opposition. Even the environment of his audiences was unfamiliar; his reputation and oratorical manner were based upon his experience with rural audiences of simple farmers, who were not deferential to authority but were grateful to anyone who opened windows upon the great world. Now he was talking to the sophisticated people of Midwestern cities among whom he was likely to encounter information, ribaldry and rowdyism. Finally the very cause which he was trying to promote cut him off from the deeper emotions of the people whom he was trying to reach. In the lives of all whom he addressed the greatest event had been war; for many this had meant personal loss, and their most profound emotion was conviction that the sacrifice should not be in vain. Against this Johnson could put into the scale the preservation of the Union, but this alone was not enough, for the Northern people had a deep psychological need to believe that they had made a more perfect Union. Across this chasm Johnson could not communicate with his audience; whatever arguments he might use were buried under an avalanche of ridicule and disapproval, and his evident failure was a stimulus to Republican morale.

* * * *

The magnitude of the Republican victory left no doubt that the President's policy had been defeated. The Northern electorate had certainly given its verdict against the admission of the Southern States without conditions. It had decided that the conditions imposed by the President were not enough. It had decided that Congress and not the President should decide what conditions should be imposed. From this point there was no doubt, and the nature of the required conditions was to be a matter of bitter recrimination among Republicans. In some states, and notably in Ohio, the election had been fought on the Fourteenth Amendment and on the understanding that Southern ratification of the Amendment would qualify them for admission (with perhaps the qualification that the Amendment must first be ratified by sufficient States to become a part of the Constitution). John Bingham of Ohio might have been expected to interpret the election in this way, but he was joined by so staunch a Radical as

Ben Wade. In Congress Wade was to say, 'if they adopt the constitutional amendment, and comply with the terms prescribed by the reconstruction Committee and adopted by Congress, I should feel bound to vote for their admission. I voted for the constitutional amendment on that hypothesis'.[1] John Sherman asserted that 'Whatever may have been said in other States, in Ohio it was the only question. Our Union convention passed no other resolution except to approve and ratify the constitutional amendment. Our party went before the people on that amendment, rejecting all minor issues; and we all understood, without an exception, that if the amendment was adopted by the Southern people, it was the end-all and be-all of reconstruction'.[2] On the other hand Stevens vehemently denied that 'there is any understanding expressed or implied, that upon the adoption of the amendment by any State, that such State may be admitted. . . . It is to be regretted that inconsiderate and incautious Republicans should ever have supposed that the slight amendments already proposed to the Constitution, even when incorporated in that instrument, would satisfy the reforms necessary for the security of government. Unless the rebel States, before admission, should be made republican in spirit, and placed under the guardianship of loyal men, all our blood and treasure will have been spent in vain'.[3] Henry Raymond asserted that 'the elections of last fall turned clearly and distinctly upon the constitutional amendment',[4] but Blaine, who did not share Stevens's enthusiasm for a revolution in Southern society, replied that, with the exception of New York, 'I do not now recall a single State convention or a single congressional convention within any loyal State that made the declaration that

---

[1] C.G. 39.2.124. When Wade made this statement the following conversation with Sumner ensued:
Mr Sumner: Even with the word 'white' in their constitutions?
Mr Wade: Without regard to that.
Mr Sumner: Without regard to the rights of the freedmen?
Mr Wade: On complying with the requisitions of the constitutional amendment I should vote for them. . . . I intended to let them in on the terms we prescribed. I did not ask for more, and I would not be satisfied with less; and if now they comply with them it would be bad faith in me to refuse to admit them. Certainly, I am as much for colored suffrage as any man on this floor, but when I make such an agreement as that I always stand by it.
[2] C.G. 39.2.128.   [3] C.G. 39.2.252.   [4] C.G. 39.2.1182.

on the adoption of the constitutional amendment the Southern States should be admitted to representation here.'[1] Blaine in the House, and Fessenden in the Senate, both stressed the fact that no Reconstruction Bill had been passed by Congress, that the mode of Reconstruction could not have been before the electorate, and that nothing which had been said, before or during the elections, could dictate the future decision of Congress on the admission of States.

The part to be played by the Southern States in amending the Constitution was no nearer determination. Would ratification of the amendment by three-fourths of the States represented in Congress make it a part of the Constitution? With characteristic precision Fessenden pointed out that in transmitting the amendment to the Secretary of State Congress had not prescribed the States to which it should be submitted. Ratification by the Southern States might be accepted as evidence of their good faith, but it need not be inferred that their assent was necessary or that Congress had recognized their status as States. If they ratified, the right of Congress to inquire into the character and legality of their governments remained unimpaired, and if they rejected there had been no recognition of their right to act as States in the Union.[1]

Yet without deciding these vexed points a compromise might be found in saying that Congress was free to decide its course of action, but that there was a moral obligation to use this freedom to decide in favour of admission if the Southern States ratified. On the only occasion when the question was brought to the test in the House of Representatives those Republicans who believed that admission should follow ratification won, with the help of the Democrats, a victory over the Radicals; in the Senate a majority of Republicans would certainly have decided in the same way.[2] The question soon became a hypothetical one — because no Southern State ratified the amendment — but the argument pointed to important differences among Republicans in their

---

[1] For Fessenden's argument see C.G. 39.2.193–4.
[2] The reference is to the vote on 28 Jan. 1866. See below p. 181.

approach to Reconstruction. They could be divided between moderates who believed that the amendment contained all that was necessary, and that the political problem was to persuade or force the Southern States to adopt it; and Radicals who believed that it was only the beginning of real Reconstruction. For Radicals the great objective remained not a formal change in the law but a real change in the character of Southern society.

There was, however, one major question which might cut across the division between moderates and Radicals. A good many moderates believed that not enough had been done in the amendment for negro suffrage, and that a more positive step was necessary. Others still regarded it with misgivings, but were prepared to see it as a necessary instrument in the process of Reconstruction. What was, however, particularly noticeable in the second session of the Thirty-ninth Congress was the evaporation of those doubts which had played so important a part in the first. Nowhere had the Republican party formally adopted negro suffrage, but everywhere it had been discussed. The abolitionist G. W. Julian, campaigning for re-election in Indiana, later said that 'the suffrage question was constantly gaining in significance, and demanding a settlement. It was neither morally nor logically possible to escape it. . . . The Republicans everywhere divided on the question, while the current of opinion was strongly against the introduction of the issue as premature. The politicians all opposed it on the plea that it would divide the Republicans and restore the Democrats to power and that we must wait for the growth of a public opinion in its favour that would justify its agitation'.[1] At the beginning of the campaign even old anti-slavery men were unwilling to follow Julian, but he introduced the suffrage question into his own campaign and found that he was gaining ground 'but their fitness for the ballot was a subordinate question. A great national emergency pleaded for their right to it on other and far more imperative grounds. The question involved the welfare of both races and the issues of the war. It involved not merely the fate of the negro, but the safety

[1] Julian, *Political Recollections*, 263.

of society'.[1] By the time of the election he believed that 'the Republicans of the district were as nearly a unit in my favor as a party can be made respecting any controverted doctrine'.[2] James G. Blaine, who was not a man to make wild assertions, believed that 'the people have plainly spoken . . . and the interpretation of their voice is not difficult. They have pronounced with unmistakable emphasis in favor of the constitutional amendment with the added and indispensible prerequisite of manhood suffrage'.[3] Blaine's reasoning was devious and need have convinced no one who was not already disposed to agree, but only Raymond challenged his interpretation of the election. The hostility of the Southern States to the amendment, and the likelihood that all would follow the first in rejecting it, weighed heavily upon the minds of moderate Republicans. Garfield's private reflection upon the situation was probably typical: if the Southern States ratified he would feel morally bound to vote for their admission, but if they rejected 'then I am in favor of striking for impartial suffrage, though I can see that such a course is beset with grave dangers'.[4] In February Bingham and Blaine quietly incorporated negro suffrage in the 'moderate' plan of settlement; the Radicals had anticipated them by only a few weeks.

*   *   *   *

Andrew Johnson allowed no man to open windows into his soul, and one can do no more than imagine the bitterness with which he surveyed the political scene as the election results came in. The people had failed him; there was now no chance of his policy prevailing, and he would have to accommodate himself, not only to the celebration of their triumph by Republicans in the second session of the Thirty-ninth Congress, but also to two further years of the still more hostile Fortieth Congress. For a moment he seems to have contemplated a retreat, and the first version of his annual message contemplated a tacit acceptance of the Fourteenth Amendment and an invitation to Congress to turn its attention to pressing problems of economic recovery and

[1] Ibid., 264 ff.   [2] Ibid.   [3] C.G. 39.2.53.   [4] T. C. Smith, *Garfield*, I.396. 1 Jan. 1867.

growth.[1] He would have found a good deal of support in such a change of course. Henry J. Raymond had tried to organize the National Union Movement on this basis, and men like Sherman and Bingham, though bitterly offended by the President's intransigence, might have responded to an invitation to work out a compromise policy. It was not necessary for the President to admit that he had been wrong — he could still maintain that the Southern States ought to have been admitted a year before — and concessions could be justified by deference to the will of the people. It was true that the Southern whites had not spoken, but nor had the Southern blacks; and, even if two deficiencies added up to nothing, the door was open for Johnson to retreat without loss of honour. On the Democratic side he could perhaps have received some sensible advice from Reverdy Johnson, an old, experienced congressman, who was to explain his eventual vote for the Reconstruction Acts by saying that 'Consistency in a public man can never properly be esteemed a virtue when he becomes satisfied that it will operate to the prejudice of his country'.[2] Unfortunately Andrew Johnson placed the virtue of consistency above the duty of mediating between the sections. Having dismissed the thought of conciliating the Northern majority he chose to stand, in his annual message, upon exactly the same ground as that which he had occupied a year before. On 17 January, in response to a request for advice from Alabama, where a movement was on foot to rescind an earlier refusal to ratify the Fourteenth Amendment, he telegraphed: 'What possible good can be obtained by reconsidering the constitutional amendment? I know of none in the present posture of affairs; and I do not believe the people of the country will sustain any set of individuals in attempts to change the whole character of our government by enabling acts or otherwise. I believe on the contrary, that they will eventually uphold all who have patriotism and courage to stand by the Constitution, and who place their confidence in the people. There should be no faltering on the part of those who are honest in their determination to sustain the several co-ordinate departments of

[1] Beale, *The Critical Year*, 400–2.   [2] C.G. 39.2.1937.

the government in accordance with its original design.'[1] In this telegram the extent of the President's misunderstanding of the past and miscalculation of the future reached a new pitch. At a time when some gesture from the South would have greatly strengthened the hands of those in Congress who were fighting for a moderate settlement he advised no action. He told the Southerners that they had no need to fear that Congress would pass acts altering the character of Southern government, though Congress was to pass two such acts within the next two months. He repeated his pathetic faith that 'the people' would sustain him and he claimed once more that the Executive had exclusive responsibility for settling the conditions of Reconstruction.

The tragedy of his decision was that his opportunity was still so great. He had failed as a maker of policy but he still had a unique opportunity to act as a mediator. In December 1865 his great strength had lain in the momentum achieved by his policy, in the reluctance of Republicans to disrupt their party by a breach with the Executive, and in respect for the strong and temperate way in which he had taken up the unexpected responsibilities of the supreme office. Most of this strength had been destroyed, but in the meantime Johnson had gained something in the prestige which he now commanded in the South. No other man was in a better position to bring Southern leaders to face the facts of a situation in which Congress backed by Northern opinion would demand 'guarantees'. He alone could have explained to Southerners the price of re-admission and have urged them to pay it quickly. On the other side he could have impressed upon selected Northern leaders the need for some conciliatory statements. Southerners wanted to know whether acquiescence would really be followed by re-admission, and whether the disabilities imposed upon their leaders were likely to be permanent or temporary. Whatever Stevens might say, a number of leading Republicans would have been ready to promise early admission, and some might have been prepared to indicate that the perpetual disqualification of Southern leaders was not their intention. It is true

[1] Beale, *The Critical Year*, 402–3.

that it was impossible to commit the whole Republican party and that the attempt at mediation might have failed; but it would have been an honourable failure. Anything would have been better for all concerned than the position which the President actually assumed. By his annual message and the Alabama telegram he abdicated from all control over Reconstruction policy while retaining the power and the will to obstruct what others proposed. Other Presidents have felt that their constitutional duty compelled them to resist the will of Congress, but a wiser and more flexible man might have discovered a course of action aimed at reconciliation rather than at emphasizing the unfortunate divisions in the nation. Whatever the future had in store it was certain that war and the election had rendered obsolete the constitutional doctrine to which Johnson adhered and that the Northern majority would never accept a settlement based upon the State rights theory which many believed had led the nation to disaster. In the North, as in the South, the war left its legacy of bitterness, but this could not be exorcised by obstructing a policy to which the Northern people had become committed, or by encouraging the Southerners to stand firm against a decision which they had not the means to resist.[1]

* * * *

When Congress assembled it had a decision but no policy. The result of the election had provided a foundation upon which Republican policy should be based, but it had not said what that policy should be. It soon became apparent that the Republican leadership was sharply divided about what should be done. In the House one group was led by Thaddeus Stevens and the other by John A. Bingham. In the Senate the Radical group lacked leadership, for Sumner was not the man to direct congressional tactics; Fessenden now leaned, in his cautious way, more

[1] Senator Sherman said, 'it seems to me the saddest, the most foolish act of the Southern people for them to reject the constitutional amendment. I shall never cease to grieve that the President of the United States has committed himself against that important proposition. He never could have done anything more injurious to the people of the Southern States than his course in encouraging them to refuse to ratify the constitutional amendment' (C.G. 39.2.128).

definitely towards Radicalism, but poor health weakened his former influence; on the other wing of the party John Sherman was coming to the fore as the main architect of moderate and harmonizing policies.

As might have been expected the Stevens policy looked to a thorough reorganization of Southern society. The bill which he offered early in the session recognized the existing governments in the South 'for municipal purposes only' and ordered them to hold elections on 1 May 1867 for a new constitutional convention. The elections were to be supervised by three Federal commissioners in each State and the voters were to be all adult male citizens. But those who had been of full age on 4 March 1861 were deprived of citizenship, and were forbidden to exercise voting rights until five years after they had filed their applications for restoration of citizenship. In other words the mass of the Southern whites were to be treated as though they were resident aliens, under the protection of the law but unable to exercise the full rights of citizens until they had gone through the process of naturalization. To this sweeping disqualification there was, however, an important exception in favour of those who would take an oath that on and after 4 March 1864 they 'would willingly have complied with the requirements of the proclamation of the United States, issued on the 8th day of December 1863 [the "ten-per-cent" plan], had a safe opportunity been allowed,' and that thereafter they had been 'opposed to the continuance of the rebellion, and to the establishment of the so-called confederate government, and voluntarily gave no aid or encouragement thereto, but earnestly desired the success of the Union, and the suppression of all armed resistance to the United States'. This provision indicated a recognition by Stevens of the practical objection to previous Radical schemes: that the exclusion of all who had been 'disloyal' would denude many Southern districts of all leadership. Those who were prepared to turn their backs upon the past, and to declare that despite formal obedience to the Confederacy they had been Unionists at heart, were now invited to participate in Reconstruction. The Constitution made by the convention was to be submitted to the legal voters for ratification and, if accepted by a majority, would be submitted to Congress. No constitution could, however, be submitted 'which denied to any citizen any right, privileges or immunities, which are granted to other citizens in the State. All laws shall be impartial without regard to language, race, or former condition'. These were to be treated as fundamental conditions for membership of the Union and any subsequent alteration or abrogation of them would automatically disbar the State from representation in Congress. Even if all the conditions were complied with, the right of Congress to accept or reject was safeguarded.[1]

As with other policies proposed by Stevens this one was practicable, so long as the national government had the will to enforce it, but contained provisions so outrageous that moderate opinion was unlikely to accept it without a fight. Stevens was too experienced in the ways of Congress to be unaware of this. He was probably using tactics which he had tried before with some success. The idea was to mark out for Radicals the objectives which they must keep in mind, to draw the fire of moderate opposition upon certain striking features, and to make the ground which he really intended to occupy appear moderate and uncontroversial. The first thing on which opposition was likely to fasten was the proposal to deprive men of citizenship. The second was the implied abandonment of the Fourteenth Amendment as the basis of Reconstruction, and its replacement by the proposal to make equality under the law a permanent and fundamental condition of statehood in the Union. Stevens was not opposed to the amendment and was quite prepared to argue that its rejection by the South was a justification for a thorough programme of Reconstruction; but he had never concealed his view that it was inadequate. He valued the clause which deprived Confederate leaders of office, and would probably have been prepared to use this if his admission to citizenship of 'reluctant Confederates' opened too large a gap in the fence, but he completely rejected the idea that acceptance of the amendment alone could qualify a

[1] C.G. 39.2.250 ff., 3 Jan. 1866.

State for admission. There was one other twist to his plan. Suppose that the convention refused to act on the lines laid down or if the Constitution were not ratified? The Southern States would still be unable to ward off negro suffrage, for so long as they were out of the Union they would be treated as Territories, and during the previous session Congress had enacted impartial suffrage in all Territories.

Stevens was now uninhibited in his advocacy of negro suffrage.[1] He stressed the need for the negro vote as a means of protection for the freedmen, for the white Unionists, for the Union itself, and for the party of the Union. 'I believe, on my conscience,' he said, 'that on the continued ascendancy of that party depends the safety of this great nation.' In the past there had been great national questions which cut across sectional divisions, but now there was only one division — that between loyalists and dis-loyalists — and the weakness of one meant the strength of the other. If the negroes were excluded from the suffrage 'you will be the perpetual vassals of the free trade, irritated, revengeful South'. Turning to the general question of racial equality 'of which so much is said by knaves, and believed by men who are not fools', he explained that it meant no more and no less than that 'every earthly being who has an immortal soul, has an equal right to justice, honesty, and fair play with every other man; and the law shall secure him those rights'. Those who feared negro competition had only to compete fairly with him and under existing circumstances the white man was likely to win, though the man who was taken in by the outcry about negro equality certainly stood in some danger, for he had never seen 'even a contraband slave that had not more sense than such a man'. To those who admitted the ultimate justice of negro suffrage but argued that it was premature, he said, 'This step

[1] He observed that the rebel States 'having now no governments, they must have enabling acts. The law of last session with regard to Territories settled the principle of such acts. Impartial suffrage, both in electing the delegates and ratifying their proceedings, is now the fixed rule'. C.G. 39.2.251, 3 Jan. 1867. This was a piece of elaborate casuistry: Congress had passed a law prohibiting discrimination in Territorial suffrage on grounds of race, creed or colour, but nothing had been said about enabling acts. Stevens had not voted on the discrimination clause and he had voted against the bill as a whole. The Southern States still had governments when he spoke, and Congress had not accepted Stevens's favourite proposal that they should be treated as Territories.

forward is an assault upon ignorance and prejudice, and timid men shrink from it. Are such men fit to sit in the places of statesmen?"[1]

Thus Stevens put the Radical cards on the table. He and his followers would fight to place Reconstruction in the hands of the 'loyalists', black and white, they would now advocate negro suffrage without equivocation, and they would press for certain fundamental and unalterable conditions for membership of the Union. As he drew this Radical manifesto to a close, he touched a chord of idealism and a sense of destiny in words which do something to explain the extraordinary dominance achieved in Congress by this vigorous, bitter, and clear-headed old man. 'There are periods', he said, 'in the history of nations when statesmen can make themselves names for posterity; but such occasions are never improved by cowards. In the acquisition of true fame courage is just as necessary in the civilian as in the military hero. . . . We may not aspire to fame. But great events fix the eye of history on small objects, and magnify their manners. Let us at least escape that condition.'[2] His natural life could not be long prolonged, his public life might well be shorter still, and no possible outcome of events could yield him any material advantage; immediate success he would enjoy, but it was on the stage of history and under the judgment of posterity that Stevens now played his part. A vindictive insistence upon past wrongs could have relegated Stevens to oblivion; as a prophet of the future he was an immense and driving power.

Any man fighting such a programme was bound to be at a disadvantage — particularly when he had already accepted many of the Radical premises — but John A. Bingham was no political weakling. On 16 January 1867, in a speech of outstanding ability, he met Stevens head on. He made a devastating attack upon the plan to deprive men of the citizenship which probably ended the usefulness of the proposal as a matter of practical politics. He ridiculed the idea of imposing by congressional Act perpetual conditions for membership of the Union. 'It is in vain that gentlemen say it is only to protect the freedmen in their rights. God

[1] C.G. 39.2.253.　　　　　　　　[2] Ibid.

knows I am ready to go as far as he who goes the farthest under your exclusive legislative power in those disorganized States ... to protect every one of them in all their rights: the right to enjoy the fruit of their toil; the right peaceably to assemble and petition this Government for a redress of grievances; the right to participate in the reorganization of the governments of the insurgent States; but I am not going, under the pretence of a mawkish humanity, under the pretence of throwing guards about the sacred right of liberty, to take away the right of a free people to amend and alter their constitutional government at their pleasure, subject only to the limitations of the Constitution of my country.'[1] Bingham was employing phrases which might sound clear to advocates of State rights — he even quoted the Tenth Amendment — but in fact his position was a good long way down the Republican stream. He believed that Congress had the power to act 'in these disorganized States' to protect these freedmen's rights, and, in a most significant addition to earlier moderate policies, he included the right of negroes 'to participate in the reorganization' of the Southern governments. Shortly he was to add the grant of impartial suffrage as a necessary condition for re-admission. Moreover the rights of States to amend and alter their constitutions were subject to the Constitution of the United States which would shortly include the Fourteenth Amendment and its civil rights clause for which he had so valiantly and successfully striven. Indeed the Fourteenth Amendment was the centrepiece of his Reconstruction policy; if the Southern States accepted it and if it became law, they should be admitted; if they refused it, then the Congress could declare that it had become law with the consent of three-fourths of the loyal States and the national government could continue to govern the South under its existing powers over 'disorganized States'. And the Southerners could come in when they were ready to give allegiance to the Constitution as amended.

The crucial difference between Bingham and Stevens was not therefore in their concern for human rights, but in their view of

[1] Ibid.

the way in which Reconstruction must be initiated and sustained when complete. Bingham believed that the existing governments in the South must take the necessary steps, and that if they did not do so Congress should simply bide its time, playing from a position of strength. But when the Southerners had taken the necessary steps, including acceptance of national responsibility for civil rights and the political disabilities imposed upon their leaders, they should resume their position as equal States in the Union, experiencing no restraints which were not borne by the others. Stevens believed that the existing leaders in the South could not be trusted and must be displaced; Reconstruction must be in the hands of 'loyal' whites and blacks, together with those 'disloyal' whites who would publicly disavow their past. Stevens was well aware that this programme entailed not only a political but also a social revolution, and it was for this very reason that he fought for it. He still nourished the hope that the more Radical Fortieth Congress would respond favourably to confiscation and land redistribution. Beyond the revolution one had also to guard against counter-revolution and he imposed equal rights in the States as a fundamental condition for congressional representation. Bingham saw no reason to change the existing power structure in the South, Stevens believed that it must be destroyed. Between these two concepts was waged the great battle of the second session of the Thirty-ninth Congress.

The contest was opened by a motion from Bingham to refer Stevens's bill to the Joint Committee on Reconstruction. Stevens wished to keep the discussion on the floor of the House, where he believed that it had a chance of success, and not to refer it to the committee of which Bingham himself was a member and where the bill was almost certain to be modified if not rejected. He knew too that his bill was likely to come under fire in the Senate but if it went to the committee it might never reach the Senate at all. After lengthy debates Bingham's motion to refer was brought to a vote on 28 January and carried by 88 to 65 with 38 not voting.[1] A small majority of Republicans had voted with

---

[1] This vote is analysed on pages 70–73.

Stevens, but Bingham had carried his motion with the help of the Democrats, while the unusually large number of members not voting on an important division probably indicated that a number of Republicans, whose sympathies were with Bingham, had abstained to avoid the wrath of Stevens. On the face of it Bingham had won a striking victory; the vote was understood at the time as a vote against Stevens's bill, and though Bingham did not relish dependence upon Democratic help this demonstration of strength might bring some of the abstainers openly to his side. In the event the Stevens bill was killed by the vote of 28 January and never re-appeared on the floor of Congress.

The moderate position was, however, much weaker than might have appeared, and it was being undermined by events in the South itself. The most damaging factor was the overwhelming majority, in every Southern legislature, against the Fourteenth Amendment. Had the fate of the amendment been a close run thing in the South, Bingham's idea of standing firm upon it and awaiting Southern action would have been plausible. It was far less hopeful to suggest that the huge Southern majorities against ratification could be upset either by a change of heart or by a new calculation of political prospects. The reaction of moderate Northerners to this situation had been anticipated by Senator John Sherman, who was by instinct opposed to drastic measures, in a speech on 14 December. He said that the Fourteenth Amendment contained 'all that is vital, and all that is necessary to secure peace and quiet and harmony in this great country of ours' and lamented that the President had committed himself against ratification. He went on, 'if they do not accept it, then what is left for us? We have either got to be ruled by these people or we have got to rule them. . . . They shall never enter here until they have entirely changed their tone and manner. They will drive the people of the Northern States, unwilling as they are, to organize new governments there, and they will have to submit to those governments, whether they are organized upon the black basis or the white basis or the loyal basis. We have made them a liberal offer; if they reject it, it is their own fault, not ours.'[1] The logic of this argument appealed strongly to Republican minds; they had committed themselves to certain objectives in Reconstruction which they believed to be just and necessary, they had asked the South to accept these objectives voluntarily, and they could not absolve themselves from blame if coercion took the place of persuasion. Thus moderates struggled against Radicals with their hands tied: they had already accepted some of the premises of Radicalism and were prepared to admit that stronger means than those already employed might be necessary. Before December 1867 two Southern States had thrown out the amendment; five more did so during that month, and the remaining three in January and February. In the two last States, after all the warnings given in the North, the decision was unanimous in both Houses, and in all Southern legislatures only thirty-two votes had been given for ratification and eighteen of them had come from two States (North Carolina and Alabama). The figures delivered a devastating blow against those Northerners who argued for caution and for dealing with the existing Southern régimes; they also proved that the white South was solid and seemed to prove that the one great division in the nation was, as Stevens had said, between the loyal and the disloyal.

The second factor which made it impossible to hold the moderate position in Congress was the flood of alarming reports on the condition of negroes and white Unionists in the South. Ever since the summer of 1865 the unprotected condition of the freedmen had been a persistent theme in Republican thought, but since the massacre at New Orleans Northerners had become increasingly disturbed by the thought that Southern authority was not only negligent but also actively engaged in persecuting the freedmen. It was of little use for Southerners to argue that over large areas, and amongst the majority of men, racial relations were good and social order preserved; it was clear that the Southern notion of harmony was one in which the white men set the tune and negroes had to sing it. Many Southerners seemed

[1] C.G. 39.2.128.

intent upon proving their contention that the negro was less
secure than under slavery, and there were all too many incidents
of casual and unpunished violence. Northern newspapers were
filled with reports of this nature — some doubtless exaggerated,
few considered against the proper background of a broken society,
but impossible to dismiss as a whole — and in December Congress
had before it the official reports from the generals commanding
in the South, which contained several disturbing passages.[1]
General Sheridan was the most outspoken when he said that 'the
trial of a white man for the murder of a freedman in Texas would
be a farce', and he ironically contrasted the local outcry against
the Indian danger on the frontier ('gotten up in some instances by
frontier people to get a market for their produce, and ... by
Army contractors to make money'), with their indifference to the
killing of many freedmen in the settled districts. General Wood
from Mississippi was far more hopeful and thought that it was
'not going too far to say that substantial justice is now adminis-
tered throughout the State by the local judicial tribunals to all
classes of persons, irrespective of race or color or antecedent
political opinions'. It was, however, fair to ask, in view of the
careful instructions against discrimination which General Wood
had been compelled to make, whether even-handed justice would
be admitted when States controlled their own criminal jurisdiction. Wood also added that 'many outrages and crimes have
been committed by the vicious and criminal or the weak, and
these crimes have in many cases gone unpunished'. He sensibly
drew attention to the vast and disturbing changes in the South
and observed that 'it should not perhaps be a matter of surprise
that so many crimes occur and go unpunished, but rather a matter
of marvel that so few occur'. Here as elsewhere the obvious
explanation for violence might also demonstrate the inability of
the State governments to maintain order and protect legal rights
without military aid. In fact the Southerners and their Northern
friends were driven to claim that crime was just as prevalent in the
North, rather than to attempt a defence of their own State records.

[1] These reports can be found in C.G. 39.2, Appendix. 28ff.

General Sickles reported in a way which was in general complimentary to the good sense and behaviour of the people of South Carolina, and said that the local authorities had usually 'shown a proper disposition to do justice between man and man and to afford protection to all good citizens'. But there were unfortunate exceptions and in six counties a freedman had 'little security for life, limb or property, apart from the protection of a garrison of United States troops', and conditions were almost as bad in some Western districts. Sickles pointed out that in these rural areas there was a long tradition of illegal violence, and that where white men had assaulted each other with impunity they could hardly be expected 'to yield with any grace to arrests for assaults and outrages upon negroes'. He went on to cite one case of organized murder and one of organized terrorism in which no action had been taken though local people knew the perpetrators. He had had to make use of his power of military arrest, and had kept cases involving offences by whites against negroes in the military courts because the laws of South Carolina did not permit negro testimony against white men.

The reports of the generals commanding in the South therefore presented neither a picture of complete anarchy and insecurity, such as extreme Radicals liked to draw, nor an orderly society in which the legal rights of all could safely be left to the civil authorities. If the Northern majority took seriously their obligation to the freed negroes they could not ignore the evidence that the laws of some States still contained provisions which discriminated against them or that in some districts the civil authorities failed to supply adequate protection for life, liberty and property, or that, where an attempt was made to do so, the white population did not co-operate in securing the arrest of white criminals. At this juncture the Supreme Court delivered a decision which seemed to strike at the whole structure of military protection. This was the celebrated case of *ex parte Milligan*.

Milligan was an Indiana copperhead who had been arrested for subversive activities during war, and tried by Lincoln's order before a military court. He had been convicted and sentenced to death. His appeal was taken to the Supreme Court, and its historic decision was given by Mr Justice Davis. The gist of the decision was given in the phrase: 'It is the birthright of every American citizen when charged with crime, to be tried and punished according to law ... If there was law to justify this military trial, it is not our province to interfere; if there was not, it is our duty to declare the nullity of the whole proceedings.' The Court found that at the time of Milligan's trial the civil courts of Indiana were open, and that the State was not a theatre of war. If it were possible under such circumstances to bring a civilian before a military court, the guarantees of the Constitution were destroyed and 'there is an end of liberty regulated by law'. Martial law could not be justified by a threat of rebellion, but 'the necessity must be actual and present; the invasion real, such as effectually closes the courts and deposes the civil administration'. The Constitution provided safeguards for the individual, and 'not one of these safeguards can the President, or Congress, or the judiciary disturb, except the one concerning the writ of habeas corpus'. Even if invasion had justified military jurisdiction its continuance 'after the courts are re-instated ... is a gross usurpation of power'.[1]

When the judgment was announced few people were thinking of the fortunate Milligan, but of the military courts in the South and of their protection for the negroes against violence and the deprivation of rights. It was clear that the Court's argument would apply directly to the South where there was no longer war, where the civil courts were functioning, and where Congress had recently enlarged the jurisdiction of military courts under the Freedmen's Bureau Act. 'That decision,' exclaimed Thaddeus Stevens, 'although in terms perhaps not as infamous as the Dred Scott decision, is yet far more dangerous in its operation upon the lives and liberties of the loyal men of this country. That decision has taken away every protection in every one of these rebel States from every loyal man, black or white, who resides there. That decision has unsheathed the dagger of the assassin, and places the

---

[1] 4 Wallace 2, 1866. The significant passages in Mr Justice Davis's opinion can be found in Commager (ed.), *Documents of American History*, II, and in many other documentary collections.

knife of the rebel at the throat of every man who dares to pro-
claim himself to be now, or to have been heretofore, a loyal
Union man'.[1] The Problem now presented to Congress was a
straightforward one. Was the white or the black man to be
deprived of his safeguards under the law? For most Republicans
there would be only one answer: protection for the negro deprived the white man of nothing which he ought to have;
exemption of Southern whites from military jurisdiction would
deprive the negro of rights which he had acquired with his
freedom. The problem had long term implications; but it was also
one of urgency, calling for immediate action.

It is doubtful whether white Unionists were in quite the
danger which Stevens depicted, but their political and social
plight was dire. Those who had co-operated with the Federal
authorities during the war, had responded to the invitation
extended under Lincoln's plan of Reconstruction, or had proclaimed their hostility to the Confederacy when Federal
occupation made this possible, were now marked men. Their fate
was that of a minority which had backed the wrong horse, and
they suffered not only the penalties of defeat but also the odium
of treason. This was, in essence, a more difficult problem to solve
than that of the negro, though its solution might have less far-
reaching effects. What steps could or ought to be taken to save a
minority from political oblivion and social ostracism? And how
could the right of a majority in the States be reconciled with a
moral obligation to the Unionists incurred by the national
government?

The attitude of Johnson and his supporters to this problem is
illustrated by an incident from the diary of Gideon Welles. On
13 December he received a visit from the loyalist Governor
Pease of Texas ('one of the Southern committee to excite the
Radicals into the adoption of measures for subverting the
constitution of the United States').[2] Pease said that three-quarters
or four-fifths of the white Texans were hostile to United States
and to the Union men of the State, and 'he said that the Federal

---

[1] C.G. 39.2.251.   [2] Beale (ed.), *Diary of Gideon Welles*, II, 641–2.

Government must send troops there to control the rebels and prevent them from grasping all power'. Welles replied that the way to change a government was to do it openly. 'Let the people decide.' And if the people chose a government which Pease disliked, then he must 'be patient, forbearing, submit to the majority. Do not organize against them and keep up antagonism'. Welles did not explain how a government could be changed openly without organizing against the party in power, and his replies had completely missed the point in the pathetic history of the Southern Unionists. It was not surprising that Pease left without further comment.

*　　*　　*　　*

Negroes and Unionists presented together a powerful argument for congressional action, and Bingham was prepared to see military protection continued until the Southern States were re-admitted. The weak points in his case were that in the interim initiative would rest with the existing Southern Governments, restrained but not controlled by the military commanders, that the Milligan decision might be used to disarm the military courts, and that even with the Fourteenth Amendment in the Constitution no one could guarantee that the existing régimes in the South would not discover numerous means of evading the spirit of its civil rights clause. Thus Bingham seemed to have blunted the Radical drive with his congressional victory on 28 January, but pressures were building up which moderate Republicans would find hard to resist. Indeed many of them were already half prepared to move with the tide.

On the day when Stevens lost the first round to Bingham G. W. Julian of Indiana delivered a speech of considerable ability and future significance.[1] Julian spoke as an extreme Radical, but his arguments were well chosen and carried much weight. Indeed, at a time when debate was becoming stale with repetition, he approached the problem with refreshing clarity. He began by emphasizing how little had been done. Nearly two years after the

[1] C.G. 39.2.79.

end of the war the South was still without governments recognized by Congress and no loyal man was safe. 'Even the conquered rebels themselves, who are supreme in this general reign of terror, seem to be growing weary of their term of lawlessness and misrule.' But he argued that the remedy was not a hasty plan of Reconstruction which would simply confirm in power those who had already abused it, and he even criticized vigorously the Stevens proposal to allow those who had not willingly supported the Confederacy after 4 March 1864 to participate in Reconstruction. This simply invited men to commit perjury (which would be difficult to detect) in order to retain power. Even if the oath were honestly taken 'the nation ought to withhold the ballot from its enemies till they have proved themselves fit to cast it. No such proof can be adduced'. So far Julian worked on familiar Radical themes, but he then went on to demonstrate that no plan now enacted would remedy the ills which he had described. 'No theory of government, no form of administration, can be trusted, unless adequately supported by public opinion.' The Southern 'aristocrats' if unrestrained by external power, would soon find ways of reasserting themselves. Not quick restoration was required, but *government* 'the strong arm of power, outstretched from the central authority here in Washington'. 'States *grow*,' he said, 'and to that end their growth must be fostered and protected. The political and social regeneration of the country made desolate by treason is the prime necessity of the hour, and is preliminary to any reconstruction of States.' He believed that the proper answer was to treat them as Territories and 'when local supremacy shall defy the national authority in any of these Territories, let it be effectively cured by the military power of the United States'. Julian's remedy was harsh but its object was humane: 'Under this educational process I would have these rebellious districts trained up in the way they should go ... while in the meantime every inch of their soil will be subject to national authority, and freely open to the energy and enterprise of the world. This policy, by nationalizing the South, would render life and property as secure in Louisiana as in Maine. It would tend powerfully to make our whole country homogeneous.' Small farms, prosperous agriculture, free schools, social independence, stable communities, respect for honest labour and for political rights would grow under such a policy. 'All these blessings must flow, if only the nation, having vanquished its enemies, will now resolutely assert its power in the interests of loyal men, over regions where nothing but power is respected.' In pointing out that the 'regeneration', which must precede Reconstruction, would be a slow process, Julian anticipated criticisms which have been made against the later course of Radical Reconstruction, but his immediate attack upon rapid restoration had considerable effect. He had said that the immediate need was not for a plan of restoration but for a resolute exercise of military power. The most attractive feature was that it provided a way out of the stalemate between Radicals and moderates; the former would be content to defer their plans until the Fortieth Congress, the latter could still believe that they were standing upon the Fourteenth Amendment, and both had admitted the need to protect the freedmen in the South.

A military bill, as a compromise, appealed also to the Committee on Reconstruction. The committee had begun by considering Stevens's bill without apparent enthusiasm, while Bingham had made a significant move towards the Radicals by offering impartial suffrage as well as the Fourteenth Amendment as a condition for re-admission. No vote was taken, and when the committee met four days later both proposals were dropped in favour of a military protection bill which Senator Williams, a member of the committee, had introduced into the Senate. In several respects the bill merely defined the position which already existed. The South was to be divided into military districts, and the commanders were empowered and instructed to 'protect all peaceable and law-abiding persons in their rights of person and property, to suppress insurrection, disorder and violence, and to punish or cause to be punished all disturbers of the public peace and criminals'. For this purpose they could set up military tribunals if the civil courts were inadequate, and 'all legislative or judicial proceedings or processes to prevent or control the proceedings of the said military tribunals, and all interference by the said pretended state governments with the exercise of military authority under this act shall be void and of no effect',[1] which disposed of the Supreme Court and *ex parte Milligan*. This military bill was to be the hinge upon which Reconstruction policy turned, and its acceptance by the committee was to have far-reaching consequences.

After making some amendments in detail the committee instructed Stevens to report the bill to the House, and adjourned for three days. When it reassembled on Saturday, 9 February, only five members presented themselves, and this being less than a quorum it adjourned to meet again when called by the chairman. The call was never made and in this unceremonious way the Joint Committee of Fifteen passed from history. Its deeds and decisions had been of momentous consequence for the future of the nation, but the final determination upon Reconstruction policy was to be made by the Thirty-ninth Congress in the month of life which remained to it.

In introducing the bill on 7 February Stevens observed that Congress had just fifteen days to act upon it if it was to be passed and re-passed over a veto. Bingham refused to be bullied into silence, but the amendments which he offered touched the form rather than the substance of the bill; he wished to alter phrases which implied that the Southern States were not States, to allow Federal courts to issue writs of habeas corpus for Federal crimes which would run against the military courts, and to insert explicit denial of any intention to continue military jurisdiction once the States were restored to their proper relationship in the Union. He concluded: 'I am sure of this: that the American people will have rule, civil or military in those insurgent States until they shall be fully restored to their constitutional relations. And in so far as they may be able under direction of law and the authority of law enacted by their Congress, they will protect all men in those States in life, liberty and property until they can be fully protected under accepted constitutional State governments.

[1] Kendrick, *Journal* 124–9, Ch. VIII *passim*, and especially 379–82.

When men in those States shall have fulfilled their obligations, and when the great people themselves shall have put, by their own rightful authority, into the fundamental law the sublime decree, the nation's will, that no State shall deny to any mortal man the equal protection of the laws — not of the laws of South Carolina alone, but of the laws national and State — and above all of that great law, the Constitution of our own country, which is the supreme law of the land from Georgia to Oregon and from Maine to Florida — then by assenting thereto those States may be restored at once. To that end I labor and for that I strive.'[1] Thus Bingham announced his acceptance of the principles of military protection, his continued faith in the idea of nationalizing rights, and his intention to fight for the freedom of States to ratify the amendment and of Congress to accept ratification as the condition for re-admission.

On 13 February the bill finally came to the vote. By this time Bingham had enlarged his proposal. He now wished to enact a Reconstruction bill and to tack the military bill on to it as an interim measure for preserving law and order until such time as the Southern States had fulfilled the conditions laid down. In the course of debate on 13 February Bingham accepted an amendment proposed by Blaine which achieved his object by the addition of a single section to the military bill. Both Bingham and Blaine laid down conditions which were by now familiar — ratification of the Fourteenth Amendment, the framing of a new constitution in accordance with it, ratification by a majority of qualified voters, approval by Congress, and admission when the amendment had become part of the Constitution — but both made a significant addition. The Constitutions submitted by the States must now provide for impartial suffrage. Blaine proposed to refer the whole bill to the Committee on Judiciary with instructions to report back immediately with his amendment as a part of the bill. This brought about a strange and unexpected alliance in Congress. Stevens and his Radical supporters wanted the military bill without amendment, and were immovably opposed to any

[1] C.G. 39.2.1083.

Reconstruction bill which would leave the initiative in the States with the existing governments. The Democrats were opposed to making negro suffrage a condition of admission to the Union and saw an opportunity for exploiting Republican divisions. Thus Radicals and Democrats joined together against a motion to bring Blaine's proposal to the vote, but they were defeated by 85 to 78 with 27 not voting. Stevens now roused himself to a supreme effort. In a short speech against the motion to refer he was as eloquent and as blunt as ever, with an added emotion which made a profound impression upon the House. 'If, sir, I might presume upon my age, without claiming any of the wisdom of Nestor, I would suggest to the young gentlemen around me, that the deeds of this burning crisis, of this solemn day, of this thrilling moment, will cast their shadows far into the future and will make their impress upon the annals of our history, and that we shall appear upon the bright pages of history, just in so far as we cordially, without guile, without bickering, without small criticisms, lend our aid to promote the great cause of human and universal liberty.' Of the Blaine amendment he said that it 'lets in a vast number of rebels and shuts out nobody. All I ask is that when the House comes to vote upon that amendment it shall understand that the adoption of it would be an entire surrender of those States into the hands of the rebels'.[1] When the vote was taken sixteen Republicans had changed sides, the Democrats continued to vote with the Radicals, and the vote stood at 69 to 94 with 27 again not voting. The Republicans now rallied to prevent the complete loss of the main bill, which was carried by 109 to 55, without the Blaine amendment, and with nearly all Republicans voting for it. It was perhaps the supreme congressional triumph of Thaddeus Stevens and the old man knew it; 'I wish to enquire, Mr Speaker,' he asked when the vote was announced, 'if it is in order for me now to say that we indorse the language of good Laertes, that Heaven rules as yet and there are gods above?'[2]

The bill had yet to pass the Senate, and time was running short. It soon became evident that a number of Republicans

---

[1] C.G. 39.2.1214.   [2] C.G. 39.2.1215.

would not accept the bill unless something like the Blaine amendment was included in it. A party senatorial caucus was held on 16 February — a Saturday morning which showed the urgency of the matter — and a committee of seven presided over by John Sherman was appointed to draw up an acceptable bill. At this late hour there was an attempt to eliminate negro suffrage from the bill and a majority of the Sherman committee voted it out; Sumner, who was a member of the committee, then appealed from it to the Republican senatorial caucus where negro suffrage was carried by a majority of two.[1] Sherman reported the same evening with a bill which was virtually the military bill with the Blaine amendment. Sherman defended the bill because 'it points out the mode by which the people of those States in their own manner, without any limitation of restrictions by Congress, may get back to full representation in Congress.' At a little before twenty minutes past six on Sunday, 17 February the Sherman bill passed the Senate by 29 votes to 10, with thirteen absent including Sumner who had left the Senate.[2] In the House Boutwell and Stevens immediately fought to reject the Senate's amendment. A comment by Stevens offers a sharp contrast to that of Sherman: 'What is the fifth section of this substitute? Why is it incorporated here? It is that we may pledge this Government in future to all the traitors in rebeldom, so that hereafter there shall be no escape from it. . . . We are promising them, we are holding out to them a pledge that if they will do certain things therein mentioned they shall come into this House and act with us as loyal men.'[3] On the other hand a Democrat described it as 'a declaration of war

[1] Authority for this statement rests upon Sumner's own account during a speech given in the Forty-first Congress (C.G. 41.2.640); it was not disputed by Trumbull, who was a member of the Sherman committee and who was then under attack from Sumner. Sumner said that in the committee 'I was over-ruled, the Senator [Trumbull] opposing me with his customary determination. I was voted down. The chairman observed my discontent and said, "You can renew your motion in caucus" '. In caucus Sumner's motion was carried by a majority of two ('Senators rising to be counted'), and, according to Sumner, Henry Wilson cried out, 'This is the greatest vote that has been taken on this continent'.

[2] His absence was explained by his enemies as the result of baffled fury at the passage of a bill which did not displace the Southern leaders; he himself said that he was tired and knew that the bill was sure to pass, though he did think that it lacked a provision for public education and was angry because he had been prevented from introducing this by the action of the caucus (C.G. 41.2.640).

[3] C.G. 39.2.1317.

against the Southern people; it is at least a revival and continuation of the war which we had hoped was forever ended'.[1] After a lengthy and angry debate the House refused to accept the Senate amendments by 98 against 73 with the Democrats once more voting with Stevens against the majority of Republican members. The disagreement was then referred to a committee of conference of the two Houses, and it was the morning of 19 February with eleven working days left for the Thirty-ninth Congress.

When the House reassembled in special session at 7.30 it was greeted by a message that the Senate had refused a committee of conference and adhered to its amendments. The situation was now desperate for it was clear that no bill would be passed unless the House accepted something akin to the Senate proposal (which was also the Bingham and Blaine proposal) for tacking a Reconstruction measure on to the military bill. Congress might well end without doing anything to protect the loyal men whose plight had been the constant theme of Republican oratory, and the urgent need for some formula of agreement was apparent. Wilson of Iowa came forward with a proposal that no person whom the Fourteenth Amendment intended to disqualify from office should be eligible for membership of the State constitutional conventions or qualified to vote for delegates. The Wilson amendment was clearly a compromise offer to which the moderates had already agreed, for immediately it had been read Blaine moved the previous question and attempted to force through a vote against the obstruction of both Democrats and Radicals.[2] In effect the moderates insisted upon a Reconstruction bill which would have some chance of speedy effect and were prepared to accept as a price the exclusion of the Southern gentry from the process of constitution making both as delegates and voters. So far as the convention was concerned the proposal anticipated the effects of the Fourteenth Amendment, which the State was bound

---

[1] C.G. 39.2.1324. Remarks by Eldridge of Wisconsin.

[2] Wilson usually acted with the Radicals. He later explained his vote for the Sherman-Blaine Bill on the ground that he thought it the best which could be obtained, but thanked the Democrats for having helped to defeat it and his own amendment (C.G. 40.1.64). From the course of the debate, however, it is clear that his proposal had been agreed with Blaine and was disliked by the Radicals.

to accept, and disenfranchised the same people for the convention election alone. This was not good enough for the Radicals, and on a motion to adjourn Stevens, Boutwell, Ashley and most of the other Radicals voted in the minority with the Democrats for adjournment. The House finally agreed to adjourn upon the understanding that a vote would be taken immediately the House resumed on the following day. When the House re-assembled Blaine attempted to bring the bill with the Wilson amendment to the vote, but his call for the previous question failed by 76 to 72. It was clear that the Radicals were still combining with the Democrats to prevent a vote upon the bill as it stood, and it was also clear that something was afoot for Samuel Shellabarger had already been on his feet in an attempt to offer a further amendment which Blaine had refused. With the failure of the call for the previous question Shellabarger was able to announce his amendment which was to add to the Wilson amendment a declaration that the existing governments of the Southern States were 'provisional only, and in all respects subject to the paramount authority of the United States, at any time to abolish, modify, control, or supersede the same' — thus keeping open the question of the status of the States which was a principal object of the Radical manoeuvres — and went on to propose the disqualification from office and from voting under the provisional governments all whom the Fourteenth Amendment intended to disqualify from national and State office. The Shellabarger amendment aimed to break up the existing régimes in the South, by driving from office most of their leaders, and to disenfranchise them until the States had been re-admitted to the Union. This did not, of course, go so far as Stevens's original proposal to deprive all ex-confederates of citizenship, but it went far enough to put an entirely new complexion on Reconstruction. It was in effect the charter for Radical Reconstruction, for it transferred the initiative from 'rebels' to 'loyal' men. Immediately after his amendment had been read Shellabarger called for the previous question, and this was carried by 80 to 41. The Speaker refused to put a motion that it should be referred to a committee, and a vote on the main question was immediately taken. This time it was the turn of Bingham, Blaine and other Republican moderates to vote in opposition with the Democrats, but a sufficiently large number of moderate Republicans had decided to join with the Radicals, and Shellabarger's amendment was carried by 99 to 70 with 21 not voting. The Speaker now took the ground that the House had agreed to the Wilson amendment as amended and that no further separate vote on the amendments was possible; it must be the whole bill with the amendments or no bill. Faced with the choice between accepting the Shellabarger amendment or leaving the Radicals in the field without any Reconstruction Act to control the policy of the Fortieth Congress moderate Republicans voted in the affirmative. United at last in an uneasy harmony the Republican party voted solidly to carry the bill by 126 to 46 with 18 not voting. In the Senate the same logic prevailed. Sherman made no secret of the fact that he disliked the House amendments, and pointed out with some bitterness the role of the Democrats in the House debates. 'If these amendments are harsh and hard upon any portion of the Southern States, they are put there, not by the Union party, but by the Democratic party: and from that position no logic can enable gentlemen to escape.'[1] For moderates, however, any bill which provided both for military protection and for Reconstruction was better than no bill or one which provided for the first alone; for Radicals a bill which drove Southern leaders out of the existing governments was much better than one which left the initiative in their hands; in the Senate therefore, as in the House, the Republicans without the Administration supporters but with one Democrat, combined to give the first Reconstruction bill a resounding majority.

As tempers cooled some were perhaps aware that a bill of vital importance for the nation, had been drastically altered at the eleventh hour by amendments which had been considered by no committees, passed without debate in the House and with little in the Senate. Men who had kept clear heads, and had tried to steer a sound course through all the tides and shoals of Reconstruction,

[1] C.G. 39.2.1640.

had been swept away by the plea of urgency to pass a measure which many of them disliked, and which no Republican group accepted as more than a second best. It was in all a sorry performance which reflected little credit upon Congress. The feeling that something must be done, and the rigid timetable of the American Constitution, had carried men to the point at which political judgment dissolved into political expediency or sheer ignorance.[1] Within a few hours decisions had been taken which would affect the future of the nation without adequate discussion and without real knowledge either of the South or, in some instances, of the meaning of what had been done.

Andrew Johnson still had a decision to make. He could kill the bill by refusing to sign it, for it would lapse automatically when Congress adjourned on 4 March; he could send in a veto and give Congress time to re-pass the bill; he could send a veto but so late that there would be no time to act upon it; or he could sign. If he killed the bill by a 'pocket' veto, it would certainly be introduced as soon as the Fortieth Congress met and an act had already passed that it should meet immediately the Thirty-ninth dissolved. The new Congress would have a larger Republican majority and a marked strengthening of the Radical element. It was therefore probable that in a new bill further Radical proposals would be incorporated. There was a slender chance that a well-argued veto message might shake a sufficient number of moderate Republicans in the Senate, and that the bill would fail to secure the necessary two-thirds in that house; and a bill which had been lost in this way would have a much poorer chance of revival. It is possible that Johnson calculated in this way, but it is more likely that he decided to deliver his veto to posterity rather than to Congress as it was. Having lost all influence upon the formulation of Reconstruction policy, and having been repudiated by the electorate, his vindication must come from the future if at all.

[1] Sherman did not know how many would be disqualified from office under the Fourteenth Amendment or from suffrage under the Reconstruction Act. He guessed at from six to ten thousand, but was corrected by Senator Buckalew of Pennsylvania who estimated 60,000 or more. (C.G. 39.2.1626, 1627–8). It is clear that Sherman was thinking of those who held office in 1860, but the Fourteenth Amendment disqualified all who had *ever* taken the oath of allegiance and subsequently supported the rebellion.

There was indeed a strong case for reconsidering the measure but a veto from Johnson no longer carried weight, and his disapproval was more likely to unite than to divide the Republicans. Moreover it was in the nature of the man to use precisely those arguments which would stir up opposition and to ignore those which might encourage a desire for second thoughts. The vulnerable points in the bill were its treatment of the Southern ruling class and the doubtful efficiency of the political mechanism which it provided. Moderate Republicans had insisted that the existing governments in the South must be allowed to initiate the process of Reconstruction, and they wished this not so much from any love for the Southern gentry, but because they knew instinctively that the stability of Reconstruction would be enhanced if they did not assume responsibility for it. The bill ousted the ruling class from control of the provisional government, excluded them from the convention to be called, and added temporary disenfranchisement. It provided, however, no mechanism by which the process of Reconstruction could be initiated, and assigned to no one the responsibility for setting it in motion. Behind this procedural defect lay the impossibility of conjuring out of the Southern people a new 'loyalist' leadership which could command the prestige or ability to shoulder such responsibilities. Johnson's veto message ignored these practical difficulties because their very discussion would have admitted the right of Congress to control Reconstruction and to provide the legal machinery for it. The veto message fastened first upon the powers given to military commanders, which every Republican believed to be justified by the plight of the negroes. He then argued that the sole purpose of this was to force upon the South conditions of Reconstruction — and in particular negro suffrage — which they would not adopt of their own free will. He then stressed the dictatorial power given to the military commanders and their subordinates, concluding that 'no master ever had a control so absolute over the slaves as the bill gives to the military officers over both white and coloured persons'. This was inaccurate and exaggerated, and the President evaded the main issue, which was the existing violence and terrorism. By implication he admitted that these things must continue until such time as the Southern whites were minded to stop them. He emphasized the right of every American citizen to trial by jury, when the white Southern jury was the heart of the problem with which Congress had been contending. Finally he attacked the provision for negro suffrage as a violation of that 'manifest, well-known, and universally acknowledged rule of constitutional law which declares that the Federal Government has no jurisdiction, authority, or power to regulate such subjects for any State. To force the right of suffrage out of the hands of the white people and into the hands of the negroes is an arbitrary violation of this principle'.[1]

The answer to Johnson's veto message came not from a Republican but from a Democrat, Reverdy Johnson, whom Gideon Welles called 'an old political prostitute . . . governed by mercenary considerations . . . with a good deal of legal ability, but . . . not overburdened with political principles'.[2] In fact Reverdy Johnson was experienced, respected, and his speech came as near to statesmanship as any utterance in this second session of the Thirty-ninth Congress. Senator Johnson made no secret of his dislike of the whole course of Reconstruction policy since the war; he still took his theoretical stand upon State rights and a belief that neither President nor Congress had the authority to impose conditions for membership of the Union other than those contained in the Constitution. The policy of Congress had, however, been sustained by the people and there was no hope that the majority would change their opinions in the near future; under these circumstances a friend of the South ought to get the best possible terms for restoration and stop trying to fight on ground which had been lost. Whatever the constitutional objections to the bill they were not greater than those to other measures which had become a part of the law of the land. Military power had been used ever since the peace, and even the decision in *ex parte Milligan* gave no assurance that the Court would not

---

[1] Richardson, (ed.), *Messages and Papers*, VI, 498 ff.
[2] Beale (ed.), *Diary of Gideon Welles*, III, 56. Reverdy Johnson's speech is in C.G. 39.2.1972 ff.

justify the policy of Congress as 'a political question to be decided exclusively by the political department of Government, by Congress, to whom alone is entrusted the power to declare war and suppress insurrections'. The advantage of the present bill was that it did provide a way in which the Southern States could resume representation and end military control; if it were rejected 'one of a more harsh and unjust character would be adopted, one founded upon the hypothesis that the people of the South were to be esteemed legally as conquered enemies, and their land and other property on that account liable to confiscation and forfeiture'. Reverdy Johnson went on to describe feeling in the South. He said that his views were shared by intelligent and reflecting men and 'they tell me it is their purpose to organize under the bill. They are taking lessons from experience. The constitutional amendment heretofore proposed to them, if they had adopted it, would I firmly believe, before this have given them representation in Congress. Of that I am in no doubt, but they rejected it, and now to adopt it would not have that result'. He disliked the amendments which the House had added to the bill, but had concurred in them because they seemed to present, under the circumstances, the only terms upon which a congressional majority could be persuaded to agree to the restoration of the Union.

The bill being repassed by more than the required two-thirds in both Houses of Congress it became law on 2 March 1867, the last working day of the momentous Thirty-ninth Congress; to the reasons given by Reverdy Johnson for his reluctant concurrence with the Reconstruction policy which that Congress had evolved, a few points may be added. He was certainly correct in believing that a failure of the bill might lead to a more drastic measure in the future. The whole history of Reconstruction policy had illustrated this, and the Radicals had achieved a drive, cohesion and success in the second session which they had failed to develop in the first. Territorial status formally declared, confiscation, and 'education' on the lines proposed by Julian lay just round the corner, if the Southerners did not organize as soon as possible on the lines determined by Congress. It is possible that the South would be a happier place today if a period of 'education' and 'tutelage' had followed, but, from the point of view of the Southerner who wished to preserve as much as possible of the existing social system, the Reconstruction Bill offered some hope. The exclusion of disqualified leaders from the provisional governments was likely to remain as much a threat as a reality. The needs of the government, and the impracticability of doing everything with the comparatively small number of troops available, would keep many of them in power. Their position would be analogous to that of English dissenters in the eighteenth century; formally debarred from office but in fact exercising much influence and continuing in many offices out of the public eye. They would continue to enjoy local prestige and the support of the white people, so that their influence upon affairs would remain; and though a strict interpretation of the Act and of the Fourteenth Amendment would exclude every 'rebel' who had ever held national or State office (down to minor local offices), a new generation was coming forward who had been too young for office before 1861 but were now ready to carry on the work of their fathers. The disenfranchisement was unpleasant and insulting, but its effect could be exaggerated. It ceased to operate once the State was restored to the Union unless the State conventions themselves made further restrictions. And though the number disqualified and disenfranchised might be a large part of the Southern gentry, the number deprived of the vote in any one district would not be large enough to affect the result of an election. It was not white disenfranchisement but negro enfranchisement which altered the political balance, but negro suffrage was inescapable, might well be controlled to Southern advantage, and secured a black majority in few districts. A removal of political disabilities under the Fourteenth Amendment was most unlikely during the Fortieth Congress but, as soon as the 1868 election was passed and political tempers cooled, the ordinary generosity of American people might well demand their removal. In all, the Reconstruction Act, unwelcome as it was and unwise in some particulars, was not so bad as it could be painted. The

World, which was the most influential of Democratic newspapers and circulated widely in the South, joined Reverdy Johnson in urging the South to comply and organize under the Act. It was able to quote a large number of selections from Southern editorials which took the same line.[1]

The weakness of the Reconstruction Act was not that it imposed impossible conditions but that it invited the Southerners to organize while alienating their leaders from the wider and more humane objectives of the Northern people. The Wilson, and more particularly the Shellabarger amendment, added insults which did little to facilitate Reconstruction and nothing to win over those whose good-will was necessary for success. The presumption behind the argument for compliance was that once restoration had been achieved the Southerners would regain the power to resist Northern pressure for further changes in their society, and that 'regeneration' would be avoided. The defects in the machinery of the Act exposed some points at which the Radical screw could be turned still tighter as — was to be immediately apparent in the Fortieth Congress — but whatever happened re-union would be based upon calculations of expediency and not upon a consensus of opinion about the moral bases of the nation. In providing the machinery for Reconstruction the Act did nothing to heal sectional bitterness, and in some respects increased it. Southerners remained convinced that too much had been done, while many Northerners continued to regard the South as an alien and inherently vicious society.

*   *   *   *

[1] On 4 Mar. the *World* spoke of the act as 'this abominable and tyrannical law'; but it went on to point out that it 'will stand for four years at least. . . . the indications are that the South must ultimately submit, therefore it should do so quickly. . . . Good policy requires that the submission should be prompt enough to prevent the Radicals from getting control of the new State organizations. The planters can control the negro vote, if they begin in season; and by accepting at once what they will be constrained to submit to at last, they can help their friends in the North elect the next President and rescue the government from Radical domineering and insolence'. On 12 Mar. the *World* was alarmed by reports that qualified white voters might abstain at the elections in protest against the Act and commented that 'if the majority of the Southern whites stay away from the first polls by choice, they will be kept away from all future polls by disenfranchisement'. On 15 Mar. the *World* reprinted a large number of Southern editorials giving similar advice. E. Merton Coulter, *The South During Reconstruction*, 122–4 refers to individual Southerners who advised acquiescence.

Immediately the Fortieth Congress met, Sumner proposed a further Reconstruction measure. The bill just passed was not enough; he said that, 'it is not what the loyal people of the South have a right to expect from Congress. It contemplates reconstruction but it does not supply the proper machinery. Then again such machinery as it does employ is left in the hands of the existing governments which the bill declares to be illegal'.[1] He was, of course, quite right in pointing that the procedure for initiating Reconstruction was defective and he gave notice that he would press for the complete transference of power to 'loyal' men. At the same time Kelley, in the House of Representatives, carried a motion instructing the Committee on Judiciary to report a bill 'declaring who shall call conventions for the reorganization of the rebel States' and 'to provide for the registration of voters'.[2] The outcome of this was the second Reconstruction Bill which pressed home the advantage which the Radicals had won with the acceptance of Shellabarger's amendment. The significant fact in the comparatively brief discussion which followed was the collapse of moderate opposition.

The bill proposed as a consequence of Kelley's motion placed the initiative firmly with the military commanders. They were to register voters, admitting only those who could take an oath that they had not been disenfranchised for rebellion; that they had never held State or national legislative, judicial or executive office and subsequently engaged in the rebellion; and that they would now support the Constitution of the United States and 'encourage others so to do'. They had next to arrange for elections at which the voters would be asked to vote for or against a constitutional convention, and to choose delegates to such a convention. If a majority of the votes cast were for a convention it should then be called, but only if a majority of all registered voters had voted on the question. The convention should then frame a constitution, and this had to be submitted for ratification to the registered voters. The Constitution could be submitted to Congress only if approved by a majority with at least one half of

[1] C.G. 40.1.10.   [2] C.G. 40.1.17.

the registered electors voting. Congress was empowered to inquire into the conditions of the ratification election and to ascertain that votes had been cast 'freely and without restraint', and to determine whether the proposed Constitution was in accordance with the provisions of the first Act.

It is interesting to compare this measure with the original Radical proposals under the Wade-Davis Bill. Then the initiative had been in the hands of a provisional civil governor, and the process of Reconstruction could be started when a majority of white male citizens had taken an oath of loyalty to the United States. Now the initial decision was to be made with the addition of negro males and without the disqualified whites. Then the convention was to be chosen by and consist of only those who could take the 'iron-clad' oath of 1862, that is, by consistent Unionists. Now former Confederates could vote for delegates and be members of the convention provided that they had not previously held State or national office. Then the convention had to incorporate in the Constitution the disenfranchisement in State elections of those who had held office under the Confederacy; now, by accepting the Fourteenth Amendment, no one would be disenfranchised but the net of disqualification would be thrown more widely and applied to national as well as to State officers. There was nothing to prevent the conventions from disenfranchising in State elections those whom they wished to penalize. The constitution under the Wade-Davis Bill was to be ratified only by those qualified to vote for convention delegates, but a majority of votes cast would be sufficient for ratification; now the qualifications for voting on ratification were more liberal but a majority of the registered voters had to participate before the act of ratification was valid. From this comparison it can be seen that the Radicals had succeeded in enacting essentially the same procedure which they had originally supported. From the Radical point of view the essential elements in this procedure were initiation by a person appointed by the national government, the consent of a carefully screened electorate to the constitution-making process, and ratification by a substantial body of the same electors. The vital point was the exclusion of Southern leaders from the whole process. The Reconstruction Acts added negro suffrage and this made it possible to be more generous over voting qualifications, but whereas it had been proposed earlier to leave ratification to the 'loyalists' strictly defined, now a majority of all registered voters was required. Throughout the dual object was to place the initiative in Reconstruction with the Southern Unionists, but to make as many white Southerners as possible assent to their work; in the Wade-Davis Bill assent was obtained before the beginning of the process, under the Reconstruction Acts at the end.

The debates in Congress on the second Reconstruction Bill had little of the tenseness of those on the first. Bingham tried to amend by providing for ratification by a majority of votes cast not by a majority of registered voters. He pointed out that under the bill the sick, the indolent or those absent from their States would be counted as votes against the Constitution, and that even under the most favourable conditions it was hard to get a fifty per cent vote in rural districts.[1] Wilson replied that whites might keep the blacks away from the polls and thus secure ratification of an undesirable constitution, and, when Bingham pointed out that Congress had still the power, under the Act, to review the Constitution and the conditions of the election, Boutwell brought out a quite different argument. If ratification by a majority of votes cast were allowed, the whites might voluntarily absent themselves; a loyalist minority might ratify but this would not be real evidence of loyalty in the State. This was the authentic Radical conviction that Reconstruction could not be real until a majority had accepted a new concept of loyalty which included not only Union but also equality under the law. After this brief discussion the bill passed the House without amendment.

In the Senate Fessenden tried to challenge the military initiative. He thought that the provisional governments ought to be asked to act so that 'we leave it, or pretend to leave it, to the people to decide that question'. He went on, 'I do not wish to take control

[1] C.G. 40.1.62.

of these people or force them back into the Union against their will, before they wish to come. I have not that degree of anxiety on the subject, because if we do that we shall have a very unhappy and disunited family after they have come back.'[1] He said that he had it in mind to offer an amendment, but in the event he did not do so. Sumner also disliked military government, and would have preferred something on the lines of the abortive Louisiana bill, which gave dictatorial powers to an appointed civil governor and council.[2] The difficulty confronting moderate opinion was that, much as they might dislike the idea of military government, it would provide for certain and speedy restoration of the Southern States. Fessenden's proposal to leave it to the provisional governments might lead to more delays, and if those governments refused to act the stage would be set for more Radical extremism. No one had anything to say for Sumner's idea of a dictatorial civil government; this would have authority to make extensive changes in Southern society, which moderates did not like, and would entail lengthy discussion before such an innovation could be launched when everyone was now anxious to get a Reconstruction policy launched. Thus the moderate Republicans in the Senate were ready to accept the military initiative, because it made it certain that something would be done, and to concentrate upon those aspects of the bill which made for delay. They succeeded in fighting off an amendment which would have required approval of a majority of registered electors, given as a separate referendum, before the convention could be called. They also succeeded in modifying the ratification requirement; in its final form the Bill no longer required a majority of all registered electors but a majority of votes cast provided that at least half the registered voters had voted.

The President delivered the expected veto. He had by now evolved a theory of Radical Reconstruction which has commended itself to some historians. 'What ... in the opinion of

---

[1] C.G. 40.1.96.

[2] C.G. 40.1.165. Sumner also tried to make the provision of free public education without racial discrimination a condition for the admission of States. This proposal led to a tie in the Senate with 13 absent (20–20).

Congress is necessary to make the constitution of a State "loyal and republican"? The original act answers the question: It is universal negro suffrage — a question which the Federal Constitution leaves exclusively to the States themselves. All this legislative machinery of martial law, military coercion, and political disenfranchisement is avowedly for that purpose and none other.'[1] It is doubtful whether, in reviewing the history of the 'radical conspiracy', he understood how much he himself had contributed to its success.

Before the Thirty-ninth Congress dissolved it had done its best to tie the hands of the President so that he had no option but to execute the will of Congress. It had passed the Tenure of Office Act which forbade him to dismiss, without the consent of the Senate, any Federal appointee for whose appointment that consent was necessary. It had also added to the Army Appropriations Act a clause which made it obligatory for the President to transmit all orders to the army through the General of the Armies (Grant), who was not to be removed except at his own request or with the consent of the Senate. It soon became apparent that the President's remaining power to issue orders to civil authorities could be used to obstruct if not to defeat the aims of military protection and Reconstruction. Behind the scenes there was growing confusion and perplexity among the responsible army officers, and this placed the Secretary of War, Stanton, in a peculiarly difficult position. Politically Stanton might be described as a moderate Republican with Radical leanings. He had come to interpret his position in the Cabinet as that of intermediary between the administration and the Radicals. There was, of course, nothing unusual in the idea of Cabinet representation for the various factions of a party, but Stanton was hardly the man to play so delicate a role of mediation. Energetic and able he had also a reputation for duplicity and a fixed habit of saying one thing and doing another. As the gulf yawned between the President and the main body of the Republican party, the position

[1] Richardson (ed.), *Messages and Papers*, VI, 531.

of a man, whose formal loyalty was to the President but whose sympathies were with the party, became increasingly difficult. It was made more difficult because most of the leading generals shared these sympathies, and intended to administer congressional policy as it was generally understood. Stanton's own position, and that of the soldiers under his direction, would become much easier if Congress cleared away any ambiguities which remained about the intent and direction of policy, for Johnson soon showed that he would use every loophole in the law to defeat its purpose. Accordingly Stanton conferred with various Republican leaders to draft yet one more Reconstruction Act which became law on 19 July 1867.

The new bill was introduced in the Senate by Lyman Trumbull and in the House by Thaddeus Stevens, demonstrating that both wings of the party were now resolved to make Reconstruction work.[1] The two bills were not identical in wording but both had the same purpose. It was declared that it was the intention of the first and second Reconstruction Acts to subordinate the civil governments in the Southern States to the military commanders; that these commanders had authority (subject to the approval of the General of the Army) to remove civilians from office; that acts of removal already carried out were confirmed; that boards of registration had the power to inquire into the past and present conduct of persons offering to take the prescribed oath before registering them as voters; and that the true intent of the oath was that all persons who had ever held State office and subsequently engaged in the rebellion were ineligible for registration. The last clause was necessary when it was discovered that in 1849 Virginia had abolished the oath of allegiance to the United States for State officials. Finally the new bill ordered that the military commanders, and those acting under their orders, were not bound by the opinion of any civil officer of the United States (thus preventing Johnson from using his Attorney-general to find further loopholes in the law). The logic of this Reconstruction

---

[1] Trumbull's speech introducing the new bill is in C.G. 40.1.506 and Stevens's ibid., 545.

Act was unassailable. Congress having agreed upon a policy must ensure the means to carry it out, but the formal declaration that the civil authorities were subordinate to the military power of the United States finally vindicated the oft-reiterated Radical theory of Reconstruction and the status of the States. As Stevens triumphantly explained, 'They are conquered territory of the United States, that being the case, all the rest of reconstruction is as easy as any problem in Euclid.'[1]

Why did the first session of the Fortieth Congress see the Radical impulse surge forward without protest or serious hindrance in Congress? Moderate Republicans who had fought against the Radical plan a few months earlier, were now almost silent and the whole party voted solidly for each new twist to the Radical screw. A part of the explanation lies simply in weariness. The leading men had been in session since December, engaged in a fatiguing and perplexing series of debates. At the last gasp agreement had been reached, and re-passage over the veto had emphasized the fact that there were to be no second thoughts. It is a familiar phenomenon in deliberative assemblies that once such a decision has been reached, even the most doubtful will join in making it work. Once the hump of disagreement has been surmounted men will eagerly combine in helping forward policies for which they had previously expressed dislike. No one was prepared to go back to the beginning, and the only alternative was to follow where the logic of revolution might lead. It was also true, as has already been pointed out, that the Radicals had operated from a position of strength — even though they may sometimes have lacked numbers — because their opponents had already accepted the most important of their premises. There had been moments at which moderate opinion could have rallied and defined a position which stopped short of Radicalism; but every opportunity had been lost. It would, however, be wrong to account for the moderate collapse merely by weariness of the flesh, or by these somewhat hypothetical arguments. If the First Reconstruction Act had been greeted with disapproval by

[1] C.G. 40.1.746.

Republicans in the country, if there had been cries for reconsideration, there can be little doubt that this would have been
reflected in Congress. On the contrary, the Republican Press
gave approval, and opinion generally seemed to accept and
commend the Act as the best that could be obtained. Even the
advice of Reverdy Johnson and of the *World* to the South contributed towards this impression. Under these circumstances it
was likely that any further obstruction would be regarded with
impatience and perhaps with contempt in the country. Thus the
impression grew that, in some way, the Reconstruction policy
devised by Congress responded to forces at work amongst the
Northern people. It is now necessary to inquire what those forces
were.

· VI ·

The Forces behind Reconstruction

In order to interpret Reconstruction one startling fact must be explained. The Republican party attained and maintained a solidarity which was without precedent and which was not to be equalled in the future. The nearest parallel is found in the early days of the New Deal, but the Democratic party was then acting with its President, with all the apparatus of executive influence on its side, and with a powerful conviction that the country demanded action. During the Reconstruction crisis the Republican party acted consistently against the President and without access to the normal instruments by which the loyalty of doubtful members can be secured. Moreover this solidarity was maintained in spite of a progression which took the whole party nearer and nearer to the extremes which had, at the outset, been represented only by the Radical minority. The impression then is one of power and coherence such as the American political system seldom produces, and this cannot be explained without an assessment of the forces in Northern society which the politicians served or to which they responded.

At the opening of the second session of the Thirty-ninth Congress Garrett Davis, former Kentucky Unionist and vigorous opponent of Republican policy, asked, 'What are the incentives to the enormous, continuing, and increasing wrongs and outrages of the northern Radicals against the people of the South?' He answered his question by pointing out that before the war the South had 'resisted the policy to make her and other parts of the country tributary to build up and enrich the northern lords of the spinning jenny and the loom. This resistence of the South continued and brought down upon her the active and envenomed enmity of the North. She commenced and her whole people soon united in assaulting the great property interest of the South in slavery, which the northern traffickers had been . . . so instrumental in building up'.[1] Reconstruction was simply the continuation of this policy. This explanation would have been rejected as an atrocious and partisan caricature by contemporary Republicans, but it has become fashionable with modern historians. It is the theme of Charles Beard's account of Reconstruction, and it has been expanded and vigorously argued in H. K. Beale's *The Critical Year*. It owes, however, more to abstract analysis and to hostile inference than to concrete evidence, and some of its errors have resulted from an attempt to read back into the period the aims and ideas which characterized the depression years after 1873.

Loss and anxiety breed a different political mood from prosperity and confidence, and the economic axioms of a crisis are not those which men emphasize during a boom. One pamphleteer in 1865 professed to have been in business for half a century and had 'no recollection of any season during that time that would bear a comparison', and as an owner of New York tenement houses could report that in spite of increases the rents were punctually paid 'which never was the case in former years'.[2] 'In 1865 and 1866', said W. D. Kelley when he looked back regretfully from the depression years, 'every man in America who had the skill and the will to labor could earn wages to support his family and lay something by. All industries were quick and active. Production ran on. The American people waked each new morning to feel that there were great duties before them, that there were mines to be opened, forges and furnaces to be erected to work the iron, the copper, the silver and the gold of our mines. New houses were to be built. Skill, energy, science and genius were taxed to quicken and cheapen productive processes. Our wealth grew as it, or that of any other people, had never grown.'[3] Another pamphleteer observed in 1867 that 'There never was a time in the history of the Northern States when churches, colleges, hospitals, hotels, club-

[1] C.G. 39.2.81, 12 Dec. 1866.
[2] 'Pliny Freeman,' *Letter to H. McCulloch* (New York, 1865).
[3] W. D. Kelley, *Money and the National Finances* (Philadelphia, 1876), 29.

P

houses, manufactories, stores and store houses, private dwellings, barns, sheds etc, were being erected in so great numbers. . . . There never was a period in which the workmen and laborers of this or any other country on the face of the globe were so busily and profitably employed as they are at the present moment'.[1] In the same year David A. Wells, Special Commissioner of the Revenue, was able to report that there was 'great activity — industrial or speculative — in nearly every section of the country, . . .' and that the 'spirit of enterprise seemed to redouble with every additional burden placed upon it'.[2] Even the interests which had formerly depended upon the Southern trade had found the war almost a blessing. It forced them to cultivate what proved to be the more profitable markets of the West, and Newark, New Jersey, which had once specialized in production for the South, now claimed a remarkable increase in business which had made it the first manufacturing town in the country.[3] Whatever the economic foundations of Reconstruction may have been, it can therefore be asserted with confidence that they were not the product of adversity.

For many Northern Americans the political revolution launched by the Civil War, and the economic progress of the age, were but two sides of the same coin. Moral and material advance were both characteristics of one great movement for the betterment of man. This attitude towards economic change was fundamental to the Northern society, but it did not mean that its members agreed upon all aspects of economic policy or that there was a uniform appreciation of economic needs. There was rather a great variety of economic interest and concept. This diversity is found within the Republican party as well as outside it, and economic views divided the Radicals as much as any other body of men.

This diversity was most apparent in the vexed question of the greenback currency.[4] The domestic expenditure of the war had

---

[1] 'Patriot', *Our National Finances, No. 13* (New York, 1867), 14.

[2] Quoted E. C. Kirkland, *Industry Comes of Age* (New York, 1961), 3.

[3] 'Patriot', op. cit. Statement based on an article in *Newark Daily Advertiser*.

[4] The most recent treatments of the currency question, to which I am greatly indebted, are Robert P. Sharkey, *Money, Class and Party* (Baltimore, 1959) and Irwin Unger, 'Business Men and Specie Resumption' in *Political Science Quarterly*, 1959, p46ff.

been financed partly by loans and partly by the issue of inconvertible paper currency which was made legal tender for all purposes except foreign payments, customs duties, and the payment of interest on certain government loans. The government notes or greenbacks were popular in the country; in spite of depreciation and rising prices the United States had for the first time a currency which was uniform in value, which circulated everywhere and which was backed by a government guarantee. They were particularly popular among small business men and manufacturers who were anxious to expand; on the other hand they were bitterly unpopular with metropolitan bankers and importers who were both forced to purchase gold for their international transactions. The premium on gold in terms of greenbacks rose in 1865 to a peak of 185 and, as the rise in domestic prices in terms of greenbacks had been considerably less than this, imported goods were being priced out of the American market. The paper currency was increased by National Bank notes; though these were tied to deposits of government securities in the Treasury, and to cash reserves amounting to not less than 25 per cent of the issues, their issue did add to the inflationary pressure in the commercial centres. It is not therefore surprising that strong pressure developed after the war for a restoration of specie payments, and, as a preliminary to this, for the contraction of the greenback currency until its reduced quantity forced up its value and brought it to a par with gold. The doctrine of gold payment drew additional arguments from two very different sources, from British classical economists who had conquered the intelligentsia of the Western world and from Jacksonian hard money policy. Metallic standards formed the thin but tough cord which linked the rank and file of the Democratic party with the great financial and mercantile houses of New York.

The sound money men had in Hugh McCulloch a Secretary of the Treasury after their own hearts. He repudiated the Jacksonian idea that only metallic currencies should circulate, but he was an ardent believer in metallic standards. 'By common consent of the nations,' he was to write later, 'gold and silver are the only measures of value. They are the necessary regulators of trade. I have myself no more doubt that these metals were prepared by the Almighty for this very purpose, than I have that iron and coal were prepared for the purposes for which they are used.'[1] In December 1865 he asked Congress for authority to withdraw between 100 and 200 million dollars of the greenbacks, and the House, with only six dissenters, approved the principle of contraction 'with a view to as early a resumption of specie payments as the business interests of the country will permit'; as the Ways and Means Committee of the House was under the control of sound money men the prospects of an enabling act were good. But at this stage strong opposition began to develop to contraction, and the committee's bill, presented by Justin Morrill was at first defeated by 70 to 65 with 49 not voting; the size of the adverse vote was partly explained by the feeling, on the part of men who were in favour of specie resumption, that too much discretion was given to the Secretary, and on a fresh trial a revised bill was passed by 83 to 53 with 47 not voting.[2]

The opposition to contraction was almost entirely Republican. The Democrats, true to their hard money doctrines, voted 27–1 for contraction, but the Republican party was cut almost in half with 56 for and 52 against. Prominent among the opponents were Thaddeus Stevens and William D. Kelley. From this it might be argued that Stevens wished to keep the Southerners out of Congress for fear of recruiting further strength for the Democratic hard money forces; it is equally plausible to argue that the currency issue had nothing to do with political Reconstruction. The association of easy money with political Radicalism can, however, tell us something about the character of the movement.

What Radicals like Stevens and Kelley wanted was a flexible paper currency, issued by the Government and by no one else, made legal tender by law, and available in sufficient quantities to meet the needs of expansive business. They were hostile to banks and believed that their functions ought to be strictly limited by

[1] Quoted Sharkey, op. cit., p. 59, from H. McCulloch, *Men and Measures.*
[2] An analysis of the congressional votes on the currency question is given in Sharkey, op. cit., Ch. III.

law. 'In my judgment,' said Stevens, 'this whole national banking system was a mistake. I thought so at the time, and I think so still. I think every dollar of paper circulation ought to be issued by the Government of the United States.'[1] Kelley explained that the operation of the national banking system stimulated unwise and discouraged wise investment: 'Men with surplus capital deposited it in a local bank, this in turn deposited it in one nearer the commercial center, and from there it went to commercial center ... so that there are from ten to fifteen people operating on a single deposit. The men who enter into wild adventures are stimulated by the bank directors to borrow their deposits. Shrewd, capable, business men, men of capital, see dangers around them and will not embark in business; they find it more profitable to let their funds lie in the bank at interest. ... Banking on accumulated deposits is what gives us undue expansion and those periods of speculation whose termination is a crisis and a crash.'[2] Stevens thought that the contraction bill was 'calculated to destroy all the interests of the country except those of a few metropolitan bankers which seek to absorb all the business of the country'.[3] Kuykendall of Illinois argued that 'reducing prices by raising the rate of interest and increasing the power of money is simply robbing labor for the benefit of non-producing capital'; he thought that the whole contraction policy originated with bankers and businessmen of New York, Boston and Philadelphia, and that this was true of every financial measure adopted by the government since 1861 'excepting alone the legal tender, and this was the measure which sustained the credit of the Government and carried us through the darkest hours of our troubles, and which was opposed by these bankers and intelligent business men at every step, and which they now demand shall be blotted from our statutes'. These 'intelligent business men' were not 'the energetic, enterprising portion of our community who are engaged in the development of our resources ... [But] the speculators in stocks, food, clothing, and all the products of labor'.[4] This distinction

---

[1] C.G. 39.1.4153, 25 Jul. 1866.   [2] C.G. 39.1.4153-4, 25 Jul. 1866.
[3] Ibid.   [4] C.G. 39.2.580, 18 Jan. 1867.

between the productive and unproductive forces was not new in
American political and economic thought, but it was a powerful
and pervasive concept. Indeed it was essential to the social theory
of the Radicals and enabled them to picture themselves in the van
of a fight which drew together skilled labour, enterprising farmers,
manufacturers, and businessmen directly engaged in promoting
production.

An analysis of the supporters of contraction was made in more
detail by Cullom of Illinois: 'Importers desire it because they
could then make a greater profit on the goods which they buy
abroad ... men who have their capital largely in government
funds desire it ... men with large capital, who are holding it
waiting for a chance to invest it in real estate, storehouses, fine
lands or town lots; they are sure upon a sudden resumption of
getting whatever they desire at half-price.'[1] And a pamphleteer
of 1867 identified the authors of a letter from New York to
McCulloch urging weekly sales of government gold as 'foreign
merchants, bankers, shippers, gold speculators and gamblers', and
McCulloch did not act upon the advice because he 'had a wholesome fear of our Radical Congress'.[2] He listed the opponents of
the greenbacks as 'Democrats, lawyers who expected increased
business as a result of contraction, retired merchants and others
living on interest, and Republicans who wanted office or feared
newspaper attacks.' In the Western States opinion reacted strongly,
and as one correspondent of E. B. Washburn observed from
Illinois, 'There may be some here who are in favour of contraction, but if there are, they are so small a part that they are never
heard of ... That Illinois is bitterly opposed to this contraction
policy there is not a shadow of doubt.'[3]

In March 1866 the New England Republicans voted 15 to 3 for
contraction, and New York 10 to 4; but in Pennsylvania it was
8 to 6 against, in Ohio 11 to 3 against. Illinois (in spite of Wash-

[1] C.G. 40.3.653.
[2] 'Patriot', op. cit. If the government had put more gold on the market the premium on
gold would have been reduced, while the greenbacks received in payment could have been
withdrawn. On the connection between the gold premium and protection see p. 231 below.
[3] L.C. *Washburn Papers*, A. A. Tyrell, Stirling, Illinois, to E. B. Washburn, 27 Jan.
1868.

burn's friend) was 7 to 4 in favour, Indiana and Wisconsin were equally divided, Minnesota gave two votes for and none against, but Michigan and Iowa each gave 4 to 1 against. Except for New England the Radical strongholds — Pennsylvania, Ohio, Michigan and Iowa — also gave the strongest votes against contraction (27 to 11 against in these four States). Of congressmen who took a leading part in Reconstruction Blaine, Conkling, Garfield, Justin Morrill, E. B. Washburn and John Wentworth voted for contraction, and Bingham, Julian, Kelley, Stevens, Hayes, Griswold, and J. F. Wilson were against. In the Senate it was strongly supported by Fessenden and opposed by Sherman, Wade, Zachary Chandler, Howard and Howe.

In 1868 the greenbacker forces in Congress seemed to have won a striking victory over the Secretary of the Treasury and his contraction policy. In 1866 Alley of Massachusetts, introducing the resolution supporting McCulloch, had said that 'Today an immense majority of the sound and substantial business men of the country are in favor of a reasonable contraction and an early resumption of specie payments. Wait a few months, even before you begin to look in that direction, and you will find the business interests of the country all against you if you attempt contraction'.[1] This was presented as an argument for a quick commitment to contraction but it was also a shrewd prophesy. In 1867 business ran into a sharp recession, and greenbackers were not slow to point the moral. For J. H. Ela of New Hampshire, one of the few New England congressmen who supported the greenbacks, the effects of contraction were that 'Business became paralysed, and labor began to be unemployed. Every manufacturer and producer saw his goods steadily decline while in process of production. So rapid was the decline in values that they often found no profit, and in many cases serious loss. Production was at once reduced, business became stagnant, and Congress was visited by committees from all sections of the country clamorous for relief.'[2] Some slackening of the post-war boom was probably inevitable, but deflation exaggerated it, and there was evident sincerity in the

[1] C.G. 39.1.1610.   [2] C.G. 40.3.886, 4 Feb. 1869.

cry which now arose against the contraction policy. It was one thing to commit oneself to vague and comforting generalizations about the desirability for specie resumption, and quite another to face the effects of tight money with loans refused, interest rates high, and prices falling. The agitation for greenbacks did not come from the debtor farmers so dear to American historiography but from farmers who had done well out of the war, from merchants engaged in domestic trade and particularly from manufacturers.[1] Even the commercial magnates of New York were not entirely untouched and in 1869 George W. Opdyke, an influential merchant of New York, wrote an open letter to Senator Conkling in which he asked, 'What then, is the proper remedy for the existing defects in our currency? I answer "Masterly inactivity." I cannot join Mr McCulloch and others in their denunciation of that currency. It has but two serious defects, namely: its depreciation and the uncertainty as to the future action of Congress in reference to it. With these exceptions it may justly be regarded as the best circulating medium that any nation has ever possessed.' He suggested a gradual contraction, and no further issues of National Bank notes, in place of the sharp contraction, and thought that the increasing demand for currency through the rising tide of business would bring the greenbacks to par in about seven years. He also thought that the Secretary of the Treasury should keep a reserve of greenbacks for emergencies to meet government liabilities in time of depression and to aid solvent bankers threatened during panics; in other words small doses of inflation should be kept in hand to treat the ills of depression.[2]

These conditions made the Fortieth Congress more hostile to contraction than the Thirty-ninth, and some largely fortuitous changes in committee membership led to a strengthening of anti-contraction among the Republican leaders. A notable addition to the House was Ben Butler who had won in Massachusetts as a

---

[1] *Garfield-Hinsdale Letters*, B. A. Hinsdale to Garfield, 9 Dec. 1867. 'Business men are hungry for more money. The Phillips Bros. took dinner with me yesterday; they join in the common cry — greenbacks, greenbacks or the country is ruined. They say you are trying to govern this country according to the precedents of history and the trouble is there are no precedents for it.' The Phillips were oil refiners.

[2] George W. Opdyke, *Letter to Senator Conkling* (New York, 1869), 19.

Radical Republican against the opposition of bankers who, he said, would have preferred to 'have a Democrat elected by withdrawing the Republican votes from myself than to have so pestilent a greenbacker as myself represent that solid old Republican district in Congress'.[1] Schenk of Ohio, new chairman of the House Committee of Ways and Means, introduced a bill in December 1867 withdrawing from the Secretary of the Treasury the power to take greenbacks out of circulation. One hundred and three Republicans voted for this bill with 18 against, and the Democrats 24 to 18 against. Even the New England Republicans now opposed contraction by 12 to 9, and New York by 14 to 1. In the Senate only four votes were cast for continued contraction.[2] The defeat of contraction was, however, less of a victory for the greenbackers than might at first appear. The aim of an eventual return to specie was not abandoned, and a vote to substitute fiat currency for one with a metallic standard would have produced a very different result. For men like Thaddeus Stevens, Kelley and Butler the greenbacks ought to be the currency of the country and their value the only standard, and as ardent economic nationalists they believed that the United States could maintain its own currency whatever the gold standard countries might do. Sherman who was becoming the most influential man in the Senate and Fessenden who was just relinquishing that position knew that this was impossible. Fessenden remained in favour of an early resumption, but Sherman was unwilling to put a monetary brake upon the economy. He professed himself in favour of specie standards but added, 'Let no man be too confident of his own opinions until he has examined those of others, and he will find that many have travelled this path before, but no man has found an easy road to the resumption of specie payments.'[3] The compromise to which the Republicans finally moved, with protests both from hard money men and greenbackers, was neither to contract nor to expand but to wait until the increase in production brought the existing paper currency to par with gold. Five, six or

---

[1] Butler, *Butler's Book*, 920–1. [2] Sharkey, op. cit., 110 ff.
[3] C.G. 40.3.630.

seven years was suggested as the period of waiting, but it was to be over ten years before specie payments were resumed.

Four main groups had emerged during the currency debates. The men who were committed to rapid contraction and early resumption. The men who believed in a regulated paper currency under Government control, and who developed the theory of fiat currency. The men who had little grasp upon currency theory but knew from experience in their constituencies the evils of a currency shortage. And finally the men who believed that the gold standard was the eventual goal but feared the disruption which might be caused by rapid deflation. If these four groups are related to political Reconstruction it will be found that the hard money men were the most conservative with the exception of some New England Radicals, that the most vocal greenbackers were Eastern Radicals and that the men who protested most vigorously about currency shortage were the Western Radicals. Outside Congress the Republican intelligentsia — men such as Schurz and periodicals such as *The Nation*—were devoted to the metallic standard but Radical on Reconstruction; and since the intelligentsia were the most articulate the impression was conveyed that hard money and Radicalism were identical.[1] Nothing was further from the truth.

The question of the National Debt was, however, a severe embarrassment to the Radical friends of the greenbacks: its inviolability was one of the cardinal conditions to which the South must agree, yet the debt included the so-called 5–20 bonds on which Congress had agreed to pay the interest in gold. This was

---

[1] Schurz claimed Sumner as a hard money man (*Eulogy*, 78–9). He took no part in the currency debates in 1866 and 1867, but seized the opportunity when the Democrats adopted the 'Ohio Idea' (see p. 223 below) to come out emphatically for the gold standard in principle. The horror and bewilderment of the Republican intellectuals at greenbackism is well expressed by Schurz in a speech of 1874 (*Writings*, II, 473): 'The Senate has been during these weeks of debate presenting a most extraordinary spectacle. In the second half of the nineteenth century, with the uniform experience of ages before us, in a period of profound peace, with no public dangers pressing upon us the necessity of exceptional measures, with ample resources to defray the expenses of the government and to develop the resources of the country, the highest legislative body of this Republic, which is proud of calling itself the most progressive state of the world, is seriously debating the question whether new issues of irredeemable paper money shall not be resorted to in order to promote the prosperity of the nation; and such an incredible proposition is supported by arguments which will make the civilized world stare if ever they become widely known beyond these precincts.'

coupled with the provision that import duties must also be paid in gold to provide bullion for the interest payments. This official recognition of a dual standard was a vital blow at those who wished for a single paper currency issued and guaranteed by the Government. In 1876 Kelley recalled how Stevens had reacted to this betrayal of the greenback position: 'I remember the grand "Old Commoner", with his hat in his hand and his cane under his arm, talking to myself and another, when he returned to the House after the final conference, and shedding bitter tears over the result. "Yes," he said, "we have had to yield; the Senate was stubborn. We did not yield until we found that the country must be lost or the banks gratified, and we have sought to save the country in spite of the cupidity of its wealthier citizens." ' He believed that the Legal Tender Act created money and at the same time declared its depreciation; 'it makes two classes of money — one for the banks and brokers, and another for the people.'[1] During the Reconstruction controversy Stevens avoided reopening the question, and it was a section of the Democrats who, in 1868, put forward the 'Ohio Idea' which demanded the payment of all interest charges in greenbacks, and President Johnson recommended the same plan. This shocked the body of the Republicans into an affirmation that the national debt must be honoured according to contract, but Stevens remained faithful to the greenbacks and refused to endorse a Republican campaign promise to pay the interest in gold.

*   *   *   *

In their fight against contraction the Radical greenbackers pictured themselves as representatives of the productive classes — employers and working men, manufacturers and farmers — against the non-productive classes of bankers, importers and men living on invested capital. This was a conventional mid-nineteenth century classification of economic interests, had a strong appeal in a land of opportunity, and was often combined with a conventional attitude towards monopoly. The greater railway companies

[1] Kelley, *Money and the National Finances*, 21.

such as the Illinois Central, the Chicago and Northwestern, and (most heinous of all because every congressman coming to Washington from the North felt its power) the Camden and Amboy were favourite targets.[1] The telegraph monopoly, set up by a working agreement between the Western Union and the American Telegraph Company, attracted much unfavourable comment, particularly when it became known that the combination had an agreement with the Associated Press which set up a stranglehold over the dissemination of news.[2] Mammoth consolidations such as the Standard Oil Company were not yet political issues, but the small entrepreneur was already beginning to feel the weight of overwhelming competition and his fears were reflected in the party which represented his interests.

This hostility to big business was characteristic of a mid-nineteenth century reforming party, and it would hardly be necessary to make the point if the Radicals had not been so widely misrepresented. They did not think of themselves as the agents of the masters of capital but of the small businessman, the active farmer, and of the enterprising working man. They believed in 'free labour' not because it would be free for exploitation by employers but because, oddly enough, they thought it preferable to forced labour. There was indeed a strain of social radicalism which mingled with the political Radicalism of Reconstruction. In 1869 Senator Henry Wilson in an article for the Radical New York *Independent*, subsequently reprinted as a pamphlet entitled, 'The New Danger', wrote that 'The power of wealth, individual and

---

[1] Elihu B. Washburn was regarded in his own State of Illinois as 'the leader in this Anti-Monopoly movement' (*Washburn Papers*, 19 Dec, 1866.) The Illinois Central 'that bloated and pampered and merciless monopoly' (C.G. 39.2.392) and the Chicago and North-western ('a great mammoth consolidated corporation') attracted his particular enmity. In Mar. 1865 he persuaded Congress to include in the Army Appropriation Bill a proviso that money was not to be paid to the Illinois Central for troops carried during the war.

[2] L.C. *Washburn Papers*, Horace White (of the *Chicago Tribune*) to Washburn, 4 Jun. 1868. 'The fact is that the Western Associated Press, ourselves included, are bound by a written contract with the Western Union Telegraph Co. till Jan 1, 1869, not to advocate measures hostile to the interests of the said telegraph company. This was a part of the machinery by which we are emancipated from the New York press monopoly. Whether right or wrong in principle (and I do not defend the principle), it seemed then to be necessary to enable us to secure independence of the New York ring, who are in my judgement more unprincipled than the telegraph monopolists.'

associated, concentrated and diffused, constitutes the *new danger* that is threatening us with its portentous and increasing dimensions.' In this power he saw not only the abuses of monopoly but also 'the greater and more disastrous evils of bribery and corruption'. He cited railways which 'like the Camden and Amboy Company buy up a State and control its legislation for a generation' or which like the New York and Pennsylvania 'by log rolling and purchase, command votes enough for the purpose'.[1] There is nothing original in such statements, but their source in the inner citadel of Radical Republicanism may be unexpected to those who have been taught to believe that Radicalism was the political weapon of the 'masters of capital'.

An attempt to absolve some politicians from the charge that they were 'tools' does not absolve all of them; nor does it suggest that business interests were not eagerly attempting to influence legislation. G. F. Hoar said that when he entered Congress in 1869 'the corridors of the Capitol and the Committee rooms were crowded with lobbyists' and he believed that among congressmen too there were 'adroit and self-seeking men . . . able in the multitude of claims which must necessarily be disposed of by a rapid examination, to impose on the committees of the two Houses'.[2] Senator Sprague, himself a large textile manufacturer though a somewhat inefficient one, attacked the politicians 'who are engaged in a particular class of business. . . . Imperceptibly to themselves they will introduce into legislation measures that harmonize with the idea they have formed in the past in carrying on a prosperous business; and especially do I object to it when their honored associates are willing to take their word as law and approve a proposition which may be submitted to them'.[3] Then as now the influence of business was felt in Congress through professional lobbyists and through congressmen with personal interests to serve and the complex and diffuse methods by which bills are drafted have always favoured their operation. It does

---

[1] Henry Wilson, *The New Danger* (New York, 1869, reprinted from the *Independent*, 10 Jun. 1869.
[2] G.F. Hoar, *Autobiography*, I.307.　　　　　　　　　[3] C.G.39.1.809.

not follow that major measures of policy were determined in this way. Even in economic questions the experienced politicians recognized the kind of influences which might be brought to bear upon them and made their own choice among the many courses of action which were pressed upon them. 'From long experience in this House', said John Wentworth of Chicago, 'I have no confidence in the profession of a lobby man anyhow. He is like a lawyer, he works for his client: and when a man comes into this House and tells me his story, I regard him just like a lawyer. He has got his fee and is working for the men who sent him here.'[1] The business affiliations of many congressmen could be recognized with equal ease. In politics men with axes to grind will usually grind them, but it is usually an error to credit them with success in rigging great national policies. It may even be charitable to accept Hoar's verdict that 'in general the men elected to the Senate and the House were honest and incorruptible', and to respect their own assertions that they were engaged upon a quest for security and justice. During Reconstruction the political temperature was far too high for accurate estimates of profit and loss, and it is above all a period during which ideas were in the saddle. To say this is not to deny that men's views may have been profoundly influenced by the economic condition of the society in which they lived, and to this point it will be necessary to return later.

Some Radicals with old abolitionist roots carried over the struggle for negro freedom into that for the rights of labour. A leading example was Wendell Phillips, but Ben Butler, announcing his support for the eight hour day, also asserted that 'what shall constitute a day's work should be defined by law is as desirable as a definition of what shall be the standard weight of a bushel of wheat'.[2] G. W. Julian described in his memoirs the evolution of an anti-slavery man into a social radical. At the request of 'intelligent working men in the employ of government' he introduced a bill for an eight hour day in the navy yards. 'This', he

[1] C.G. 39.1.3399.
[2] L.C. *Butler Papers.* Draft reply to an invitation to attend a mass meeting in favour of the eight hour day.

said, 'was the beginning of the eight hour agitation in Congress. I had not given much thought to the necessity of such legislation in this country, but the proposed measure seemed to me an augury of good to the working classes. . . . While I was a believer in free trade I was not willing to follow its logic in all cases of conflict between capital and labor. My warfare against chattel slavery and the monopoly of the soil had assumed the duty of government to secure fair play and equal opportunities to the laboring masses.'[1] A few years later Kelley, speaking upon a proposal of 1871 to set up a Federal Labor Commission, said that 'It is the failure of Governments to consider the condition of the masses of the people that is upheaving society in all lands and has brought about an international association of the bone and muscle of the world, the action of which is teaching Governments and privileged classes that with the laborers, notwithstanding their hard condition, there are also intellect, culture, and energetic and disciplined will'. He feared that America 'was walking in the ways of old nations' though saved at present from social crisis 'by reason of the extent and freedom of our public lands'.[2] The interest in and concern for the condition of labour shown by some Radicals was significant, but they would have rejected what they called 'class legislation' on either side of the fence; what they believed in was harmony between employer and employed, secured mainly by enlightened self-interest, but fostered in a limited number of cases by government action. This coincided with their demand for the positive action of government to protect the civil rights of negroes. They did not regard themselves as Hamiltonians — by which they would have understood support for legislation to give privilege to an élite — but as Jeffersonians who had enlarged the virtuous classes to include not only the cultivators of the soil but also the small entrepreneurs and the enterprising workmen. The labourers whose interests

[1] Julian, *Political Recollections*, 274.
[2] C.G. 42.2.104 ff. See also Wendell Phillips, *The People Coming to Power* (Boston), 8–9. 'We protected the black laborer and now we are going to protect the laborer North and South. . . . I believe that the Republican party ought to hold the United States for the next ten years, but it never can hold it, unless the party embraces these new issues.'

they had at heart were the skilled workmen of industry and they
showed little concern for the unskilled masses of the urban poor
who were largely foreign-born and generally mainstays of Democratic city machines. And as on the currency question there were
sharp differences between Radical leaders and Radical intellectuals.
The Nation summoned all its editorial scorn to assert that 'It is
enough to condemn the scheme of this eight hour labor league to
say that, if executed, it would diminish production.... There
never was a time when the plans of this labor league could have
been more injurious to the working-men than at present'.[1] *The
Nation* was prepared to concede the justice of a ten hour day
because this was the natural limit set to labour by the hours of
light and by physical endurance, but an eight hour day was
'simply an attempt to set aside or nullify one of the natural economic laws by a law of a State, and all such attempts must fail;
and to cast imputations on people's humanity for pointing this out,
is about as sensible as to abuse a doctor for discouraging a patient
from taking a delightful-looking house in a malarious district'.[2]

The role of poor man's friend may appear inconsistent with the
protectionist doctrine of a high tariff. This question must, however, be seen in the traditional context of American protectionism
and not through the eyes of free traders whose potent arguments
have succeeded in blinding posterity to the popular basis of the
protectionist case. The United States had, since 1787, been the
largest free-trade area in the world, and nowhere else was the
dream of economic self-sufficiency nearer to realization; thus the
English argument for the necessity of imported food and imported
raw material gave way to the American argument that a high
standard of life must be protected against the competition of cheap
labour overseas. It was equally plausible to argue that the potential
of American industrial growth could not be realized unless it was
protected against the competition of foreign industries which had
established a lead when America was still a purely rural country.
For the American protectionist the question was simply whether
the people as a whole were ready to pay a modest price for the

---

[1] *The Nation*, I, 517.   [2] Ibid., 615.

development of an industrial system which would serve them all and for the high wages which the industrial workers deserved.[1]

In 1865 most of the moneyed men of the country were either hostile to or unenthusiastic about high protection.[2] Bankers, importers, and those engaged in the cotton trade were low tariff men. Even the New England textile manufacturers did not want to increase the tariff on manufactured imports to the extent that it would foster domestic competition, and they were definitely opposed to increased protection for iron which would raise their production costs. Railway promoters and operators were strongly opposed to protection which would raise the cost of rails, engines and rolling-stock. It was thus possible to represent the protectionist argument as one directed against the big money interests in favour of small mining and manufacturing concerns and of skilled labour. In December 1866 the *Iron Molders International Journal*, representing one of the best organized groups of skilled workmen, observed that 'It is a well-known fact to every intelligent man, that there exists among us a "ring" or combination, composed almost exclusively of foreign importers, and agents of foreign manufacturers, who have millions of dollars to spend to defeat any effort made by Congress for the protection of our industry'.[3] In Pennsylvania the tariff always had been a popular and vote-winning issue, and men like Stevens and Kelley with their high tariff enthusiasm merely reflected the long established interests of their constituents. A special case for protection was presented by the wool interests of Northern New England: wool growers were threatened by cheap imported wool, wool manu-

---

[1] Protectionists could, on occasion, represent their cause as a corollary of the fight against slavery. In Feb. 1865 (C.G. 39.1.808) Senator Sprague of Rhode Island was opposing a proposal to extend the time during which imported goods could be left in bonded warehouses without payment of duty. He said, 'The measure that is now endevoured to be perpetuated upon the industry of the country is one of the same system and plans that produced the monopoly of slavery upon your political system. For years you gave liberty some strength and slavery some strength, and you continued to keep them about even until you know the result. You had a policy of tariff and a policy of free trade ingrafted upon your industrial system. You must accept one or the other.'

[2] For this discussion of the tariff I am indebted to Stanley Coben, 'Northeastern Business and Radical Reconstruction; A re-examination', *Mississippi Valley Historical Review*, XLVI (Jun. 1959), 67 ff.

[3] Quoted Sharkey, op. cit., and see Ch. V *passim* for labour attitudes towards economic problems.

Q

facturers by high grade imported woollens, and the complexity of the wool argument haunted every attempt to construct a logical tariff schedule. In the Midwest, and particularly in Ohio, the infant industry argument had strong appeal. Thus the high protectionist case was a tripod with its three legs planted in Pennsylvania, Maine and Vermont, and Ohio, but its advocates were found in every Northern state, and their argument derived its strength from an appeal to national interests.

'England is the foe of the laborer in every land', exclaimed Kelley. 'To maintain her monopoly she must undersell other nations in their own markets, and to effect this must depress the wages of labor to the lowest possible point.'[1] 'Is there a Senator . . . who would reduce the laborers of our country to the level of the pauper labor of Europe?' asked Senator Catell of New Jersey, and linked up his argument with the anti-slavery movement, 'There was once a class of men in these Halls who might have consented to this. Under their "peculiar institution" . . . labor was degraded by chains and fetters, and the bold announcement was made that "capital should own its own labor". They resisted with blood the higher civilization which taught the sublime truths of the universal brotherhood of man, and the rights of all men to the just rewards of their labor.'[2] Arguments over the tariff have seldom brought out the best in men and there is ample scope for hypocrisy and for self-interested appeals to higher law, but the 'pauper labour' argument was a real one to many Americans not least to the industrial workers themselves. Protection might appeal

[1] C.G. 39.2.256.

[2] C.G. 39.2.640. Industrialization could be pictured as an agent of human progress in all fields, and protection had therefore results which were not purely material; thus Senator Sprague said, 'If I can ever see the time when the New England system of industry becomes the system of every State in the Union, it will be the happiest day in my life; and whatever aid it may be in my power to give, I shall always be ready to extend, and to devote my time and attention to that purpose. I desire that, because I desire to extend the prosperity of my own State and section, and to introduce that prosperity into every State in the Union. I know the benefit that it confers upon the people in whose limits those interests are carried on and protected. I know that every interest of that people is made better, that their morals, their religion, their education, their desire to occupy higher grounds and positions in life, everything that goes to ennoble men and women, receives a start from those industrial occupations; and it is because of that reason, among others, that I would, if it was in my power, push every manufacturing and mechanical interest of New England into the western and middle States that they might enjoy the benefits and the strength which those States are receiving today' (C.G. 39.1.808).

to established manufacturers anxious for higher profits, but it could appeal with equal force to those who were making no profits at all, and it is a mere perversion of history to assume that every advocate of a high tariff was a servant of the 'masters of capital'.

High tariff men were often easy money men and the two causes were connected in their minds. Thus the pamphleteer 'Patriot' wrote that 'The great manufacturing monopolists of New England ... whose stock is owned by millionaires in New York, Boston, Providence, Portland, etc., prefer free trade and hard money, or a limited circulation of paper money, to protection which covers the raw material, and a free circulation of Government money which increases the price of labor, and restricts the number of hours the laborers are compelled to work. With cheap water power, complete machinery, and abundant accumulated capital, independent of Treasury notes, all they require for their prosperity is cheap raw materials, cheap coal, cheap labor, and long days. With the aid of these they can thwart the enterprise of men who own small manufacturing establishments or who attempt to establish new ones'.[1] There was indeed a direct connection between protection and easy money. The premium on gold automatically raised the cost of imported goods, sold by British exporters who demanded gold, because the greenbacks were depreciated more in international exchange than in relation to domestic prices; this meant that the importer had to sell for money which was undervalued abroad and to find the difference by raising his prices.[2] Conversely the American manufacturer with surplus goods found it easier to sell abroad as his products were relatively cheap in terms of gold. After the war the falling price of gold offset the effect of the war tariffs, and though the average level on dutiable imports was 47 per cent it did not prevent large importations of foreign goods. In addition the price of domestic manufactures was increased by high taxes. The connection between protection and the gold premium was widely recognized, and the equation between the two was expressed concisely by the editor of the *Bulletin of the American Iron and*

[1] 'Patriot', op. cit. [2] Sharkey, op. cit., Ch. IV *passim.*

Steel Association in October 1867 when he said, 'If gold is at a premium, then iron can be made to profit, but if it descends much below its present point, then can the British come in at prices that render its production unprofitable.'[1]

For the Radical exponents of high tariffs their cause was linked with the ascendancy of the Union and the Reconstruction of the South. Their attitude towards the South cannot be explained by their protectionist doctrine, but this doctrine made them more receptive to the political and moral arguments of Reconstruction; the moral obligation to the negro and the hatred of the leading secessionists was not spun out of tariff schedules, but the tariff did form a part of the Radical's social picture which made their attitude towards the South logical and consistent. This combination of Radical Reconstruction and high protection was found, however, only amongst a minority of the party. If New England Republicans were not free traders their understanding of what should be protected differed sharply from that of the Pennsylvanians. The majority of the intellectuals in the party were free traders, at least in theory, and strongly opposed to further increases in the tariff. Horace Greeley of the *Tribune* was an exception, and the place of his journal in Republican history and his consistent support (on purely theoretical grounds) of high protection have misled some into seeing party unity where none existed. It was indeed a large part of Greeley's purpose to convert members of his own party.

The most important opposition to high tariffs within the party came from the West, and the increasing doubts of the Westerners were directed not only against the forward pressure of the iron interests but also against the longer established protection of cotton textiles. The protectionist doctrine had had great attraction for many Westerners when their industry was in an embryo stage, but protection could do little to help meat packing or milling, while other local manufactures were already receiving some protection through the transport costs of Eastern and European goods, and conversely the consumer did not see why high

---

[1] Quoted Sharkey, op. cit., 158.

transport costs should not be offset by cheap goods when these were available. Cotton textiles were not produced in the Western States, and iron as yet in very small quantities. The increasing number of Western railways and the growing ability of local businesses to finance ambitious projects without government aid deprived protectionists of the old argument for infant industries. Under these impulses the volume of Western complaints about the tariff increased, though it took some time for these complaints to sort themselves out into a real low tariff movement. The mood is expressed by an Illinois merchant who wrote to E. B. Washburn in 1865, that 'educated a protectionist, since 1847 a subscriber and constant reader of the New York *Tribune*, all my predeliction and sympathies have been towards that school. But during the past summer, considering what is for the interest of the people of Illinois and the Western agricultural States, every examination drives me farther from my early views. In my own business I see clearly the effects of the tariff upon the cost of iron to our farmers and mechanics. Its price is regulated not by the cost of production at the American mine and of freight to the place of consumption, but by the cost of delivery here of English iron'. The great money earning trade of the West was the westward movement of grain to the East and to the Atlantic ports; 'let us get in exchange for it as cheaply as we can the products of other regions and if the English importers will sell us in New York more iron or other commodities for it, than the manufacturers of the Eastern States, let us buy of him.'[1] In other words the Western States were moving towards the classic ideas of exporting economies which depend upon others for some necessities. In Congress, and among the influential leaders of Republican opinion, these views had a spokesman in J. W. Grimes of Iowa. In January 1867 he attacked the move for a higher tariff and said that 'It means that two or three large manufacturing interests in the country, not satisfied with the enormous profits they have realized during the last six years, are determined at whatever hazard to get more money

[1] L.C. *Washburn Papers*, K. C. Burchard, Freeport, Illinois, to Washburn, 16 Nov. 1865.

into their pockets; and to this end they have persuaded some and coerced other manufacturing interests to unite with them in a great combination demand for what they call protection to American labor, but what some others call robbery of the American laborer and agriculturalist'.[1]

In March 1866 Horace White of the *Chicago Tribune* wrote to Washburn that 'You and I (Old Whigs as we both are) know that the North West is being bled at every pore by the existing tariff for the benefit of New England and Pennsylvania'. He had obtained from England a few copies of the *Catechism on the Corn Laws* and sent one of them to Washburn with the wish that it should be passed on to General Grant so that the man who expected to be the next President might have his eyes opened to the free trade argument.[2] In May 1868 Medill, also of the *Chicago Tribune*, wrote that 'The tariff is now *excessive* ... every cent of addition to it is a tax on our people',[3] and in distant Minnesota Ignatius Donnelly came out for low tariffs.[4] Not far ahead was the Western upheaval which would lead to Liberal Republicanism in 1872, and this was in inception a low tariff movement. But while the Westerners were developing their doubts about protection the majority of them were giving consistent support to Radical Reconstruction. For some of them there was a conscious subordination of economic to political aims, and in the letter already quoted Horace White added that 'this tariff question will not and cannot become a vital one while the reconstruction question remains unsettled'. The Westerners were not fools, particularly where their own sectional interest was concerned, and the real

---

[1] C.G. 39.2.696.   [2] L.C. *Washburn Papers*, 12 Mar. 1866.   [3] Ibid., 1 May 1868.
[4] The key speech by Donnelly was at Winona on 15 Oct. 1869. In 1892 he commented that 'This was an important speech and had an important effect on the politics of the States for years afterwards'. The local Republican organization tried to read him out of the party and he replied that it 'had been organised on the basis of opposition to slavery, and that the Tariff question was merely an incidental issue, upon which every man has a right to think for himself' (Diary in Minnesota State Historical Society). A friend wrote that 'hope you will not go so far on the road to free trade that your old friends cannot accompany you. We are nearly all in favour of a reduction in the tariff which is your position as I understand you (not free trade)'. (*Donnelly Papers*, loc. cit., D. Bassett to Donnelly, 16 Nov. 1869). These comments illustrate the way in which protectionism was still the official doctrine of the Western Republicans; what was protected, and how well, were points which might be disputed.

problem is not whether their interest in Reconstruction enabled Radical protectionists to manipulate their votes, but why they considered that the political question justified the leadership of men with whom they would otherwise have quarrelled.

*   *   *   *

This review of the economic controversies current during the Thirty-ninth Congress has shown the diversity of opinion within the Republican party. On the two leading questions of the day — currency and the tariff — four different combinations were possible and all were found in the party in some strength. These were high tariff and easy money, high tariff and hard money, low tariff and easy money, and low tariff and hard money. The most vocal Radicals in the House were high tariff and easy money men, but their monetary theories were regarded with horror by some eminent Republicans, and their tariff views with distaste by many others. In the Senate Sumner was a hard money and low tariff man, and when Henry Carey wanted to attack the unsound views of New England on protection his chosen target was Henry Wilson, Sumner's colleague from Massachusetts who was opposed to taxation on raw materials. Fessenden was for high tariff and hard money, but his friend Grimes who worked so closely with him on Reconstruction inclined to moderately easy money and lower tariffs. In Ohio Garfield was an unyielding hard money man, but Sherman and Wade were against violent deflation. Attitudes to these two questions of the day were also symptomatic of deeper divisions about the role of banks, money power, monopoly, and labour legislation. Orthodox classical economy was firmly entrenched among the intellectuals and rather less firmly held by many of the politicians; but amongst a small but politically influential section the ideas of Henry Carey were dominant, while the old Whig tradition of positive government participation in promoting economic activity modified the *laissez-faire* attitudes of many members. At several points many leading Republicans expressed their hostility towards the 'money power' in various forms, and the leading merchants of New York

responded in kind by giving their support to Andrew Johnson.[1]
It was not until the election of Grant became certain that 'conservative' businessmen sank their doubts about Reconstruction
and rallied to the Grand Old Party.

If it is difficult to discover any unity of economic purpose
among the Republicans it is equally difficult to see what economic
gain any of them can have expected from Reconstruction. As
some intelligent Southerners realized, the negro, if he ever voted,
was more likely to vote as a Southern man; there was no real
reason to suppose that the poor black would show any more
enthusiasm for tariffs and internal improvements than the poor
white had done. It might be assumed that gratitude and organization would keep the negro voting Republican if he had a free
choice, but in the party he was more likely to add strength to the
Western than to the Eastern wing. Nor was Reconstruction a
necessary prelude to the economic penetration of the South by
Northern capital; leading Southerners were crying out for
Yankee capital to repair their shattered economy and it was easier
to deal with the established ruling classes than to embark upon
perilous political experiments. At this point it can perhaps be
argued that the 'masters of capital', though suspicious of Stevens
and impatient of the moral tone of the old abolitionists, nevertheless realized that economic subjection could not be complete
without political hegemony and that to this end they used the
Radicals as willing tools. No one has, however, identified these
'masters of capital' or demonstrated any means by which their
influence was exercised, and until this is done the theory seems
unpromising.

Indeed it is an error to suppose that the big businessmen of the
North were moved by ambitions either to dominate or to exploit
the South. If they had wished to do so the instrument lay close at
hand in the provision of that economic aid without which the

[1] Coben, op. cit., 88. For the attitude of New York businessmen to Reconstruction,
and their differences with Boston and Philadelphia see also G. R. Woolfolk, *The Cotton
Regency: The Northern Merchants and Reconstruction 1865–1880* (New York, 1958).
This work contains much useful information about the attitudes of businessmen but its
political inferences are unreliable.

Southern recovery would be impossible; but most of them preferred
to look for quicker and safer profits elsewhere. Two large moneyed
interests had a direct interest in the South. New England merchants and manufacturers engaged in the cotton trade had an
immediate interest in the recovery of cotton production, and
several important New York mercantile and financial interests
were anxious to renew their former Southern connections and in
some cases to restore the value of their Southern assets. The
Boston merchants were alarmed by the idea that the freedmen
would desert the plantations and that production would be
abandoned. They were humanitarian enough and realistic enough
to know that mere coercion would not work, and that some
incentives must be provided to introduce the negro to useful
labour. The answer seemed to lie in a labour policy planned by
the national government and executed by the Freedmen's Bureau.
In November 1865 Edward Tobey addressed the Boston Board of
Trade on *The Industry of the South*. He pointed out that Southern
capital was insufficient and Northern capital unwilling to set the
Southern economy on its feet and that 'this deficiency in capital
and the protection and organization of labor now there can . . .
be provided for by the government, and at the present moment,
by it only'. With enlarged powers the Freedmen's Bureau might
be able to lease or purchase land and 'organize and employ such
portions of the laborers there as cannot otherwise be employed
for want of capital in private hands, and thereby secure to the
laborer the rewards of industry and to the national wealth, the
results of that industry'.[1] This idea acquired a considerable
following among Boston merchants and they hoped for a favourable result from Lyman Trumbull's new Freedmen's Bill. This
bill did not envisage government organization of production on
quite the scale contemplated by Tobey, but it did provide for
the allocation of land, in lots not exceeding forty acres, to freedmen and white loyalists, and it was hoped that the combination of
civil protection with economic security would stimulate cotton
production and the failure to do so was one of the counts against

[1] Woolfolk, op. cit., 50–2. Coben, op. cit., 85.

Johnson's veto. The bill was passed at the second attempt but by then it was too late to do much about the crop for 1866 which was a dismal failure. In his veto message Johnson did not refer to the economic aspects of the bill but by the time of his 'swing around the circle' he was insisting that 'the freedmen's Bureau was a simple proposition to transfer four millions of slaves in the United States from their original owners to a new set of taskmasters. I have been laboring for years to emancipate them; and then I was opposed to seeing them transferred to a new set of taskmasters, to be worked with more rigor than they had been worked heretofore. Yes, under this new system, they would work as slaves, and call on the government to bear all the expenses, and if there were any profits left, why they would pocket them'. The argument that it is better for men to starve than to earn money in organized production has always a certain attraction.

The veto of the Freedmen's Bureau Bill was therefore a setback to certain groups of Boston capitalists, and strengthened the Radicalism of such men. In this instance it is therefore possible to detect the 'masters of capital' at work behind political Reconstruction, but their interest plays a comparatively minor part amidst the reactions produced by the veto. The political implications have already been emphasized, and the economic implications went beyond the schemes of the cotton merchants and manufacturers. The veto hit at the theory of 'free labour' as understood in the North. Of course the labourer must work, and the case for political equality rested upon social utility. 'Free labour' glorified productive effort but it demanded that the labourer should share in the profits of his industry; moreover his share should take the form of cash wages which he could then use freely. As the labourer was relatively weak he was protected by political and civil rights, and though this protection did not go so far as most modern social theory demands it was a great advance for a labourer to be the equal of his employer under the law. The reward of honest labour was the attainment of property, and once the labourer became a property owner he had a bulwark against the injustice of employers. The veto struck squarely at this theory so far as it concerned Southern negroes: they were not to receive the equal protection of the law, not to be able to command the wages which their work would earn in the free market, not to be given property, and were to work under such rules as their former masters decreed. This may not have been what Johnson intended but it was the way in which his veto was interpreted. Later rationalizations about preventing the transfer of the slaves from one taskmaster to another seemed to be nonsense — and spiteful nonsense into the bargain.

There were more demands for the investment of Northern capital in the South than takers, but there was a group of New York bankers and merchants who were anxious to raise money for Southern investment. To these men Radical Reconstruction was a nuisance; they favoured a restoration, which would place the Southern States under the control of the same type of planter businessman as they had known in the past, and active support for the President was easily found among wealthy men of New York city. In February 1866 they organized a public meeting to express support for the veto of the Freedmen's Bureau Bill, and the painful experiences of the 'swing around the circle' were relieved by a splendid dinner for the President at Delmonico's which had been organized by Alexander T. Stewart, known as the 'dry goods king', and by Henry Clews, who was second only to Jay Cooke in the realm of government financial operations. It was attended by many leading businessmen, and three weeks later the same business groups were trying to launch the pro-Johnson movement with a great National Union meeting.[1]

*   *   *   *

This brief and selective review of economic controversies and influences during the Reconstruction period is, perhaps, sufficient to confirm the verdict of a close student of the problem that 'The Reconstruction program of the Radicals cannot be explained as an

[1] Coben, op. cit., 88. In January 1868 Marcus L. Ward wrote to Elihu B. Washburn criticizing a proposal to send Kelley to New York to see what could be done about securing aid for Grant. He said, 'Mr Kelly [*sic*] is a good man for some things, but not for this purpose. He is tariff, radical and enthusiastic, whereas the solid men of New York are the reverse' (L.C. *Washburn Papers*, Ward to Washburn, 27 Jan. 1868).

organized attempt by the business interests of the Northeast either to preserve and promote their own economic advantages or to obtain protection for the economic exploitation of the South. Actually northeastern businessmen had no unified economic program to promote'.[1] In any complex economic society it is unlikely that the leaders of business will agree upon policies when confronted with a novel situation, and even less likely that they will succeed in persuading the politicians and the electorate to adopt such a policy if conceived. Occasionally the economic consequences of a policy may appear to businessmen to be so clear that they unite in support of or in opposition to it — such, for instance, has been the modern businessman's reaction to socialism — but no such clear and over-riding considerations presented themselves in the Reconstruction crisis. The majority of business interests would probably have been well served by a speedy return to business as usual; a minority with vested interests in high protection hoped to get their tariffs through before the Southerners were able to resume their traditional opposition, but many others had lived profitably in the past under Democratic tariffs with Southerners in the Union; a good many were concerned and divided over the currency question, but it was impossible to forecast how this might be affected by Reconstruction. Economic interpretations may, however, have been applied to Reconstruction at the wrong level; a confusion of economic aims when men calculate their interests in the immediate future is compatible with the determination of basic political attitudes by the economic character of a society. If one goes beneath the superficial arguments over means one may well find a uniformity over ends.

Though economic controversies had figured prominently in all the major political conflicts of the American people there was little fundamental difference of opinion about the kind of economic society which they desired. Most Americans believed consciously or unconsciously in a natural economic order and, though the use of economic power might be attacked, the nature of that power was a part of the divinely ordained plan. They

[1] Coben, op. cit., 89.

believed that the right of property was one of the basic rights which government existed to protect, that the general welfare was best served by private enterprise, that the motive force in economic life was and ought to be individual decision, and that these decisions should be left as free from restraint as possible. They believed that society could not exist without the unremitting labour of the majority of its members, but they also believed that their system provided the opportunity by which those labourers possessed of prudence and ability could escape from dependence upon others. From this fundamental agreement two traditions had developed which placed different emphases upon its implications, and this led to different views of the role of government, and particularly of the national government, in economic affairs.

The emphasis of the Democrats was upon freedom, and they regarded government intervention as its necessary enemy. If the public interest required action it should be made by the government which was closest to the individuals concerned. They believed that the economic functions of the national government were few, strictly defined in the Constitution, and ought not to be enlarged by interpretation. The theory of State rights was the traditional bulwark against unconstitutional activity by the national government, and this negative view was reinforced by the laws of political economy — by free trade and by hard money — which reduced the discretionary power of government or of moneyed men. The Democrats were not hostile to business provided that it had established its position by 'natural' means, without privilege conferred by government, and in the few cases in which it was necessary to confer privilege by incorporation this should be done exclusively by State governments. They resisted the argument that men could be made happier by giving them economic advantages which nature had not conferred, and they believed that a man could be happier in a backward society, provided that he was his own master, than in an advanced society if dependent upon somebody else. This attachment to freedom stopped short at the negro who was happier under control because of his child-like and inferior character.

The Republicans inherited the old Whig doctrine which had grown out of the experience of developing communities during the early nineteenth century. They believed that moral and material progress were intertwined, and, though men could be good without economic success, communities required a measure of prosperity in order to provide churches, schools, cultural activities and charitable institutions. For them 'general welfare' meant the development of the separate communities but they believed that the needs of these communities could be treated as a national problem and not in isolation from each other. Localism was an obstacle to progress, and State rights had been interposed between the people and the material development which they deserved. They did not believe in unlimited national government or in the annihilation of local authority, but they believed that limited government and divided sovereignty were the means and not the ends and should yield when they obstructed useful economic development. While Democrats opposed all national economic action which was not positively sanctioned by the Constitution, the Republicans believed that when the utility of an action was demonstrated it was legitimate unless positively prohibited. The great contested points had been the tariff and Federal aid for internal improvements, and these two test cases were the symptoms of different attitudes towards the role of the national government. The Democrats believed that the government must do no more than permit the development of economic life along lines chosen by the people in their States; the Republicans believed that the national government had a positive function to perform as the architect of beneficial growth and as the regulator of economic harmony. To these cardinal tenets the Republicans had added the abolitionist doctrine of free labour. Most Republicans were not prepared to give the negro equal status in their own communities, but they did believe that he should have the same opportunities of development as the white man. Moreover they believed that the existence of servile labour degraded labour everywhere.

For Republicans the South had been, in the past, the main

obstacle to economic growth along the desired lines. Southerners had opposed the tariff and internal improvements; they had imposed the concept of negative government upon the nation, but had also supported a system of land monopoly and servile labour which was the negation of free enterprise and free labour. The experience of war had confirmed the picture of the Southerners as the enemies of human betterment, and as a consequence of their secession it had been possible to enact a protective tariff, to pass a homestead law, to grant land for transcontinental railways, and to abolish slavery. 'Southern aristocracy', 'State rights' and 'slavery' had become symbols which evoked strong negative responses amongst Northern Republicans, and during the Reconstruction period this image of the South as the enemy of healthy economic progress had a powerful influence upon Northern minds.[1] Thus the threat of a restored and unreconstructed South was in part an economic threat; but the impetus in Reconstruction came not from what Northerners wanted to do with the South but from their fear of what the South might do to them. This picture of the South in peace and war was more powerful than the prospect of gain, and imagination was more potent and pervasive than calculation.[2]

[1] In 1866 Stevens sponsored a bill to authorize the building of a new railroad from Washington to New York; when the rights of States were urged as an objection he replied, 'As to this States' Rights notion, I have no respect for it. . . . It has got us into mischief enough already. If the Constitution means anything it expressly declares that Congress shall have power to regulate commerce among the States.' He argued that the power of Congress should be used to break monopolies 'and one of the monopolies chartered by Maryland adds thirty cents to each fare for the benefit of the State. There is a monopoly beyond it. There is a monopoly in the Camden and Amboy railroad which makes everyone bend to its will. . . . This is an attempt on the part of the people to get rid of these odious monopolies which have been grinding us to the earth for years' (C.G. 39.1.4250–1).

[2] It could be argued too that the political resistance of the South, in the past and in the present, to Northern policy had brought disaster to the section. Economic co-operation would soon obliterate political differences. Cf. a speech by Kelley on 3 Jan. 1867 (C.G. 39. 2.260), 'The imminent want of the people of the South is not "political status." That would not enable them to settle the "labor question." What they want is capital and currency and a willingness to permit loyal men, whether white or black, native or foreign, to dwell among them, and by their labor quicken into commercial value the boundless and varied natural wealth of the land they occupy, but which they will neither work themselves nor permit others to work in peace and safety. When in obedience to a healthy national sentiment or the promptings of their own interests they will make capital secure, opinion free, and give peaceful scope to enterprise within their borders, . . . new enterprises will be transferred to the South to develop her production and taxable power, and make her populous and prosperous beyond the wildest dreams of the visionary theorists who involved her in a war as causeless as it was disastrous.'

The economic aspects of Reconstruction must be seen in this context, and one passes immediately from economic aims narrowly conceived as expected profits to fundamental social aims. What was at stake was the kind of society which was to exist in America, and the 'blood-stained hands of traitors', the black codes, the denial of civil rights, the persecution of loyalists were the symbols of a society which the Northern majority wished to reject. It had been proved by the secessionists themselves that the two societies could not co-exist, and it became necessary to remodel the defeated society on the lines laid down by the victorious. The Union must be indivisible and this implied social homogeneity.

To understand the power of these ideas in the Republican party it is necessary to imagine the kind of constituency which its members served. The typical constituency is perhaps a fiction, but it is not beyond the bounds of reasonable fiction to construct a constituency which has the largest number of possible common factors. This typical constituency was largely rural but included one or two small towns which served as market and commercial centres, perhaps as railway junctions and certainly as the place of business for bankers, real estate dealers, and lawyers. There might be a little manufacturing industry and probably a good deal of agricultural processing. At a distance was the metropolitan centre through which passed most of the strings which controlled the local economy, and somewhere beyond the metropolis were the distant markets and distant suppliers. If the constituency was not in New England it would probably have a strong flavour of New England transported. If the Church was not Congregational it probably had the same emphasis upon communal organization, and only very poor villages did not have their schools. It was not improbable that the town centre of the constituency would have a college or other establishment for higher education. It probably depended much upon communications which owed more to artifice than to nature and was linked by railway with the outside world.

In such a constituency the emphasis was upon development,

and development was the result of energy and enterprise. In all constituencies west of the Appalachians there still lived pioneers of early settlement, the rise from small beginnings was a part of living traditions, and so was the knowledge that growth had followed upon the application of the instruments of capitalism to virgin resources. The successful farmers had not been content with subsistence agriculture but had aimed at increasing land values by commercial production; the businessman had not come into the agricultural community as representative of an alien civilization but in response to indigenous needs, and nowhere in the world did he enjoy higher prestige. There was little class antagonism or class consciousness because the idea of community development embraced the interests of all sorts and conditions of men. The idea of the harmony of interests appeared as a real statement of fact and not as a theoretical abstraction, for the fruit of productive labour was multiplied by the services of an advanced business system. By contrast the typical Democratic constituency was either a large city with a mass of low-paid and immigrant labourers, or a rural area of scattered farms and backward agriculture. In these city or rural Democratic constituencies the poor in worldly possessions were strong in votes and felt themselves alienated from the dominant trends in Northern society.

The Republican congressmen had usually made their early career either as small business entrepreneurs or, more commonly, as lawyers. They belonged to the community which they represented; if businessmen they were conscious of the part which they had played in its progress and anxious to promote its interests on the national stage; if lawyers they represented their communities as they had once represented their clients and the two were often indistinguishable. The political magnates — the senators or the more powerful members of the House of Representatives — might have acquired an outlook which transcended the interests of a particular community, but when they thought of the State or the nation it was as the community enlarged.

R

The kind of community which has been sketched was an amazingly successful institution; nowhere else had pioneer societies produced so high a standard of material and educational achievement, and nowhere else was so general a level of contentment compatible with so advanced an economic organization. The constraints, tensions and stratification of Old World societies had been by-passed, and the Old World transplanted to the New (which was how they viewed the South) had been rejected and defeated. Nowhere else was it possible to combine intense individualism with a realization of mutual dependence within the community and, beyond the community, upon the outside world. Yet success had exacted a price, and men who were not indigenous to this society could be shocked by the self-righteousness of its members, by their apparent hypocrisy in the combination of high moral sentiment with sharp business practice, by the contempt bred of ignorance with which they regarded all other peoples, and by the dull conformity of their thought and custom. All their virtues combined to make them the last people in the world to understand the difficulties of others or to tolerate the existence of those whom they regarded as harmful. These limitations had not been removed but reinforced by the experience of war; lives and material had gone to preserve the society of the North, moral indignation had sprung readily to the support of military effort, and participation in an epic struggle had sublimated the quest for material betterment.

A description of the social aims of the Northern Republican community cannot be couched solely in material terms. The social and economic environment made certain beliefs attractive and relevant to experience, but the beliefs themselves had an independent history which made them more potent as factors of union in the Republican party than economic aspirations. The principles of the American revolution, finding a fertile soil in regions where there was no ready-made ruling class, had fused with the older traditions of New England Puritanism. The exclusion of slavery and abundant land had prevented the formation of an upper class based on large estates, while the emphasis upon communal development and the dependence of individual fortunes upon the prosperity of regions as a whole had made businessmen the natural leaders of society. At the same time dependence upon commercial agriculture had prevented any sharp division of interest between the countryside and the towns. In the West settled from New England and Northern Europe it had been necessary to rely upon the developed capitalism of the East, and the mutual interest of the two regions became one of the axes upon which American politics revolved. The fact that this community of interest depended upon man-made communications had led through the history of internal improvements to an expectation that the national government must act as a positive factor in national growth. In New England itself, in western New York, and in western Pennsylvania these attitudes had been ingrained at an early stage and persisted with the stimulation of manufacturing and mining. Here the tariff emerged as the leading popular economic issue. Finally the Philadelphia region retained the imprint of early Quakerism with its anti-slavery tradition in a city which was one of the emporiums of Western trade.

Working in these regions there had been, since the early thirties, the strong ferment of the anti-slavery movement, which had identified the slave power as the fount and origin of all those policies and ideas which the Republican North had come to dislike. The anti-masonic movement, with its strong reaction against the idea of privileged groups, also formed a background to Eastern Republicanism; but anti-slavery had proved the stronger influence because it gave men a positive ideal as well as a negative response. Anti-slavery also forged an abiding link between the popular democracy of the community and the men of letters and intellect, and the prejudices of humble men were voiced in elevated language by Emerson, Whittier, Lowell and Whitman, in penetrating oratory by refugees from European oppression such as Carl Schurz and in the sermons from a thousand Northern pulpits. Widespread popular emotions, powerful economic forces and a committed intelligentsia made the Republican party one of the strongest political combinations of modern times, and unlike most American parties it had an ideological backbone.

It is as ideology that one must interpret the real force behind Radical Reconstruction. Prejudice and emotion was there in strong measure; but so also was a coherent view of what America ought to be and an appeal to ideals which transcended while they expressed popular aspirations. As with other ideologies it arose from the needs and experience of the society which accepted it; and as with other ideologies it was blind to the merits of differing systems. To the Northern Republican the logic and the justice of his society seemed to be self-evident, and it was the peculiar triumph of old abolitionist and new Radical propaganda to convince him that negro freedom was an intrinsic part of this logic. The proposition was easier to accept because few Northern communities contained many negroes, but those who are not in the immediate presence of a problem can often appreciate best the principles involved. Fear of restored Southern domination was a spontaneous result of the war and the commitment to protect the rights of the negro as a citizen was reached by more subtle means; but as the passions of war slowly subsided fear of the Southerners took second place to the obligations arising from the abolition of slavery.

The progress of an ideology is not to be stopped in mid-course, particularly when it has been blessed by the heroism of war. The premise of the revolution had been stated and largely accepted, and thereafter conservative objections were likely to come tumbling down. Opposition and checks did not argue men out of their beliefs, but led them on to insist upon their realization. Northern opinion, faced with the choice between sacrificing through compromise some of the gains of the war and pushing forward to find new ways of securing them, almost inevitably chose the bolder course; and in general the people at large moved faster than the politicians. Here was the dynamic force which unified the Republican party behind Radical leadership and endorsed Radical Reconstruction; it was not a force which could be exorcised or ignored, and its consequences were disturbing and profound. As the ideological revolution rolled forward one question was presented which was vital to the American system of government: how would this powerful and popular force affect a government of checks and balances designed to blunt the impact of majority rule? To a consideration of this question the next chapter is devoted.

· VII ·

Reconstruction and the Constitution

In January 1866 Fessenden explained that 'Whether you call it war power or some other power, the power must necessarily exist, from the nature of the case somewhere, and if anywhere, in us, to provide for one of the results of the contest in which we have been engaged. All the world would cry shame on us if we did not. . . . I cannot work the problem out, and nobody else can, to show that in the Constitution itself there is a clear power; but I can work the problem out so that the power may be found when the positive necessity of the thing is apparent, where the thing must be done, and must be done by the Government as a consequence of other things that it was compelled to do, and that it had a perfect right to do. Otherwise . . . we are a Government without the necessary powers to carry out and effect our own objects'.[1] These sentences contain the whole problem of the Constitution and Reconstruction, and emphasize the dilemma of any government of checks and balances 'when the positive necessity of the thing is apparent'. The law provided for obstruction, for delays and perhaps denied powers which were essential for the attainment of desired objects; but was there a reserve of power in the nation which could overcome these obstacles and 'to carry out and effect our own objects'?

For Charles Sumner the problem presented no great difficulty. For him the power to secure justice had always been inherent in the Constitution though suppressed by the slave power. 'By the adoption of the Constitution the people of the United States constituted themselves a *nation*, one and indivisible, with all the unity and power of a nation. . . . The sovereignty then and there

[1] C.G. 39.1.365.

established was the sovereignty of the United States, where the States were only "parts of one stupendous whole". The powers then and there conferred upon the nation were supreme. And it is those very powers which I now invoke, in the name of the Union, and to the end that pretensions in the name of State rights may be overthrown.'[1] On a later occasion he was to elaborate his theory of latent national power by saying that 'the Constitution is full of power; it is overrunning with power'. Power was in the original text but the war had established 'a new rule of interpretation for the Constitution, according to which, in every line and every word, it is to be interpreted uniformly for human rights. Before the rebellion the rule of interpretation was precisely opposite. The Constitution was interpreted always, in every clause and line and word, for human slavery'.[2] There was a good deal of sympathy for this sweeping assertion of national power. Newell of New Jersey thought that the one question settled by the war was that 'once and forever the United States is a nation, not a simple confederacy of States'.[3] Yates of Illinois said that 'I had in the simplicity of my heart supposed that "State Rights," being the issue of the war had been decided. I had supposed that we had established the proposition that there is a living Federal Government and a Congress of the United States . . . which, while it allows the States the exercise of all their appropriate functions as local governments, can hold the States well poised in their appropriate spheres, can secure the enforcement of the constitutional guarantees of republican government, the rights and immunities of citizens in the several States, and carry out all the obligations provided for in the preamble of the Constitution, "provide for the common defence," "promote the general welfare," "establish justices," and "secure the blessings of liberty to ourselves and to our posterity" '.[4]

This concept of national power invited attack. 'The Union consolidated is one thing; the Government of the Union consolidated so as to take within its own grasp powers heretofore supposed to be reserved to the States is another,' said Reverdy

[1] C.G. 38.2.791.   [2] C.G. 42.2.727.   [3] C.G. 39.2.285.   [4] C.G. 39.1, Appendix 98.

Johnson.[1] Doolittle, the leading Republican supporter of Johnson's policy, warned of a peril hanging over the Union which was 'not a separation of the territory which constitutes the Union, but the wiping out of the States, the destruction of the rights of the States, the trampling underfoot of that which is absolutely essential to the liberty of the citizen'.[2] He distinguished the right to secede, which had never been one of rights of States, from the right 'to defend and control their own domestic institutions'. Criticism did not, however, deflect but intensified the quest for national power. It was not likely that Republicans would be moved by the argument that the rights of States over civil rights was a sacrosanct, unalterable and essential part of the Constitution, but many were troubled by the implications of Sumner's theory that the nation had always possessed the power which he claimed, and an assembly of lawyers sought for an explanation which did less violence to precedent. Some of them found the answer in the Thirteenth Amendment, which had abolished slavery and had given Congress the power to pass appropriate laws.

At the opening of the Thirty-ninth Congress Henry Wilson argued from the Sumner position that the national government could nullify the 'black codes', but Sherman assured him that it was unnecessary to look further than the Thirteenth Amendment. 'The moment the constitutional amendment is adopted, then our legislation on this subject may be general throughout the United States. . . . Here is not only a guarantee of liberty to every inhabitant of the United States, but an express grant of power to Congress to secure liberty by appropriate legislation.'[3] This was challenged by Saulsbury of Delaware, the nearest approach to an unreconstructed Southerner in the Thirty-ninth Congress, who asserted that in the debates on the amendment 'no Senator . . . avowed this doctrine . . . they told us that they simply wished to amend the Constitution to get clear of slavery'.[4] But Saulsbury was silenced by the authoritative voice of Lyman Trumbull who said, 'I reported from the Judiciary Committee the second

---

[1] C.G. 39.1.2199. [2] C.G. 39.1.2493. [3] C.G. 39.1.41. [4] C.G. 39.1.77.

section of the Constitutional amendment for the very purpose of conferring upon Congress authority to see that the first was carried out in good faith, and for none other; and I hold that under that second section Congress will have the authority . . . not only to pass [Wilson's] bill, but a bill that will be much more efficient to protect the freedman in his rights.'[1] Trumbull was supported by Howard, also a member of the Judiciary Committee, who thought that 'it was in contemplation of its friends and advocates to give to Congress precisely the power over the subject of slavery and the freedmen which is proposed. . . . Its intention was to make him the opposite of a slave, to make him a free man.'[2] It was upon the second clause of the amendment that Trumbull based his Freedmen's Bureau and Civil Rights Bills, because, he said, 'I have never doubted that, on the adoption of that amendment, it would be competent for Congress to protect every person in the United States in all rights of person and property belonging to a free citizen.'[3] This assertion enlarged still further the purport of the amendment, for according to Trumbull it was not only concerned with former slaves but with every person in the United States, and every infringement by a State of civil liberty might be the occasion for the exercise of national power. Here then was a major constitutional revolution based upon the interpretation of a single clause which had been passed with little debate and without consideration in Congress of its far-reaching implications.

Trumbull's argument might satisfy men in their search for an immediate justification for measures which they felt must be passed, but it was an insecure basis for a great constitutional change which would transfer the protection of private rights from the States to the national government. Many of them may have felt that the interpretation was too strained, and there was at least some doubt whether the Supreme Court would accept it. Of more immediate concern was the knowledge that measures passed by a majority in one Congress might be repealed by a simple majority in another. Hence there arose the demand for making the responsibility of the national government explicit in a further

[1] Ibid.   [2] C.G. 39.1.53.   [3] C.G. 39.1.77.

amendment. Stevens would have preferred an unequivocal statement of equality under the law, and proposed his amendment that 'All national and State laws shall be equally applicable to every citizen, and no discrimination shall be made on account of race or color'. It has already been seen that this failed to find favour with the majority of Republicans who hoped to protect the negro without committing themselves to unqualified racial equality. But John A. Bingham, whose constitutional doubts were so serious that he voted to sustain Johnson's veto of the Civil Rights Act, fought for a civil rights clause in the Fourteenth Amendment. His original strong version of a positive grant to Congress to enact laws affecting civil rights yielded to the negative form of limitations upon State power, but even in this weaker form of amendment added a new dimension to constitutional history and was to be the bedrock of future advances towards racial equality.

*　　*　　*　　*

The first constitutional problem encountered by Reconstruction had been the need to give to the national government as a whole powers which had been exercised by the States; the second was to assert the right of the legislative branch within the national government. Legislative supremacy was not without good historical antecedents. The makers of the Constitution had assumed that the House of Representatives would be the dominant partner in government, and they had tried to provide some freedom of action to Executive and Judiciary by limitations upon the power of the majority in the House; but they did not contemplate a situation in which either President or Court would oppose decisions on policy made by Congress. The veto and the jurisdiction of the Supreme Court had been provided to prevent clear infractions of the Constitution, not to decide points on which honest men might differ and the majority had spoken. The Jeffersonians had seen the focal point of the government in the elected representatives; they had rejected the claim of the Supreme Court to decide upon the constitutionality of congressional acts, and it was not until the Presidency of Jackson that the veto had been used as an instrument of policy. The old Whig theory of government had been that of congressional government, and the Democratic successors of Jackson had been content to leave to Congress at least the appearance of initiating policy. It was not until the war that the powers of the Presidency had emerged, and even then it had been challenged by members of both parties. There were therefore good precedents for claiming that Congress should govern and that the checks in the hands of the other departments of government were not intended to obstruct the will of the majority except when there had been a clear contravention of the Constitution. The sovereign will of the people had to operate within limits imposed by the Constitution, but the Constitution should not be interpreted so strictly that it prevented the majority from achieving anything.

The theory of legislative supremacy, when applied against the Executive, confronted some special difficulties. If the President was reduced to a strict interpretation of his constitutional function of executing the laws it was difficult to see how the country could be governed. Long intervals elapsed between the sessions of Congress, and the Cabinet was not responsible to Congress but to the President. A multitude of occasions presented themselves when the President would have to act upon his own initiative during the recesses, and the ministers had no constitutional alternative but to obey their master. The Thirty-ninth Congress tried to solve this problem temporarily by bringing the Fortieth into session as soon as the old Congress expired; but the only way to achieve continuous legislative oversight was by continuous session, and even the most dedicated politician could hardly contemplate such a solution. Even while Congress was in session a major difficulty lay in the initiation of policy. During the Reconstruction period policy was initiated in Congress, but it was a cumbersome process which led in the end to no institutional innovation. However, an important precedent was almost established. The appointment of the Joint Committee on Reconstruction, with the exclusive right to consider all matters affecting

Reconstruction and to report bills or amendments to Congress, might have been a landmark in American constitutional history. Here was a congressional cabinet and though it was to deal with only one item of policy, that one was so wide in its scope that it touched upon all the functions of government. It lacked a prime minister, though Fessenden came near to assuming the role, and the inclusion of the Democrats clouded the idea of collective responsibility. But even with these qualifications the Joint Committee had some indispensable features for the development of real congressional government; it might have led the way out of the wilderness of special committees, in which policy becomes lost and through which local and special interests can operate, and it could have bridged the gap between party programmes and legislative action. It would perhaps have been too much to expect that the knot tied by the theory of separate powers could have been easily unravelled, and the Joint Committee remained as a constitutional oddity; but never again would Congress have so practicable an instrument for filling the void left by the Constitution at the point where policy is to be initiated.

However, the main drive against Presidential power attacked the use of existing instruments and did not contemplate the creation of new governmental institutions. Questions were raised as soon as Johnson began to discriminate against Republicans and Republican congressmen in the use of his patronage, and the effects were described by Sherman early in the second session of the Thirty-ninth Congress. 'My impression is that every leading office-holder in the State of Ohio received a polite notice that if he did not attend the Philadelphia convention, or did not approve of the call of the Philadelphia convention, he should promptly communicate that fact to a self-constituted committee in this city [Washington], composed of men very high in official position. . . . They were called upon to contribute money to support a new party in antagonism to the party that brought the President into power and to which they were attached.' Whatever may have been asserted to the contrary Sherman said that 'nearly every prominent office-holder in the

State of Ohio was removed, and in nearly every case for political reasons'.[1] In many congressional districts committees had been organized to supervise the distribution of political patronage, and Democrats had had a large share in advising dismissals and appointments. Congress was able to inspect a letter written by Gideon Welles on appointments in the Norfolk navy yard in which he said that 'Those who oppose the Government in its efforts to establish national amity, whether by claiming that States have the right to voluntarily withdraw from the Union by secession, or striving by arbitrary and undelegated power to exclude States from the Union, and deprive them of their guaranteed constitutional rights, are not deemed worthy of service in the the Union which they oppose and by the Government which they would subvert'.[2] It was pointed out in Congress that a Southerner wishing for employment on these terms had only to abjure the abstract right to secede while a Republican had not only to oppose the party which had secured his appointment but also to commit himself to a policy which that party had rejected.

Confronted by a President whom they did not trust, Republicans became uncomfortably aware of the scope allowed to the appointing power. The President under the existing law could appoint to Federal offices only with the consent of a majority of the Senate, but he could dismiss on his own responsibility. During recesses of Congress he could appoint, and provided that money had been appropriated for the office the new holder could be paid. The President could even appoint during the recess a man whom the Senate had rejected and, though sooner or later the appointment would have to come back to the Senate, a man rejected by the party could enjoy the fruits of office for six to nine months while party organization would have been disrupted by the dismissals of good party men. The first attempt to remedy this was made by Trumbull in April 1866 when he proposed an amendment to the Post Office appropriation which would prevent the payment of salaries to any official appointed by the President until confirmed by the Senate unless the vacancy had been caused

[1] C.G. 39.2.43.   [2] C.G. 39.2.495.

by death, resignation or expiry of the original term.[1] Sherman suggested a more general measure and asked, 'What is to prevent now the Judiciary committee from carefully framing a law prescribing the term of office of the various classes of the Government and declaring that the President shall not remove any one of those officers except for such and such causes?'[2] This was the germ of the Tenure of Office Act which Congress proceeded to enact in the second session.

In origin therefore the sole purpose of the Tenure of Office Bill was to prevent the President from disrupting the party which had elected him. In the debates on the measure another idea emerged which was more far-reaching. The establishment of senatorial control over dismissals, and the limitation placed upon recess appointments, might be used to extend the control of Congress over policy.[3] It might be extended further and establish some degree of Cabinet responsibility to the legislature. This was not at all in Sherman's original design and during the debate in April he had specifically stated that 'It would be intolerable that the President should be expected to carry on the business of this great Government with a Cabinet council over whose members he had not the power of removal, complete and absolute power'.[4] The larger idea appealed, however, to some Republicans and when the first form of the bill in the Senate specifically excluded cabinet ministers from its operation, Senators Howe and Sprague tried unsuccessfully to include them. In the House a similar move failed twice, but the advocates for the inclusion of cabinet ministers were persistent and the clause finally went into the House bill. The Senate refused to concur, but a conference agreed to include the Cabinet with the proviso that the term of ministers

[1] C.G. 39.1.2274 ff., 30 Apr. 1866.   [2] C.G. 39.1.2278.
[3] Senator Williams who introduced the bill argued that its purpose was to correct a misinterpretation of the Constitution which went back to the First Congress. He also thought that the First Congress would have regarded dismissals on account of opinions held by the office-holder as an impeachable offence, and he added, 'Pass this bill, and you may dispense with the dead letter of the impeaching power' (C.G. 39.2.17–23).
[4] The proposal was introduced as an amendment to the original bill that cabinet officers should have tenure during a presidential term with power to appoint their own subordinates. It was during the debate of this amendment, which was defeated, that Sherman made the comment quoted (C.G. 39.2.77–81).

should be that of the President appointing them and one month thereafter, so that a new President would have a free hand in dismissing his predecessor's appointees. Sherman expressed the view of senators who disliked the inclusion of cabinet ministers when he said that he continued to support the bill only because its general purpose was 'so very important, it established so salutary a reform, that . . . it ought not to be endangered by a dispute on a collateral question', and he added, 'I take it that no case can arise where a Cabinet minister will attempt to hold on to his office after his chief desires his removal.'[1] It is ironical that the impeachment of Johnson was to rest upon his dismissal of a minister who refused to resign, and that Sherman was to vote for his conviction.

The argument for the inclusion of cabinet ministers in the Tenure of Office Act brought out some perennial problems of the Cabinet in the American political system. The most consistent argument on this side was presented by Senator Timothy Howe of Wisconsin. When a Democratic senator referred to the President's 'own cabinet', Howe denied that the Cabinet was the President's, that 'it was intended to be so by law, that it ought to be so in fact'. It was, he said, 'the Cabinet of the people'.[2] He compared the American with the British system and declared that 'it is no more necessary that they should be on confidential terms with the President than that they should be on confidential terms with the representatives of the people'.[3] Howe's argument was not very popular with other senators, and had no future in American constitutional development, but it did bring out the way in which the impact of Reconstruction brought the United States to the threshold of a great constitutional revolution. The adoption of something akin to the British parliamentary system was not so remote or impossible as has usually been imagined; the instruments were at hand though the principle was rejected. The Tenure of Office Act was repealed when the succession of Grant was assured, and this attempt to write executive responsibility into the American political system is remembered only

[1] C.G. 39.2.1515.   [2] C.G. 39.2.383.   [3] Ibid.

because President Johnson's defiance of it provided the ostensible cause for his impeachment.

The impeachment was the major attempt on the part of Congress to control the Executive. In September 1867 a friend of J. A. Garfield saw what was at stake in clear though perhaps over-emphatic terms when he wrote that 'the conviction is certainly growing that Johnson must be impeached. There is to be a trial of strength between the Congress and President. The next great question to be decided in our history is this — is the National Legislature to be as omnipotent in American politics as the English is in English politics. The struggle through which we pass in reaching an answer to that question will be the parallel to that through which the British people passed in the time of the Stuarts. . . . May we not anticipate a time when the President will no more think of vetoing a bill passed by Congress than the British crown thinks of doing the same thing?'[1] When impeachment finally arrived everyone accepted the fact that the breach of the Tenure of Office Act was not the real cause of the impeachment; it was necessary to prove a specific breach of the law but the reason was the need to demonstrate that a President could not pursue a policy rejected by the legislature. An early draft in Stevens's handwriting lists the following grounds for impeachment: that Johnson had undertaken to govern the South by his own prerogatives and without assembling Congress, that he did not confine himself to military duties but undertook to organize new States, that he undertook to admit members to Congress by his own proclamation and 'when warned of the illegality of these proceedings and directed to desist he bid defiance and continued in the exercise thereof by his own single will,' and that he had 'attempted to corrupt the people by abuse of the patronage'.[2] Sherman claimed that Johnson's breach of the Tenure of Office Act must be seen in relation to his political crimes. He said that the great offence of the President was his opposition to the Fourteenth Amendment for 'he alone of all the citizens of the United States by the wise provisions of the Constitution is not to

[1] *Garfield-Hinsdale Correspondence*, 107.   [2] L.C. *Stevens Papers.*

have a voice in adopting amendments to the Constitution, and yet he by the exercise of a baleful influence and unauthorised power, has defeated an amendment demanded by the result of the war'.[1]

In his final speech for the prosecution Bingham tried to emphasize the permanent issues which were to be determined by the success or failure of the impeachment. He asserted that 'It is the head and fount of Andrew Johnson's offending, that he has assumed to himself the executive prerogative of interpreting the Constitution and deciding upon the validity of laws at his pleasure, and suspending them and dispensing with their execution'.[2] On the other hand it was seen that a denial to the President of the right to use his own interpretation of the Constitution as an instrument of policy would mean legislative supremacy. Bingham described the argument of the defence as maintaining that 'the President of the United States is invested with the judicial power to determine the force and effect of the Constitution, of his own obligations under it, and the force and effect of every law passed by the Congress of the United States'.[3] Yet if the President had not the discretionary power 'to determine the force and effect of the Constitution' someone else must exercise that power for him. When the President executed a law he must decide what it meant, when he vetoed a law he must make some judgment upon its constitutionality, when he issued executive orders he must decide how they were related to the law and the Constitution. If these decisions were to be formalized so that the President was deprived of discretion in making them, it followed that there must be some institutional way of determining his action. Was the constitutional mind of the President to be decided by the Cabinet (as in England), or by Congress, or by whom? And whatever the answer it would mean a fundamental change in the concepts and practice of the American system of government. Moreover, as impeachment was the only constitutional means by which a President could be brought to account, this cumbersome procedure might become a normal part of political

[1] C.G. 40.2.450.   [2] C.G. 40.2, Supplement 380.   [3] Ibid., 379.

mechanism. These difficulties persuaded Fessenden, Grimes, Trumbull and four other Republican senators to vote against conviction. 'Whatever may be my opinion of the incumbent,' said Grimes, 'I cannot consent to trifle with the high office he holds. I can do nothing which, by implication, may be construed into an approval of impeachments as a part of future political machinery.'[1] The one vote which saved Johnson from conviction had comparatively little effect upon the immediate history of Reconstruction, but it proved the death-blow to the emergent notion of legislative supremacy.

If one prong of the drive for legislative supremacy was directed against the Executive the other was necessarily directed against the Supreme Court. The prestige of the Court, with the odium of Dred Scott still hanging about it, did not stand high, and the whole question of its political function was brought to a head by the famous case of *ex parte Milligan*. The elevated language in which the Court expressed its determination to protect American citizens from military trials in time of peace, could not mitigate the consequences of the decision for the Southern negro, or conceal the fact that the Court had gone out of its way to deny a power to Congress when it was necessary to deny it only to the President. The decision was described by Wilson of Iowa as a 'piece of judicial impertinence which we are not bound to respect. . . . The discussion by the court was out of place, uncalled for, and wholly unjustifiable'. He compared the Court to the men who had counselled neutrality in 1861. 'The voices sound alike; both lack harmony with the constitution and the national life and both are toned by States rights teachings; both assert the superiority of the condition of the state over the necessities of the nation.'[2] *The Nation* observed editorially that 'the chief duty of the court . . . is to confine itself strictly to the matter in hand, to decide precise points before it, and abstain rigidly from the slightest discussion of political questions not necessarily involved. In *ex parte Milligan* there was not any need to touch upon the right of Congress to set up military courts. . . . Dred Scott was a de-

---

[1] Ibid., 424.   [2] C.G. 39.2.1484.

parture from the settled practice of leaving political matters to be decided by Congress. We cannot believe that the attempt will be repeated. . . . If it should be the people will have to meet it not only with contempt but with punishment'.[1] A careful writer in *Harper's New Monthly Magazine* examined the implications of judicial veto and asked whether it ought not to be possible to pass invalidated acts again, perhaps requiring two-thirds of both Houses as with the presidential veto. 'It is contended that a mere majority of the Supreme court have a right which Congress cannot affect or regulate to settle the construction of the Constitution in all cases,' and he pointed out the illogicality of such a claim when the Constitution gave Congress power over the composition of the Court, over its appellate jurisdiction, and over inferior Federal courts.[2] Already within the Constitution Congress had the authority to discipline the Court and to ensure that it did not trespass upon purely political ground. A Republican congressman observed that 'The people of this country thus far have preferred to govern the country themselves and let the court attend to its law decisions. Both its great political opinions have been reversed upon appeal to the ballot-box, and the general opinion of the bar of the country follows the popular verdict rather than the judicial decisions. The Constitution, by furnishing Congress with a mode of getting rid of both President and court, evidently intended to make it "master of the situation" '.[3] This was also the view of John A. Bingham who pointed out that all appellate jurisdiction could be swept away, and that 'if the

---

[1] *The Nation*, IV, 30.

[2] George B. Butler, *Harper's New Monthly Magazine* (1867-8), 657 ff. Throughout American history there has been an undercurrent of protest against the theory and practice of judicial legislation. The failure of the Federal Convention in 1787 to give the Supreme Court an explicit mandate to review Federal statutes indicates doubts or divisions among the 'founding fathers'. Criticism was vocal amongst Jeffersonians after *Marbury* v *Madison;* they believed that each of the 'powers' was entrusted with the right to interpret its own constitutional actions, that the Supreme Court could declare unconstitutional flagrant and obvious contraventions of the Constitution, but that it had no call to interpret where one man's opinion was as good as another's. The majority of constitutional historians have taken the line that this argument was, from the first, absurd and somehow immoral, and their anger reaches a crescendo when dealing with Reconstruction. For a rare statement of the case against the Court see Louis B. Boudin, *Government by Judiciary* (New York, 1932), and especially Vol. II, Ch. XXII.

[3] F. Pike. C.G. 39.2.255.

court usurps power to decide political questions and defy a free people's will it will only remain for a people thus insulted and defied to demonstrate that the servant is not above his lord by procuring a further amendment and ratifying the same, which will defy judicial usurpation by annihilating the usurpers in the abolition of the tribunal itself'.[1]

Various proposals were made, including a requirement that a majority of two-thirds should be necessary for voiding an Act of Congress and another that Congress should have power to re-pass Acts which had been voided, but the action taken was less drastic. It was made illegal for the Court to hear appeals from the military tribunals set up by Congress in the South. Subsequently the Court refused jurisdiction when Mississippi and Georgia sought to enjoin the President and the Secretary at War respectively from enforcing the Reconstruction Acts, and in *Texas* v. *White*, while rejecting the Radical contention that the rebel States had ceased to be States, the Court also admitted that the Reconstruction Acts were constitutional. This timely retreat put an end to plans for altering the powers of the Court, and this abortive revolution was the prelude to an era of judicial veto and judicial legislation.

In its assertion of national power and of legislative supremacy the Radical revolution remained incomplete; great changes in the constitutional balance of power had been suggested but not driven home. The Fourteenth and Fifteenth Amendments cut off the old Constitution from the new, but their existence did not prevent events in the South which the Radicals had sought to

---

[1] C.G. 39.2.502. In Mar. 1868 an amendment, to deprive the Court of jurisdiction over appeals from the military courts in the South, was tacked on to a bill extending the jurisdiction of the Court over appeals in cases concerning customs and revenue officers. The bill was vetoed by the President and re-passed over the veto. There was some impropriety in tacking a highly controversial amendment on to a non-controversial bill, but by the time the bill was reconsidered after the veto everyone knew what was at stake. The majority of constitutional historians have argued that it was an abuse for Congress to exercise a power which was specifically entrusted to it by the Constitution (Art. III, 'The Supreme Court shall have appellate jurisdiction, both as to Law and Fact, with such Exceptions, and under such Regulations as the Congress shall make'). It has been argued that the great scandal was to legislate while a case affected (*ex parte McCardle*) was *sub judice*; on this point there can be no final determination — a majority of the judges had made it clear that they would decide the case in a way contrary to the majority in both Houses of Congress, and there was thus a clear choice between judicial and congressional legislation.

avert. In spite of the care which had gone into the phrasing of the civil rights clause in the Fourteenth Amendment it was possible for the Supreme Court to evade the implications of equality under the law, to connive at racial discrimination in the South, and to read into the amendment meanings which few of those who supported it can have intended. Congress was unlikely to act unless gross violations on the part of the States were proved, and then only if the congressional majority was inclined to act, and the return of the Southern upper class to power and to Congress meant that action to enforce civil rights was very unlikely. Sumner did not help matters by trying to extend the meaning of the amendment beyond civil rights, as understood by most Republicans, to embrace discrimination in education, churches, transport and hotels; by pressing too hard he weakened the resolution of the party to insist upon a literal observance of what had been achieved. Nevertheless the great amendments were in the Constitution and could not be removed; their day was to dawn in the twentieth century and upon them was to be built the yet incomplete edifice of racial equality. Paradoxically this advance has been achieved by judicial legislation.

*   *   *   *

One reason why the constitutional revolution failed was that even its strongest advocates had reservations about majority rule. Most of them were old abolitionists who had known what it was to suffer from the tyranny of the majority and knew then that their political power might be short-lived. The sovereign people acting through a Republican Congress was to be applauded, but the same claims made by a future Democratic majority would be dangerous in the extreme. The Radical problem was therefore to demolish the idea that the Constitution imposed permanent checks upon the will of the people while resisting the proposition that a majority could do anything which it liked. The theory which they tried to establish was that the majority had all power to what was right while constitutional checks continued to prevent the majority from doing wrong. The problem was illustrated during the debates on the Thirteenth Amendment abolishing slavery. Pendleton, who had just fought the 1864 election as Democratic candidate for the Vice-Presidency, argued that even the power to amend was limited, that an amendment which destroyed the spirit of the Constitution would be void, that 'you cannot subvert republicanism . . . you cannot destroy the liberties of the States . . . you cannot decide the status of the citizens of the States'.[1] His fellow Democrat, S. S. Cox, pointed out that this was the doctrine of the higher law controlling the Constitution, which Democrats had regarded with horror when advanced by the anti-slavery men, but the Radical, George Boutwell, tried to have it both ways. He admitted that there was a limitation upon the power to amend, and pointed to the preamble to the Constitution. The great objects of the Constitution were 'to form a more perfect Union, establish Justice, insure domestic tranquillity, provide for the common defence, promote the general welfare, and secure the Blessings of liberty to ourselves and our posterity'. An amendment made in violation of these objects might be legally operative but could have no moral force, but an amendment made to further them would be legally and morally binding. Specifically an amendment to establish slavery would be inconsistent with the spirit of the Constitution but an amendment to abolish it was unassailable.[2]

This idea, that the majority had no right to do wrong, can be discovered in the speeches of Charles Sumner. Sumner was always apt to make constitutional doctrine fit the needs of the situation as he saw it. His assertion of State rights before the war, when it had been necessary to protect fugitive slaves, had been as emphatic as his assertion of national authority when it was necessary to secure to freedmen 'the Blessings of liberty'. This very inconsistency is interesting for it illustrates the difficulty of achieving objectives defined in moral terms within the limits imposed by a written Constitution. The obligation to do justice to the negro called forth the majestic might of the nation, but it also imposed a limitation upon what the nation could do. The

[1] C.G. 38.2.222 ff.   [2] Ibid.

national sovereign must not be allowed to debase the negro, to write racial inequality into the statute book, or to acquiesce in discrimination. There are indications that this point bothered Sumner during the Reconstruction debates, but it did not become explicit until the controversy over his ill-fated Civil Rights Bill in 1872. He wished Congress to pass a law which would make illegal all forms of discrimination — in public places, public transport and schools as well as in politics and the courts — and he was naturally asked to show how such a law could be consistent with the Constitution. Of course it was consistent, Sumner argued, because the Constitution itself must be consistent with the Declaration of Independence. This was the document which declared the purposes of the United States as a nation, and nothing had happened when the Constitution was made to alter those purposes and principles. 'I insist', he said, 'that the Constitution must be interpreted by the Declaration. I insist that the Declaration is of equal and co-ordinate authority with the Constitution itself. . . . Whenever you are considering the Constitution, so far as it concerns human right, you must bring it always to that great touchstone; the two must go together and the Constitution must never be interpreted in any way inconsistent with the Declaration?' If there appeared to be a conflict then the Declaration was to be preferred because it was 'earlier in time . . . loftier, more majestic, more sublime in character and principle'.[1] In other words the Constitution must be interpreted to give absolute power to ensure that men created equal were treated as such, to secure to men their inalienable rights, and to ensure that government depended upon the consent of the government. Laws which contravened the principles of the Declaration were unconstitutional, and where the law was silent and the Constitution offered imperfect guidance it must be supplemented by the Declaration. The power to enact a Civil Rights Act *must* be found in the Constitution; if it could not be found in the Constitution then the Constitution was inconsistent with the Declaration; which was absurd. But if the interpretation of the Constitution must be consistent with the

[1] C.G. 42.2.728.

principles of the Declaration, it followed that these principles restrained the people. The power to act justly did not carry with it the power to act unjustly. It is doubtful whether Sumner understood Rousseau's distinction between the General Will and the will of all, but his arguments illustrated the perennial difficulty in combining universal moral precepts with the unfortunate fact that they may not be universally accepted.

Another weakness in the Radical concept of national power was a failure to understand the nature of the tasks which modern government would be called upon to perform. They were hardly to blame, for even the Whig theory of government had been severely limited when compared with what a twentieth-century government is expected to do. In all the debates over Reconstruction there was little realization of the tasks which lay ahead in the South and in its place there was insistence upon 'protection'. The Union must be protected from its enemies, the freedom of the negro must be protected, and finally the negro must vote to protect his rights and the Union. So long as one thought of suffrage as a defence mechanism the argument that the negroes were too ignorant and inexperienced had little relevance, for, as a Radical pamphleteer observed, 'We have enough, and more than enough, to make Know-Nothings of us all, were we to give way to the idea that the lowest class, so-called, is the worst class. . . . The mal-administration of government seldom if ever springs from the influence of poverty. Men in higher life, men of means, and wealth, and affluence, commit political sins that low-down people cannot meddle with'.[1] Yates of Illinois thought that 'the masses may err but it is not to their interest to err, they are always ready to correct the mistakes which passion and prejudice have brought upon them'.[2] And Frederick Douglass remarked that if the negro 'knows as much when he is sober as an Irishman knows when he is drunk, he knows enough to vote on good American principles'.[3] The assumption behind all these remarks was that the function of democracy was to provide a means by which the errors of govern-

[1] L. Sherwood, *Democratic Platform . . . . A Republican Form of Goverment: definition, Manhood Suffrage* (New York, 1865).
[2] C.G. 39.1, Appendix 104.   [3] Douglass, *What the Black Man Wants* (Boston, 1865).

ments could be restrained, and though Radicals might appeal to the will of the people when it was on their side they had little notion that this will should sweep up from the constituencies, through elections, through parties, into Congress, and so on to the initiation and legislative fulfilment of policy. And, if a few of them seemed to talk in these terms, it was not an idea which was likely to appeal to Americans trained under a system of divided sovereignty, separate powers, and checks upon legislative majorities. They would have been still more hesitant if they could have foreseen the power and range which future democratic governments would claim.

The difficulty of envisaging real government by a national majority was deepened by a profound uncertainty about the meaning of national existence. This problem was brought to the fore by the discussion over Southern loyalty. Once Lee had surrendered, nine out of ten Southerners were prepared to take an oath of allegiance to the United States, but this did not mean loyalty to the ideals which had come to inspire the North. It was clear to most Republicans that this 'loyalty' would not prevent Southerners from using whatever political advantage they could win to restore Confederate leaders to power, pay the rebel debt, evade the obligations of the national debt, and to keep the negroes in a subservient condition. But if this kind of 'loyalty' was not enough, what could take its place? Some Radicals tried to meet this difficulty by demanding a precise definition of the word 'republican'. The Constitution guaranteed to each State a republican form of government, and it was pointed out that this was not a matter of contract between the individual States and the national government, but between all the States and every State. It not only guaranteed republican government to the people of a State but also assured each State that every other State was republican in form. It was argued that a State which disenfranchised large numbers of citizens was not republican, and that the national government had therefore the right to insist that it should become 'republican' before it was recognized as loyal. This attempt to establish an ideological criterion for loyalty soon sank beneath the waters of uncertainty, for no man could define 'republican' with either precision or historical veracity. The problem of national existence remained. 'What makes us a nation?' asked Sumner in 1871, and answered, 'not armies, not fleets, not commerce reaching every shore abroad, not industry filling every vein at home, not population thronging the highways: none of these make our Nation. The national life of this republic is found in the principle of Unity and in the Equal Rights of all our people; all of which being national in character are necessarily placed under the great safeguard of the Nation.'[1] This was to define the nation in terms of power applied to particular ends; it evaded the points that national ideals depend for their existence upon popular beliefs, and that no amount of coercion could make the unwilling Southerner believe in an ideology which he did not accept. Loyalty as defined by the Radicals could not be tested without looking into men's souls, and this the American Bill of Rights was specifically designed to prevent.

The easiest solution to the problem of national loyalty was perhaps the most brutal. Thaddeus Stevens was consistent in arguing that the conquered Southern States must be given no voice in the new concept of nationality which was being forged. In making amendments 'their aid will neither be desired nor permitted, but when they enter the Union they will swear allegiance to a Constitution to which the consent of their Legislatures will not be asked'.[2] The Southerners would be presented with a Constitution which embodied the concepts of equal rights and national protection; if they chose to live outside it they could continue under Territorial government; if they chose to accept then they would do so as a voluntary act and the principles of the Union would rest upon consent. The consent might be unwilling but it would be an overt act from which men could not in the future disassociate themselves; it would be a new contract in which the conditions would be clearly stated. This procedure would have imposed little real hardship and might have led to a clear understanding of what national existence implied; but traditional

[1] C.G. 42.1.651.　　　　　　[2] C.G. 39.1.

inhibitions preferred a compromise solution which ended by recognizing formal allegiance as the test of loyalty while leaving men free to grumble that the gains of war had been surrendered by the North and rejected by the South.

*   *   *   *

So far this chapter has attempted to consider the impact of the Reconstruction controversy upon the Constitution; it may be appropriate to conclude with some reflections on the effect of the Constitution upon Reconstruction. It can be argued that in the past the Constitution had not preserved harmony but had averted conflict until the interests piled up behind the barriers of the Constitution had burst through. Slavery might have been on the way to extinction at the end of the eighteenth century if the national majority had controlled the situation, but the division of sovereignty ensured that the economic interests could gather around slavery in the States and moral convictions followed in their train. The Constitution had encouraged Southerners to concentrate upon those political elements which would strengthen their sectional safeguards. Shielded in this way the South became increasingly a section apart from the rest of the nation and a society apart from the changing climate of the nineteenth-century Western world. If the South had not been protected by the Constitution from the storm which was brewing as a result of dynamic material and intellectual changes, it might have become a more flexible and more realistic society. Tier upon tier, the checks and balances of the Constitution protected the South against the 'winds of change' until the tempest overtook them.

After the war the Constitution continued to exert its old magic, and even devoted Unionists felt the need to protect the South against the implications of defeat and abolition. The end-product, in everyone's eyes, was a South which could once more take its place in the Union, and to this end the Southern States should enjoy as many of the constitutional safeguards as were not positively dangerous to the Union. Only the extreme Radicals led by Stevens argued that the Constitution was inappropriate to the totally new situation, and that it must be changed in essential particulars before one could define what rights the States possessed. Constitutional moderation or compromise encouraged the Southern States in their belief that they had a moral and legal right to resist the terms which the North wished to impose.

Within the national government the separation of powers made for confusion and indecision. In 1865 what was necessary, above all, was a rapid and clear decision upon the terms of Reconstruction. On the morrow of defeat the Southerners would probably have been prepared to accept any terms, and, as politically mature men, the leaders of the South could have made most terms work; but the separation of powers ensured that the terms would be neither quick nor exact. The Constitution allowed the President to proceed without summoning Congress but did not prevent second thoughts when Congress finally met. The Constitution provided the President with the means to obstruct if not to defeat the terms proposed by Congress, but also made it impossible for his policy to work without legislative consent. The bitter struggle which ensued did no one any good, and the ultimate solution was to be achieved in an atmosphere of bitterness and recrimination.

The delays imposed by the Constitution might have been expected to produce a more moderate solution, but this did not happen. If one looks only at the vexed question of negro suffrage, regarded in the South as the ultimate political evil, one can see how these delays made it politically possible. Constitutional weapons of resistance and obstruction, employed by the President and by the Southerners, ended by producing what was, from their point of view, the worst possible outcome. Because it was necessary to go back at each stage into the armoury of Radical arguments to produce the weapon with which to overcome new obstacles the Republican party was forced along the road to Radical Reconstruction. There was plenty of good sense, and for that matter a good deal of charity, among Northern leaders but both were thwarted by the constitutional deadlock. The Southerners were asked to recognize that the negro was a free citizen, but the traditions of the Constitution encouraged them to believe that they could make their own rules for his treatment. Many Northerners abandoned with reluctance the idea that whatever happened the initiative must be left to the existing leaders in the South, but the impasse into which they had been led by adherence to constitutional forms persuaded them to accept Radical Reconstruction as the only way out.

The Constitution was, is, and always has been a marvellous instrument for the adjustment of differences and for producing a workable government amongst people who are agreed upon fundamentals. Where there was fundamental disagreement it served to entrench opposing interests. When one side of the disagreement was manifested in a powerful ideology, convinced that certain moral ends must be achieved, the Constitution could obstruct and annoy but it could not reconcile. A drastic solution imposed by a simple majority unhampered by checks and balances might have shocked at the time, but it need not have left the festering sores which remained to plague relations between North and South. However unwisely individuals may have behaved their faults were magnified by the controversies and delays which were the necessary consequence of the Constitution which they tried to serve. Yet when all was said, and all recriminations had been uttered, the Constitution remained the one symbol of nationality upon which Americans could unite. Here is the major paradox among all the perplexing counter-currents of Reconstruction and the Constitution.

· VIII ·

The Waning of Radicalism

In June 1868 seven Southern States were admitted to Congress under the Reconstruction Acts. In March 1870 Mississippi, Texas and Virginia were admitted, and in July Georgia, which had been returned to military rule after the white members of the legislature had expelled the negro members, was re-admitted. In February 1869 the Fifteenth Amendment, making it unconstitutional to impose racial qualifications for suffrage, passed both Houses and was ratified by March 1870. The Radical plan of Reconstruction seemed triumphant.

In spite of this record of achievement a Radical might well have regarded the future with misgiving. The essence of the Radical case had lain in the insistence that time must elapse until the necessary transformation had taken place in Southern society, and the temporary ascendancy of Southern Republicanism was no substitute for a period of tutelage under national direction. Disquiet would soon be emphasized by Southern terrorism, conservative gains and the doubtful prospects for the Reconstruction governments. In 1870 and again in 1871 laws were passed to enforce the amendments and suppress violence, but the debates indicated the reluctance of many Republicans to contemplate that sustained exercise of national power which could alone hold counter-revolution in check. The power of the white Southern majority might have been restrained by resolute enforcement of the law, but it could not be exorcised by words alone. The course of Reconstruction policy had ensured that the bulk of the Southern upper class would form a ready-made opposition to the new régime, and the Republican majority was left with the stark alternative of conniving at Southern 'redemption' or reinforcing unpopular governments.

The record of Southern Reconstruction governments was less outrageous than is sometimes imagined for what survived was the story which Southern whites wished to believe.[1] There was much good-will and many good intentions, but also much inexperience, some rascality, and tasks which would have challenged the wisest and most popular of régimes. These untried administrations and legislatures were forced to grapple with the problems of a society in which economic growth had been retarded by the dominance of the plantation and ruined by war; there was large scale poverty, a drought of capital, savings dissipated by repudiation, few manufactures, and widespread illiteracy without a system of public education to remedy the deficiency. The governments were forced to adopt the economic and social aims of modern government without experience and in a region which revered weak government as a political benefit. They were forced to tax, borrow and spend among a people for whom frugality was identified with political rectitude. In retrospect it is possible to see that the only thing which might have saved the Reconstruction governments would have been a massive injection of capital guaranteed or perhaps supplied by the national government, and the speculative and predatory activities of small Northern entrepreneurs was a very poor substitute. Under the circumstances, and considering the impossibility of any large scale government aid for an undeveloped region, Northern enterprise came South in the only available form. Many old-style Southern gentlemen grasped the opportunity and joined in speculative ventures to revive commerce, build or rebuild railways, and foster new industries, but

[1] See B. A. Weisberger, 'The Dark and Bloody Ground of Reconstruction Historiography', *Journal of Southern History*, XXV (Nov. 1959), 427 ff. A wide range of new questions about Reconstruction in the South was opened up by W. E. B. Du Bois, *Black Reconstruction* (New York, 1935), but he laboured under the double disadvantage of being a militant negro leader and of being influenced by Marxism; his work was therefore largely ignored. One can expect an increasing volume of studies about the South during Reconstruction; not all will, of course, be 'revisionist' but all are likely to take some account of Gunnar Mrydal's remark that the memories of Reconstruction 'are in a sense cherished. They serve a vital defensive function to the white South. Even the liberal Southerner . . . has to express his abhorrence of the Reconstruction atrocities. They are, in fact, symbols of regional allegiance'. The 'horrors of Reconstruction' may well prove to be very tame when compared with more recent experiences of brutal government. John Hope Franklin's *Reconstruction after the Civil War* (Chicago, 1961), is a valuable assessment by a leading negro historian.

in a way which was less open and more discreet than the officials and legislators who accepted bribes, granted privileges, and expected to share in the profits. There were Whig precedents for using public money to subsidize private ventures, but even if this had been acceptable to the Southern population the taxable income was insufficient to pay for the vast tasks, and the only recourse was to government borrowing or to government guarantees for private bonds. From this it was easy to construct a picture of unprecedented extravagance, and the naïve enthusiasm with which negro legislators enjoyed the amenities of upper-class life added striking colours to the picture of corruption wallowing in luxury at the expense of the people. Though twentieth-century analysis may take a kindlier view, Radical government in the South looked, by nineteenth-century standards, like very bad government, and it was increasingly difficult to persuade Northern men that it must be sustained. Nothing failed like failure and the momentum of Radical Reconstruction suffered a severe and mortal check.

Even without this disillusionment true Radicalism was dying of weariness and old age. The leaders had been men who had borne the heat and burden of the crusade against slavery, and the younger men who were coming to the fore were cast in different moulds and acknowledged different masters. The Radicalism of men such as Conkling, Garfield, Hayes and Blaine was different in temper and quality from that of men like Stevens, Sumner, Wade, Kelley and Henry Wilson. The moderation of men such as Fessenden, Trumbull and Bingham — which was firmly based upon the concept of equal rights — different from the moderation of Sherman based upon the needs of Ohio and the cautious ambitions of Senator Sherman. It was not, however, likely that either the emotions or the convictions bred of anti-slavery and war would die down overnight, and there remained many men in public life who believed that the battle for equal rights had been the great battle of the century. The Republicans continued to enjoy the support of the bulk of the intelligentsia and had an impregnable hold upon the conscience of the respectable Northern middle class. A young Republican coming to Congress in 1869 found his party full of idealism and buoyant hope, and at the end of a long political life he was able to reflect that whatever their errors the Republicans had commanded all that was best in national life.[1] Yet the political atmosphere was slowly changing: American politicians were ceasing to talk about first principles and reverting to the more usual and more congenial task of arguing about tariff schedules, currency and the satisfaction of local interest. Attempts to revive the old enthusiasm would soon be branded as 'waving the bloody shirt' and seen as a cynical exploitation of old hatreds for party advantage.

The turning-point was probably the failure to impeach President Johnson. Dictated partly by personal spite, partly by the need to establish the principle that a President could not defy Congress, and partly by a fear that the President might use his executive power to wreck the policy of Reconstruction, the impeachment was a political error of some magnitude. The chance of failure was always too great, and the consequences of failure too damaging, to justify the impeachment even at the lowest level of political calculation. It belongs indeed to that class of gambles in which revolutionary movements characteristically overplay their hands. Impeachment enjoyed some wild popularity in Republican ranks,[2] but this very enthusiasm produced a reaction when the result was failure. From Chicago Medill wrote to Washburn that 'Our people are greatly disgusted and apathetic in consequence of the failure of impeachment. They have lost their zeal to win. It is a fact that

---

[1] G. F. Hoar. *Autobiography* I, 200, 245.

[2] M. M. Tappan wrote to E. B. Washburn about an election in New Hampshire in March 1868 (L.C. *Washburn Papers*, 12 Mar. 1868) 'There never has been anything in this State like the political campaign through which we have just passed. It has been contested inch by inch, foot by foot. No dodging of the issue. . . . Reconstruction — taxes — impeachment — these have been the great questions everywhere. Our people are sound to the core. Impeachment instead of hurting us has given us at least 500 votes.' A Southern Republican from Mississippi (ibid., 30 Sep. 1867) attached great importance to impeachment: 'I am of the opinion that if it is not done the Republican party will be in great danger of being defeated at the next Presidential election and such a result would be fatal to the Unionists South without regard to color' (W. H. Gibbs, Mayor of Woodville, Miss.). And cf. Julian, *Political Recollections*, 316, where he describes how, to an old anti-slavery man, 'it seemed that all the trials of the war were merged in this grand issue, and that it involved the existence of free government on this continent'. He believed that the impeachment was undoubtedly inspired 'mainly by patriotic motives', but 'the spirit of intolerance among Republicans toward those who differed with them in opinion set all moderation and common sense at defiance'.

T

there is no enthusiasm or self-sacrificing feeling among the rank and file. . . . The Democrats are hungry and anxious for office and spoil, and the Republicans seemingly indifferent on the subject'. He noticed also that economic questions were beginning to replace Reconstruction controversies in the public mind, and that if Congress did nothing on the financial questions 'it will be taken as a confession . . . that the Republicans have no financial policy except high interest, untaxed lands and gold for the bond holder with double taxation and depreciated shinplasters for the people'.[1]

Against apathy and disillusion the Republicans had one trump to play in General Grant's candidature; yet this was bound to be regarded with mixed feelings by the Radicals. Grant might be a good general but his attachment to Republicanism was doubtful and, in Radical eyes, his famous report on the South in 1865 had shown a sad misunderstanding of the true Southern problem. Greenbacker Radicals were alarmed by Grant's predilection for moneyed men and by his rumoured fondness for sound money and full repayment of the debt. Even more alarming was Grant's refusal to commit himself. Ben Butler, who had his own strong reasons for disliking Grant, preferred Admiral Farragut, another non-political hero,[2] and some of his friends pressed Butler himself to show the Radical flag. 'Is the Republican party to take Grant anyway, without his saying a word?' asked one of them, and went on, 'I am satisfied that if we have Grant on a Radical platform we have got to drive him there.' He suggested the formation of a Butler club on the manhood suffrage and greenback basis which would be a certain draw for the Radicals, would 'take all that is valuable out of the Republican party', and attract Democrats on the greenback issue. 'Would not Grant's backers be so frightened that they would have to put him on a radical platform if nothing else happened?'[3] J. H. Wilson saw that the General would be and must be nominated, but thought that 'The Union

[1] L.C. *Washburn Papers*, 10 Jul. 1868.
[2] L.C. *Butler Papers*, draft reply to J. W. Shaffer, 17 Feb. 1866.
[3] L.C. *Butler Papers*, E. J. Sherman (one of Butler's keen supporters in Massachusetts) to Butler, 8 Jun. 1868.

party must close its ranks, readjust its lenses, ascertain the main
issues, and move steadily on without allowing itself to be drawn
an inch aside to discuss side questions. Concentration should be
the policy. The country should be reconstructed upon the principle of equality, justice and right; when that is done it will be
time enough for the Union party to saddle itself with temperance,
whiskey laws, Sunday laws, etc.'[1] In the event a vote for Grant
was clearly understood as a vote for the Reconstruction Acts;
what was lacking was the idea of future development, of Reconstruction as a growing policy rather than a past achievement.
There was not even a commitment to universal suffrage, and old
man Stevens could not commend the Republican platform which
'like all those of Republicans for the last six years was tame and
cowardly'.[2] The framework of Reconstruction remained but its
dynamic force was wasting away.[3]

The Grant candidature was not merely a matter of calculation
and evasion. The General's previous detachment from politics and
his enormous prestige attracted many would-be reformers who
looked for a lead and expected a purge of abuses. 'What we want
from him', wrote one of them, 'is men who will do the work —
Some Hercules in the Interior Department, for instance, who will
take the many headed serpent of robbery and strangle it in its
various shapes — Indian rings, Patent rings, Stationery rings, and
Railroad rings. . . . General Grant has an opportunity now as great
as that which Washington had when he became President or that
which the first Bonaparte had at the battle of Marengo. He can put
upon America a policy of retrenchment in office, of dignity among

---

[1] L.C. *Washburn Papers*, 12 Oct. 1867.   [2] L.C. *Stevens Papers*, 24 Jun. 1868.
[3] The mood of the hour is described by James A. Putman in a letter to E. B. Washburn
(L.C. *Washburn Papers*. 29 June 1868): 'I think there is a large class of conservative
Republicans who will support Grant wholly irrespective of Congressional policy. I think
the Reconstruction policy involving universal negro suffrage, on general principles,
grows weaker every day with a large class of Republican voters. I think there is a growing
weariness of the struggle over the negro.' In January 1868 Albert E. Powell, who claimed
to have been 'almost constantly travelling' in the Eastern, Middle and Western States, told
Washburn that the great majority 'wish to see the Southern States in the Union — in
Congress — as soon as possible. It is generally believed that as soon as these States are
represented in the council chambers of the nation that trade will revive and the country
will be once more on the road to prosperity.' The great concern was now with heavy
taxation (ibid., 24 Jan. 1868).

office holders, or reform in the civil service and of more simplicity of Republican practice.'[1] Under the leadership of Representative Thomas A. Jenckes of Rhode Island the movement for civil service reform had been gathering support, and Grant's supposed belief in reform encouraged reformers to hail his election as a triumph. The American Social Science Association, founded in October 1865 for the advancement of education and 'the diffusion of sound principles on questions of economy, trade, and finance', added civil service reform to its objectives in December 1868, and the President-elect became a member early in 1869.[2] Civil service reform was a cause which could unite ardent spirits of the old anti-slavery stamp with hard-headed businessmen who had a natural suspicion of politicians, and, so long as Johnson was in office, the prospect of taking some Federal appointments out of the President's hands was attractive to many Republicans. When Grant's election was secured, however, the prospects of taking the civil service out of politics looked less attractive, and the new President gave no positive lead in that direction.

Thus the triumph of Grant helped to dim two of the lights which had illumined the Republican party since its birth. Grant would maintain the formal structure of Reconstruction but he would add nothing to it, and the reforming zeal of the educated middle class would waste away amidst the political professionalism of the new era. Sumner fighting for civil rights, Jenckes harping on civil service reform, and G. F. Hoar pressing for a national education system including Federal aid for Southern schools, all found that they were living in a climate which grew rapidly colder after 1869.[3] Significantly it is the old Radicals who lead off the many complaints that the distinction between parties had been lost

[1] L.C. *Washburn Papers*, J. Russell Young (of the New York *Tribune*) to E. B. Washburn, 5 Jan. 1869.

[2] Cf. Ari Hoogenboom, 'Thomas A. Jenckes and Civil Service Reform', *Mississippi Valley Historical Review*, XLVII (Mar. 1961), 636 ff.

[3] It is fair to Grant to say that Hoar regarded him as a special friend, along with Sumner, to a national system of education (*Autobiography of Seventy Years*, I, 255). 'It was defeated by the timidity, or mistaken notions of economy, of Northern statesmen. In my opinion this defeat accounts for the failure of reconstruction so far as it has failed.' Sumner told Hoar shortly before his death that when the resolution declaring the provision for public education at the national charge was defeated in the Senate by a tie vote, he was so overcome that he burst into tears and left the Senate chamber (ibid.).

and that while old principles had lost their relevance the party showed no signs of adopting new ones. In 1870 Ben Butler was explaining to his supporters that 'The Republican party, in its inception, held in fact but one principle in common; its members differed upon every other.... That distinctive idea has been taken from the Republican party, leaving it, as a party, no peculiarity of doctrine for its future aspirations upon which to rally its partisans. Its record is of the past alone. Its mission, at home, has ended save to garner the gleanings of the harvest of its great past'.[1] Ignatius Donnelly observed in his diary that 'the time was when the line between the parties was as clearly drawn as a line of battle; the banners with conflicting mottoes faced each other; no deserters moved from one to the other. Now all is confusion. The surrender under the Apple tree of Appomatox seems to have dissolved the two great parties of the country as well as the contending armies'.[2] And G. W. Julian, looking back upon the events of these years, said that by 1870 the Republican party was 'regarded by many as a spent political force although it had received a momentum which threatened to outlast its mission.... While the issues of the war were retreating into the past the mercenary element of Republicanism had gradually secured the ascendancy and completely appropriated the Presidency'.[3] As the instrument of power the Republican party — with its efficient organization, attractive slogans and tremendous achievement—remained strong, and there would always be those ready to exploit its strength; but it ceased to be a dynamic party of change and became a highly integrated and successful mechanism for the defence of the existing social structure and the emergent economic order. Within the party Radicalism lost the savour of idealism, and became the descriptive label for the preservation of carpetbag government in the South.

Thaddeus Stevens did not live to see the apotheosis of Radicalism. He died in August 1868 and was buried in a cemetery

---

[1] *The Present State of Parties* (Boston, 1870), 3 ff.
[2] Minnesota State Historical Society, Ignatius Donnelly, *Diary*.
[3] Julian, *Political Recollections*, 330–1.

which made no distinction between the races, and explained, in an epitaph which he himself had written, that

'I have chosen this that I might illustrate in my death
The Principles which I have advocated through a long life:
EQUALITY OF MAN BEFORE HIS CREATOR;'

Before burial his body lay in state in the Capitol, guarded by the Massachusetts Regiment of negro Zouaves, and it was noticed with surprise that only Lincoln's body had drawn a larger number of visitors to pay their last respects.[1] He had now only to reckon with the hostility of historians, but his Radical colleagues had to live on in a world which was growing weary of enthusiasm and becoming absorbed in the task of building a superb and successful capitalist civilization.

Several of the old Radicals were to emerge as leaders in the ill-fated anti-Grant Liberal Republican movement of 1872, and among them the most interesting and influential was Carl Schurz. A convinced supporter of Radical Reconstruction Schurz believed that it could not achieve its objectives while directed by a party which had fallen 'almost entirely into the hands of the office holders and ruled by selfish interest'. He believed that a way out of the Reconstruction impasse could be found if the younger men in the South were persuaded to co-operate in a new departure. To Sumner he wrote that 'A very large number of Southerners, especially the young men who have become disgusted with their old leaders, care nothing about the Democratic party; but they detest Grant. They are sincerely willing to uphold the new order of things *in every direction*'. He thought that Sumner ought 'to be the great leader of this movement which will create the party of the future. It is the only way in which the equal rights of all can be permanently secured in the South. All your Ku Klux and enforcement laws avail nothing if we do not find the means to control public opinion, and this is the way to do it'.[2] Though Sumner had broken with Grant amid bitter and mutual recriminations he was

---

[1] F. Brodie, *Thaddeus Stevens* (New York, 1959), 366.
[2] *Speeches, Letters and Political Correspondence of Carl Schurz.*

not prepared to lead the new movement though preserving towards it an air of benevolent neutrality, but other Radicals committed themselves to Liberal Republicans.[1] More, however, remained loyal Republicans and though the party recovered easily after 1872, the Radicals found it impossible to recover from the split between the reformers and the regulars. Some of the Radical reformers found an outlet for their energies in the service of other causes: Wendell Phillips threw into labour agitation all the enthusiasm and indiscretion which he previously devoted to anti-slavery; G. W. Julian became the congressional champion of the eight hour day for the Federal employees and of attempts to save the public domain for homesteaders. Ignatius Donnelly charted an unhappy course through various protest movements in his state until he emerged into the rough seas of Populism. Ben Butler continued as a thorn in the flesh to all respectable Bostonians and made his last public appearance as the Greenback-Labor candidate for the Presidency in 1884. A regular Republican who moved from Radicalism towards later progressivism was W. E. Chandler, once an officeholder under Johnson, then a convert to Radicalism and manager of the Republican campaign in 1868. He became a bitter opponent of Hayes's Southern policy and of Republican connivance at the restoration of white supremacy; as late as 1890 he was struggling for a new 'force bill' to secure negro voting rights, and his failure to persuade the Republican leaders of the Senate that this was more important than a tariff bill may be described as the last dying gasp of Radicalism. At the end of his life he was one of the first in New England to take up the new reform programme sponsored by the Progressives. The streams of Radicalism could probably be traced flowing through many channels in the later nineteenth century; but the movement itself was becoming diffused, the men were growing old and weary, and the concentration which had won them their victories was no

---

[1] Vice-President Schuyler Colfax remained a regular Republican but in a letter to the South Bend Register, Oct. 1871 he described Republican policy in a distinctly 'liberal' way. He wanted, (1) retrenchment, (2) no more land grants to railroads, (3) a general amnesty to Southerners, (4) civil service reform, (5) lower taxes, (6) lower tariffs. (Smith, *Schuyler Colfax*, 338).

longer possible. Fair weather Radicals, and those who had seen Radicalism merely as an instrument of power, found their natural home in the changed Republican party.

* * * *

It is comparatively easy to explain the waning of Radicalism in terms of personal failure, evaporating enthusiasm, the urgent demands of business, and the tendency of all political organizations to fall into the hands of professionals. It is easy also to see how the challenge of the new age, with its manifest problems of the relationship between private business and public authority, had a divisive effect upon the Radicals — turning Kelley into a fanatical protectionist, Schurz into a free trader, Butler into a Greenbacker, and Donnelly into an agrarian radical — while drawing together the main body of Republicans around the citadel of American capitalism. But the break-up of Radicalism may also reflect more profound weaknesses in the position which it maintained.

It has been argued that much of the Radical success was explained by the pressures from below which drove cautious politicians even further than they had intended, and that this pressure must be explained in ideological terms and not as the product of mere interest groups. The ideology had expressed in abstract but attractive terms certain propositions about man in society which, for a moment in time, seemed to epitomise the aspirations of the Northern people. Racial equality, equal rights and the use of national authority to secure both were living ideas in the Reconstruction era as they have since become, in some quarters, in the mid-twentieth century. For the first time these concepts were cast in the form of a political programme which could be achieved; but their success depended upon the response which they aroused from the Northern people. After Reconstruction the ideas persisted but failed to rouse the same enthusiasm; their formal acceptance was a very different thing from the popular emotion which could push them forward despite the usual obstacles to policies which disturb complacency and refuse to let men rest in peace. The question remains whether the slackening of the pressure behind the Radical ideology should be explained by rival distractions and changing interests or by a weakness in the ideology itself. Examination will show that the generalities of the Radical ideology — so attractive at first sight — could not stand pressure. The weapons bent and broke in the hands of those who used them.

A belief in racial equality has never won universal assent and to the majority of men in the mid-nineteenth century it seemed to be condemned both by experience and by science. The literal equality between men of obviously different physiological characteristics was an abolitionist invention and it rested upon emotional conviction rather than upon rational proof; the comparison between intelligent negroes and retarded poor whites proved little because the civilization of a few blacks did not redeem the mass from docile ignorance and the degradation of some whites did not detract from the high standards of the majority. The abolitionist argument was based largely upon pure *a priori* statements or upon experience with fugitive slaves; a mass of argument could be produced against the one, while the defiance of the occasional runaway did not prove that the mass of his fellows were not fitted by nature for a subordinate position. The behaviour of the negro was obviously different from that of the whites and, though those who knew him best granted him some admirable traits, they would also maintain that he was sadly deficient in the capacity for industry, thrift, self-reliance, enterprise, sexual restraint and the whole galaxy of virtues esteemed by nineteenth-century civilization. The abolitionist argument that the negro appeared 'inferior' because he had lived in slavery for generations failed to carry weight because no free negro society could be found to prove the proposition. Moreover there was an added complication in the mixed ancestry of so many of those who, like Frederick Douglass, were quoted as evidence of innate negro intelligence. This is not the place to enter upon the tangled problem of racial characteristics; it is sufficient to state that in the later nineteenth century racial equality was a hypothesis which was generally rejected. It was not accepted in the North any more than it was in the South and even abolitionists were anxious to disclaim any intention of forcing social contacts between the races and all shied away from the dread subject of racial amalgamation.[1] An initial weakness of the Radical ideology was therefore its dependence upon a concept which was not self-evident, lacked scientific proof, and offended popular susceptibilities.

The usual weakness of equalitarian theory lies in demonstrating that people ought to be treated as equals in spite of natural inequalities, and this difficulty is acute when dealing with people of different races. While it is possible to argue, among men of the same race, that it is necessary to treat men as though they were equal, it is far harder to do so in the face of popular prejudice that men of a different race are marked at birth as 'inferior'. The conventional Republican argument was that men were unequal in capabilities but equal in rights, and in the American context this proposition rested mainly upon an appeal to the preamble of the Declaration of Independence; but the assertions of the Declaration were not 'self-evident' to most white Americans when applied to negroes. Moreover there were some particular difficulties in equalitarian theory when applied to a mass of people, concentrated in a single region, and occupying from time out of mind a subordinate position in society. Equality demands protection of the weak against the strong and positive law to afford it; but it usually involves the assumption that given certain legal rights the due process of law will enable men to maintain their equality. With the negroes this assumption could not be made: what was required was protection, maintained by enforceable law, at every point where the power of the dominant race was likely to impinge upon the weaker. With tradition, economic power, prejudice, social custom and, in most Southern districts, numbers all entrenched on one side, protection could not be provided merely by changing the law and leaving its administration to the local authorities and courts. The concept of negro equality demanded

[1] Cf. L.C. *Stevens Papers*, Stevens to Kelley, 6 Sep. 1866. 'A good many people . . . are disturbed by the practical exhibition of social equality in the arm-in-arm performance of Douglass and Tilton. It does not become radicals like us to particularly object. But it was certainly unfortunate at this time.'

interference with the processes of local government on a scale never before contemplated in America or in any other nation. Would the Northern majority be prepared to exert continuously this kind of pressure and provide this kind of protection? In the answer to this question lay the second great weakness of the Radical ideology.

Further difficulties lay in the complexities which sheltered behind the simple word 'equality'. Whatever the moral arguments the negro was not, and could not be in the immediate future, an equal to the white man in economic life, in competition for the scarce educational facilities of the South, or in winning public office. Racial equality would have to be an artifical creation imposed upon Southern society; the negro would have to have guarantees which were not given to the white man, and the quest for equality would demand unequal incidence of the law. No other minority required special legislation to ensure equal status in the courts, or the care of a Federal bureau, or the use of force to protect the right to vote. Negro equality implied that something must be taken from the whites, and this was explicit in two features of Radical policy: confiscation and disqualification. Stevens never wavered in his belief that negro democracy must have an economic basis in negro landownership; confiscation and redistribution were therefore cardinal points in his programme. Yet the most passionate advocates of equality could not persuade the Republican majority to embark upon such a disturbance of property. Negro democracy would also be a sham if the former ruling class retained its grasp upon local and national office, and disqualification was necessary. This policy succeeded because it was supported by Northern fear of restored Southern domination at Washington, but it proved to be the most vulnerable and perhaps the least wise aspect of Reconstruction. Both confiscation and disqualification demonstrate the formidable difficulties which attend the imposition of equality upon a society in which it did not exist, and in which the beneficiaries of equalitarian policy were too weak, socially and economically, to stand upon their own feet. The price of equality was revolutionary change, vigilance and constant pressure, and who would pay the price when enthusiasm grew cold and the suspicion grew that the negroes were not yet ready to exercise rights which could not be secured without the coercion of their fellow citizens.

It is in this context that the work of John A. Bingham assumes great significance. In his fight for the civil rights clause of the Fourteenth Amendment he cut equal rights free from negro protection and made them national. The later perversion of this clause to protect the rights of corporations tended to obscure the significance of a measure which protected all citizens and all persons under the jurisdiction of the States, but once the importance of nationalized right was recognized the Fourteenth Amendment grew in stature. Conversely the Fifteenth Amendment was weak from the outset because it linked suffrage with race; it was a law for negro enfranchisement and could be enforced only so long as some people had an interest in doing so. If the Fifteenth Amendment had declared in unequivocal terms that all males over the age of twenty-one who were citizens of the United States had the right to vote it might have been recognised as a cornerstone of democracy and attracted popular support. As it was the Fifteenth Amendment enacted 'impartial' suffrage which meant that the States could impose any qualification they chose provided that it was not based on race; this meant that the white majority of the nation had no particular interest in its enforcement.

Beyond the major problem of equality by enforcement lay the vast and ramifying difficulty of definition. Was equality indivisible or if divisible which aspects were essential? The three classic definitions of equality — *in* the eyes of God, *under* the law, and *of* opportunity — each carried different implications. Equality in the eyes of God might well be an excuse for inequality on earth: Dives and Lazarus had both lived under the judgment of God, both received their deserts after death, and their inequality on earth was dramatic but irrelevant to their condition in eternity. Equality in the eyes of God implied some limitation upon the principle of subordination for it had been an essential part of the abolitionist case that the children of God should not be treated as less than human beings, but it provided no definition of the place of man in society. Many pious Northerners saw no inconsistency between Christian conviction and racial discrimination, and the brotherhood of man in Christ was no barrier to the belief that equality on earth was no part of God's purpose. It was therefore necessary to supplement the Christian concept of equality in eternity with the purely secular arguments for equality on earth.

Equality under the law had deep roots in the Anglo-Saxon tradition but in its mother country it had not proved incompatible with aristocratic privilege, an established Church, denial of suffrage to the masses, and the exploitation of low paid labour. The guarantee of equal status in the courts was a great and important addition to the rights of negroes, but it would not of itself create a political and social revolution. Beyond the formal guarantee of equality under the law lay the intractable question of who should administer the law. The legal rights of negroes might be recognized in Southern courts but they were likely to be strictly interpreted; one could be confident that the white Southern judge would administer the law scrupulously, but between the negro and equal justice stood the white Southern jury. Equality under the law was a grand sweeping theory, without which no other form of secular equality was possible, but it did not erase the notion that the negro was an inferior man to whom only a grudging recognition was extended. It might be argued that, once the groundwork of legal equality had been laid, the progress towards equality in other fields would follow, yet one might doubt the certainty of this hypothesis. It was only in 1867 that the British Parliament was to decide after centuries of equality under the law that the agricultural labourer was entitled to a vote, and millions of simple Englishmen still went unlettered to their graves.

Equality of opportunity seemed to be a more positive demand. If the racial barrier could be removed from access to education, occupation and public office the negro would have the right to compete on equal terms with the whites in most of the fields to which his aspiration might lead him. Yet equality of opportunity implied inequality of achievement and in the South its immediate result might be the confirmation of white supremacy. If the negro was to be given a real chance of equal achievement he must be given positive aids which were not given to the white man, and one was brought back once more to the basic problem of equalitarian theory: that positive government was required to correct habitual inequality. This led on to the political difficulty that, in the climate of nineteenth-century opinion, sustained and purposeful government intervention was unpopular and improbable. The comparatively modest aims of the Freedmen's Bureau aroused intense hostility in the South and many doubts in the North; any further attempt to translate the commitment to equality into governmental responsibilities might wreck the whole structure of Reconstruction, yet without this the purpose of equalitarian Radicalism could not be achieved.

Many Republicans contended that it was unnecessary to embark upon the troubled sea of racial equality if one could stop in the safe haven of guaranteed rights. The negro was a man, and as a man he had certain inalienable rights; if these could be secured the vexed question of equality could be deferred or perhaps dismissed. This theory of inalienable right had better prospects than any theory of equality. American tradition had long accepted as its cornerstone the idea of man as an atom in society, entitled to do all that was within his power provided that it did not impinge upon the rights of others. But American tradition had usually failed to recognize the fact that rights were not 'inalienable', that the exercise of legal rights depended upon the consent of the majority, or that some rights of some men could always be denied by the sovereign power of the people. In Reconstruction Americans were brought face to face with the problem of free men whose 'rights' were denied by the local majority and could be secured only by external coercion. Moreover the whole attitude of Americans towards rights had been governed by their implicit acceptance of the idea of checks and balances. The rights of the people were a check upon the enlargement of authority, and to give some rights to some people at the expense of others had been damned by association with the idea of privilege. What was the intrinsic difference between rights conferred upon a chartered monopoly and rights conferred upon a weak minority? This conundrum had always been implicit in American political discourse but Reconstruction made it explicit.

Even if these pitfalls could be avoided there remained the knotty problem of which rights should be protected and how they could be distinguished from rights which were unprotected. The Declaration of Independence referred to the rights of life, liberty and the pursuit of happiness, but these were *among* the inalienable rights and not an exclusive list; and even if one stopped short at the classic three the pursuit of happiness was so elastic an idea that it was little guide to an enumeration of rights which could be protected by law. There were three main attempts to distinguish the categories of right and to determine which could, and which could not be protected. The first was the distinction between civil rights and political rights, the second between those which were fundamental and those which could be left to the discretion of political authorities, and the third was that between public and private rights. The first proposal made by Thaddeus Stevens — that all laws, state and national, should apply equally to all persons — attempted to cut through this maze of difficulties. Later Sumner was to express the same idea when he said 'Show me . . . a legal institution, anything created or regulated by law, and I will show you what must be opened equally to all without distinction of color.'[1] This was the true Radical argument. It recognized that private prejudice could not be legislated out of existence, but maintained that discrimination could be prohibited in every activity touched by the law. Stevens and Sumner would have left people to do what they liked in their homes or in private associations, but they would have outlawed discrimination at the polls, in public places, on public transport, and in education. Sumner even hoped to add churches, cemeteries and benevolent institutions to this list. He resisted the argument of 'separate but equal' by asserting that 'Equality is where all men are alike. A substitute can never take the place of equality'.[2] At the other end of the

[1] C.G. 42.2.242.   [2] Ibid.

Republican spectrum was Lyman Trumbull who said the 'civil rights' (which should be guaranteed by law) were 'the right to his liberty, to come and go as he pleases, have the avails of his own labor, and not to be restricted in that respect'. In other respects the legal rights of negroes must depend upon the discretion of their political sovereign for these were 'all matters of privilege'. This attempted to treat the negro as a free man without treating him as an equal man, and Trumbull even regarded the right to serve on a jury as one of these matters of privilege.[1]

Before the Reconstruction controversy ended moderate Republicans including Trumbull himself, had moved significantly nearer to the Radical view of rights which ought to be guaranteed, but there remained a distinct cleavage between those who believed that wherever the law flowed it should carry with it equality of right, and those who believed that one soon reached a frontier at which a 'right' became a 'privilege' and could be withheld at the discretion of the legal sovereign. The extreme Radical position was unequivocal and relatively uncomplicated, but would require a large invasion of the traditional areas of State authority; the 'moderate' position was clouded with difficulties of definition and separation but in the nature of things it was more likely to appeal to the majority of men who disliked sweeping logic and preferred to believe that the minimum of effort would produce the best results. Under the circumstances the best which the Radicals could obtain was probably the imprecise but traditional phrases which Bingham wrote into the Fourteenth Amendment. The 'privileges and immunities' of citizens of the United States, 'the equal protection of the laws', and 'due process of law' were all expressions which could mean as much or as little as lawyers were prepared to read into them. They did not prevent the Supreme Court from legalizing segregation but they also provided ammunition for the Court's later attack upon segregation. It is possible that Bingham's first suggestion, which would have given to Congress the responsibility for initiating measures to protect rights, would have obviated some of the difficulties inherent in judicial legislation; but

[1] Beale (ed.), *Diary of Gideon Welles*, II, 489–90.

Congress, even more than the Court, would be unwilling to act until there was sufficient public interest to support action. Once the Northern majority had refused to accept the principle that wherever the law operated race must be forgotten, and had accepted the distinctions between rights which were rights and rights which were privileges, the whole idea of equality under the law was lost. Natural right became neither more nor less than the right which the majority was prepared to recognize and to protect.

Charles Sumner realized the dangers inherent in the attempt to split up the rights of man into various categories, and devoted the closing years of his life to a struggle for a measure which would have embodied the Stevens principle of equal incidence of national and State laws on all citizens. When he was accused of occupying the time of the Senate with arguments over access to hotel rooms or the exclusion of negroes from benevolent institutions he replied that 'Every question by which the equal rights of all are affected is transcendant. It cannot be magnified, But here are the rights of a whole race, not merely the rights of an individual, not merely the rights of two or three or four, but the rights of a whole race'.[1] A year after Sumner's death Congress enacted some of the provisions of the bill for which he had fought and guaranteed to the negroes equal rights in hotels, places of public entertainment, and public transport, but did nothing about education. In 1883 the Supreme Court found this Act invalid on the ground that it was intended to protect 'social' and not 'civil' or 'political' rights. In 1896 the Supreme Court upheld a State law requiring segregated facilities on railroads, and the tide of Radicalism which had once lashed so furiously against the ramparts was at its lowest ebb. Only a bold man could have predicted that the stone which the builders rejected was to become a cornerstone of liberal orthodoxy in the second half of the twentieth century.

The Radical solution to the dilemma of rights which were natural but which could only be secured by artificial means was negro suffrage. With the vote the negro would be equipped to protect his own rights, and there were Jeffersonian echoes in the idea

[1] C.G. 42.2.243.

that the cultivator of the soil would not only defend his personal rights but also act as a repository for political virtue.[1] The voting negro would protect himself against injustice and the Union against its enemies, but this concept of suffrage as a protective device proved inadequate when Reconstruction governments were compelled to assume the tasks of modern administration in a region where the best government had always been that which governed least.[2] So long as the vote was merely protective the ignorance of the negro was not a relevant argument because a poor man could understand what had to be defended as well as the best educated; but when negro suffrage became the basis for an economic and social revolution guided by positive government it was relevant to ask whether the former slave was yet equal to his responsibilites.[3]

The Radicals argued the case for negro suffrage in the context of nineteenth-century liberal thought, and they can hardly be blamed for not having transcended the ideas of their age. Moreover they were inhibited by the political circumstances in which they had to operate. It was hard enough to convince Northern public opinion that negro suffrage was safe and just without complicating the question. In the summer of 1866 a Radical member of the Reconstruction Committee told Congress that 'we may as

---

[1] Henry Wilson observed (C.G. 39.2.43) that 'I do not believe the country has suffered much from 1789 to this time on account of the ignorance of voters; it has suffered far more from the character of voters. The people of the country, the labouring men of the nation, desire proper legislation. They are for just, equal and humane laws. They are patriotic, and they have generally proved it; and you often find them by the hundreds and by the thousands voting nearer right than many of the most intelligent men in the country who have personal ends to accomplish. . . . We hear a good deal of the evils of ignorant suffrage. . . . The country has suffered far more during the last twenty years from the selfish conduct and unpatriotic conduct of intelligent men.'

[2] A curious by-product of the protective theory was seen when Senator Pomeroy spoke up for female suffrage. Senator Williams argued that 'to extend the right of suffrage to negroes in this country I think is necessary for their protection; but to extend the right of suffrage to women is not necessary for their protection'.

[3] It was not long before the question was asked even in sound Republican circles. Cf. G. F. Hoar (C.G. 42.2.1872): 'Both parties in this House agreed that the condition of the governments of the South . . . was due to the fact that, in reconstructing those States, you had based their governments upon their ignorance. The criticism is just, in part. You did, Republican statesmen, in reconstructing those States, found their government upon their ignorance. You could not do otherwise. The education of those States had proved itself unfit to govern. . . . The mistake you made was this: that you failed to see that the power to establish government on the will of the people, which you asserted, was in the nature of things inseparable from the power to require the education of the whole people.'

well state it plainly and fairly, so that there shall be no misunderstanding on the subject. It was our opinion that three fourths of the States of this Union (that is of the loyal States) could not be induced to vote to grant the right of suffrage, even in any degree or under any restriction, to the colored race'.[1] Between this time and the passage of the Fifteenth Amendment a remarkable change took place in public opinion, but in order to foster it the Radicals were forced to rely less and less upon appeals to abstract justice and more and more upon the utility of the negro vote to the party and to the Union. This stress led them to pass lightly over the tasks which negro democracy might be called upon to perform, and to treat their votes merely as a counterweight in the political balance of the nation.

Radicals themselves hesitated at times over the problem of the vote. Was it one of the inalienable rights, or was it, as everyone else said, a political right which could be granted or withheld at the discretion of the political sovereign? Among the conservative Republicans, and particularly amongst the better educated, there was genuine hesitation about mass democracy, and if they turned one eye towards the negroes of the South they turned the other to the foreign-born city vote which formed the electoral basis of Boss Tweed's New York ring. Reformers could join hands with the merely fearful in urging the case for universal literacy tests, and old Know-Nothings could make common cause with new Republicans against universal suffrage. Yet literacy tests which would exclude the mass of the Southern negro people, and could be manipulated by the ruling State authorities, were useless as a political solution in the South, and Radicals were pushed from their early caution on the suffrage question to an outright avowal of belief in universal suffrage. In a letter written for communication to a Republican meeting in New York in January 1868 Thaddeus Stevens insisted that the right to vote was inalienable, and put natural right ahead of the argument from utility, but he went on to stress the other arguments in favour of universal suffrage. 'True, I deemed the hastening of the bestowal of that franchise as very

[1] C.G. 39.1.2766.

essential to the welfare of the nation, because without it I believe that the Government will pass into the hands of the loco-focos, and that such an event will be disastrous to the whole country. With universal suffrage I believe the true men of the nation can maintain their position. Without it whether their suffrage be impartial or qualified I look upon the Republic as likely to relapse into an oligarchy which will be ruled by coarse Copperheadism and proud Conservatism. I have never insisted that the franchise should be unjustly regulated so as to secure a Republican ascendancy but I have insisted and do insist that there can be no unjust regulation of that franchise which will give to any other party the power if the Republicans are true to themselves and do not fall into their usual vice of cowardice. The Republicans once beaten into a minority by the focre of Negro prejudice will never again obtain the majority and the nation will become a despotism.'[1] Six months before his death Stevens explained that after long reflection he had 'finally come to the conclusion that universal suffrage was one of the inalienable rights intended to be inserted in (the Declaration of Independence) by our Fathers at the time of the Revolution and that they were prevented from inserting it in the Constitution by slavery alone'.[2] His reflection owed more to the exigencies of contemporary politics than to a knowledge of history, but there is no need to doubt the sincerity of his conclusion. Universal suffrage was the logical and complete answer; 'impartial' suffrage was not. With Stevens dead, however, there was no one with the same influence who could put the case so clearly and the Fifteenth Amendment enacted impartial and not universal suffrage. The Radicals failed in the first instance because they did not or could not spell out what negro democracy was to do, and the second instance because they could not resist the modification of the right to vote which let in literacy tests, grandfather clauses, and poll taxes.

Paradoxically some of the Radical arguments for negro suffrage tended to rebound. The idea that the vote would enable the negro

---

[1] L.C. *Stevens Papers*, Stevens to F. A. Conkling, 6 Jan. 1868.
[2] Ibid., Stevens to J. H. Forney, 11 Mar. 1868.

to protect himself provided an excuse for non-intervention, and for the belief that the Southern question could now be treated as a local question. In 1880 James G. Blaine, writing in the *North American Review*, justified the grant of negro suffrage by saying that 'had the franchise not been bestowed upon the negro as his shield and weapon for defence, the demand upon the General Government to interfere for his protection, would have been constant, irritating and embarrassing. Great complaint has been made for years past of the Government's interference, simply to secure to the colored citizen his constitutional right. But this intervention has been trifling compared to that which would have been required if we had not given suffrage to the negro'.[1] It was thus easy to infer that having instituted negro suffrage as an automatic regulator of the Southern political mechanism Northerners could turn their eyes away from what actually went on in the South. To be fair one should add that when Blaine wrote the extensive disenfranchisement of the negroes had not taken place, and that in some districts he could vote freely provided that he voted for the Democratic ticket.

It is not suggested that equal participation by the negro in Southern politics would have been automatically secured if the Radicals had succeeded in establishing the suffrage as an 'inalienable right', but an unequivocal statement that all adult males had the right to vote would have been easier to enforce and more difficult to evade. Nor is it suggested that universal suffrage would have done anything to solve the vexed and unexamined question of what the negro was to do with his vote. What is suggested is that the Fifteenth Amendment was a weak compromise which failed to achieve the Radical aims and, in the long run, helped to discredit that freedom of State action which moderates wished to preserve. Under the Reconstruction Acts all 'loyal' males had voted; the Fifteenth Amendment allowed States to retreat from that position while the belief that the suffrage was secured on equitable terms allowed the Northern majority to relax pressure at

[1] James G. Blaine, *Political Discussions*, 278. From an article in the *North American Review*, 1880.

the point where it was most needed. The keystone of the Radical arch proved too weak to hold up the edifice. In a sense negro suffrage was premature — though it could have been written into the law at no other time — but this was only in part the result of negro immaturity. Beneath the surface of the suffrage question lay larger problems of the role of government in a democratic State and these American society as a whole was unwilling or unready to contemplate. By 1880 *The Nation*, which had earlier given somewhat lukewarm support to negro suffrage while insisting that it should be impartial and not universal, was emphasizing that the *quality* of voters should be the primary consideration.[1] For the intelligentsia who had, for the most part, thrown their influence behind Radical Republicanism, the great national problem was no longer the protection of negro rights but the defence of public morality, social respectability and economic orthodoxy against demagogues, bosses, agitators, agrarian Radicals, and mass ignorance.

It has been argued in the preceding pages that an essential weakness in the Radical programme lay in its demand for national intervention to secure equality and protect rights, exercising a power which was unfamiliar and depending upon the support of public opinion which might well be apathetic or even hostile to its objectives. The arguments for enlarged national power were made clearly and forcibly, and there was no failure on the part of the Radicals to realize that their policy demanded the use of national authority not only on a greater scale than ever before but also upon new principles. The idea which had been presented in Sumner's 'Freedom National' speech of 1852 had germinated and grown until it was possible to see the nation newly based upon equal right and abandoning the divided sovreignty of the past. 'It certainly seems desirable', said the moderate Luke Poland in 1866, 'that no doubt should be left as to the power of Congress to enforce principles lying at the very foundation of

---

[1] *The Nation* always opposed the idea that suffrage was a natural right. It gave some pious advice about thrift ('Every deposit in a savings bank is worth ten votes') but in spite of its preoccupation with educational tests it refused to support a National Education Bureau or Federal aid for Southern education.

all Republican government if they be denied or violated by the States.'[1] This was a constant theme of the Republican party and one which brought forth the most bitter cries of anguish from their opponents. 'The time was,' said one Democrat in 1869, 'when the suggestion of grave doubts of constitutional warrant would cause the advocates of pending measures to hesitate, to reflect.... Innovation and reform, however specious and desirable, were rejected at once and finally unless clearly sanctioned by constitutional authority.'[2] Six years later another Democrat expressed the common view of his party when he charged that Republican interpretation of the Constitution 'freed from all verbiage and ambiguity ... amounts simply to the assertion of a supreme power in Congress over every subject that concerns the life, liberty and property of any person within the United States; in other words over everything that is the subject of the law'.[3] The detached observer may well ask what was wrong with the exercise of such power, and why the national government should not remedy the deficiencies of the States. The Radicals did not wish to scrap the Constitution, but they thought that its failure in 1861 demonstrated the need for greater flexibility in interpretation and greater concentration of power at the centre. This may appear to have been not unreasonable, but by and large the Democrats have had the best of the argument, and modern historians have echoed their criticisms though approving an extension of national authority during the New Deal which went far beyond the wildest expectations of the Radicals. It remains to ask why the concept of strong national government, which has proved so attractive to so many men in the twentieth century, did not gather the support which might have sustained it during the later nineteenth century.

Some of the explanations are obvious. The weight of tradition was against strong national government, and the word 'centralism' was bogey enough to frighten large numbers of people who would not stop to ask what was being centralized, by whom, and for what purpose. Increased national authority might put power into

[1] In a particularly able and temperate defence of congressional policy. C.G. 39.1.2961-4.
[2] C.G. 40.3.642 (Eldridge of Kentucky).
[3] A. G. Thurman, speech at Mansfield, Ohio, 31 July 1875.

the hands of those who were distrusted by the would-be reformers, and the professional politician might be the beneficiary from an attempt to provide the national government with a moral purpose. Roscoe Conkling had a telling point against the opponents of 'centralism' when he said that 'Every civilized government may protect its citizens in the uttermost ends of the earth, but when the United States interposes to check murders, and burnings, and barbarities at which humanity shudders, perpetrated by thousands, and overawing all local authority, it is suddenly discovered that we are in danger of "centralism" '.[1] Yet for many people the argument against 'centralism' was epitomized in the fear that it might increase the power of men like Roscoe Conkling; they could not ignore the fact that his vehemence against civil service reformers was as great as that against the perpetrators of Southern atrocities.

In their presentation of the case for national power the Radicals were inhibited by conventional American and nineteenth-century political thought. While the old Whigs, whose ideas they inherited, had believed in more positive action by the national government than their Democratic opponents, they had never thought of writing a blank cheque for government intervention. What they wanted was Federal responsibility for the performance of certain economic functions defined by the economic interests concerned, and since that time the concepts of *laissez-faire* had tended to narrow the sphere of action which business interests were likely to prescribe for government. Northern intellectuals who were attracted by the political aims of Reconstruction were precisely those who were equally attracted by the utopian elements in *laissez-faire*, by the theory of natural harmony, and by the faith in betterment through individual enterprise. The government was therefore being asked to 'secure the blessings of liberty' at the very time when it was being asked to contract its responsibility for 'promoting the general welfare', and the hope of securing civil justice for the Southern negro was not coupled with the expectation of securing social justice for the Northern farmer and worker. Thus

[1] Speech at the Cooper Institute, New York, 23 July 1872.

the Radicals' concept of national power was too wide to satisfy conservative men but not wide enough to gather support from the nineteenth-century movements of protest.

Even if the concept of national power had not suffered from these inherent weaknesses it would still have had a precarious hold upon the nation. Radical Reconstruction declared certain principles of national responsibility but it did nothing to create the institutions of government which could give these principles a permanent place on the national stage. The Freedmen's Bureau was such an institution but even its friends recognized that its life must be limited. The Fourteenth Amendment left the door open for Congress to make laws which would enforce the civil rights clause, but it did not make it mandatory for Congress to do so and the assumption was that the law would be self-enforcing through the existing machinery of government and courts. The initiative remained with the traditional instruments of government — with the President, with the judges and with the States themselves — and no new instruments of government were brought into being. One can contrast this with the experience of the New Deal with its proliferation of governmental agencies; when enthusiasm receded the administrative achievement remained, and many Americans (ranging from highly paid government servants to the very poor) had acquired a vested interest in these new institutions. When Radical enthusiasm withered away it left behind it no such institutional bulwarks, and when the Freedmen's Bureau expired there remained no new government departments, no new government agencies, and no administrative doctrine to carry out those obligations to citizens of the United States of which so much had been heard.

*   *   *   *

The arguments which have been presented in the preceding pages have attempted to show why the ideology of Radical Republicanism, which appeared so powerful during the crisis of Reconstruction, failed to gather that momentum which could have carried it forward in the years which followed. It is of course

exceedingly improbable that the Radicals of the Reconstruction
period could have conceived their problems in any other way or
that they could have gone on to produce the ideas and institutions
which would have corrected the weaknesses in their edifice.
Radicalism shared the weaknesses of all liberal bourgeois movements of the nineteenth century, and it would have required a far
more profound revolution in thought and action to make them
view their situation through the eyes of twentieth-century liberals.
In their equalitarian sentiments, in their realization that individual
rights might be incompatible with local self-government, and in
their attitude towards national power they were prophets of the
future; yet they remained children of their age and were bound by
its assumptions and inhibitions. And even if their vision occasionally transcended these limitations they were unlikely to persuade
the majority of their countrymen that the revolution which they
had initiated ought to proceed to further innovation. The failure
of Radicalism is thus a part of the wider failure of bourgeois
liberalism to solve the problems of the new age which was dawning;
but having said this it is important to remember that if the
Radicals shared in the weaknesses of their age they also had some
achievements which were exceptional.

First among civilized nations the United States had met the
problems of a bi-racial society, and first among civilized nations
they had committed themselves to the proposition that in such a
society human beings must have equal rights. If the definition of
'rights' was confused the idea that they must be recognized was
clear. The civil rights clause of the Fourteenth Amendment was in
many ways unsatisfactory, but it contained explosive material
which could shatter the lines of racial discrimination. The United
States had committed themselves to the statement that suffrage
should be colour-blind, and if the phrasing of the Fifteenth
Amendment invited evasion the principle which it enunciated
would outlive attempts to defeat it. Americans may well differ
upon the wisdom of these equalitarian ideas, but it is impossible to
deny their importance for the future. The Fourteenth and Fifteenth
Amendments could have been enacted only during the period of

Reconstruction, and without them the subsequent history of the United States would have been very different. Not least important has been their effect upon the negro race in America, for the knowledge that the goals of negro aspiration are already written into the Constitution has had the powerful consequence of turning American negroes aside from thoughts of revolution. In his quest for equality the negro appeals to established national law and not against it, and one of the most striking developments of twentieth-century history has been the failure of Communists amongst a people who had many reasons for disaffection. The constitutional amendments had an equally powerful effect upon Northern thought. If Northern opinion, in the later years of the nineteenth century, was not prepared to implement the principles of the amendments, they were not removed from the Constitution and were to become the basis for further thought about the problem of race in America and in the world at large. It is possible to attribute the modern American hostility to 'colonialism' — which so often embarrasses the European allies of the United States — to memories of the Revolution, to ingrained suspicion of Great Britain and to mere calculation about the changing balance of power in the world; but it is equally significant that during Reconstruction Americans rejected the idea that law should recognize the 'inferiority' of non-European races. These are not unimportant consequences and may serve to lighten the gloom with which Americans have been accustomed to regard the crisis of Reconstruction.

The great failure of Radical Reconstruction lay in its attempt to remould Southern society. Hypothetical arguments may be produced to show that the attempt should never have been made, or that it was not made thoroughly enough, that too much or too little pressure was applied to the white people of the South; all that the historian can do is to record that the attempt as made did not produce the immediate results for which Radicals hoped. If it is believed that nothing should have been done the responsibility of the Radicals for having done something is clear; if it is believed that not enough was done it has been argued that moderate pressure not Radical initiative laid the ground for a Southern counter-revolution. Radicals argued at the outset that compromise and conservatism were not the principles with which to meet an unprecedented situation, and though one may blame them for their determination to have a revolution it is a little unfair to blame them for being forced to stop half-way. On the other hand if the revolution was going to stop half-way it is fair to blame the Radicals for insisting upon the alienation of the Southern ruling class whose support was vital for any compromise solution. It can be shown — and it is likely that the evidence will gather weight — that the Reconstruction governments in the South were not so bad as they have been painted in the Southern picture, but no amount of argument is likely to convince anyone that they were successful governments. This book has been concerned with the ideas and motives of Northern Reconstruction policy and not with the consequences of that policy in the South. It is true that the policy cannot be divorced from its consequences but motives cannot be judged from results. The authors of Reconstruction policy did not intend that it should perpetuate racial antagonism in Southern society, discredit colour-blind democracy, and provide further ammunition for Southern attacks upon the North. They were not disunionists, as Andrew Johnson called them, but they believed that the old Union, containing elements which could not combine, must be reconstructed. They hoped that the preamble to the Declaration of Independence should become the new formula for national existence, and they hoped to endow the national government with the power to ensure this result. These ideas were not negligible, absurd or unworthy. Their presentation was marred by a bitterness which was the legacy of war but was sometimes redeemed by the idealistic impulses which war had released. They left a record of failure in the South and permanent alterations in the law of a great nation. They faced intractable problems which still vex the modern world and they anticipated many of the assumptions with which men now tackle these problems. There was tragedy in the crisis of Reconstruction, but the tragic element transcends the particular circumstances of the post-war era and belongs to the whole condition of modern man.

BIBLIOGRAPHICAL NOTE

THIS book makes no claim to open up new sources for Reconstruction history, and it is therefore unnecessary to append a bibliography. The most complete critical bibliography of the events covered in this book is that in Howard K. Beale, *The Critical Year* (New York, 1930); unfortunately the bibliography was not brought up to date when the book was reprinted in 1958. J. G. Randall, *Civil War and Reconstruction*, 2nd ed. revised by David Donald (New York, 1962), contains a thorough reassessment of Reconstruction and a useful survey of the literature on the subject. The valuable section on 'Suggested Reading' in John Hope Franklin, *Reconstruction after the Civil War* (Chicago, 1961), is devoted mainly to Reconstruction in the South but indicates the scope and range of recent 'revisionist' treatments of Reconstruction. There is a useful select bibliography, of works bearing directly upon the subject of this book, in Eric L. McKitrick, *Andrew Johnson and Reconstruction* (New York, 1960). On the economic aspects of Reconstruction there is an excellent bibliographical essay in Robert P. Sharkey, *Money, Class, and Party* (Baltimore, 1959). Other recent books which contain bibliographies are Fawn M. Brodie, *Thaddeus Stevens* (New York, 1959) and George R. Woolfolk, *The Cotton Regency* (New York, 1958).

INDEX

American Social Science Association, 280

Arkansas, 'ten-per-cent' plan in, 17

Badeau, Adam, letter on Johnson's policy, 38–9

Baltimore, 73

Bancroft, George, 39

Beale, H. K., on Johnson's veto of Freedman's Bureau Bill, 133 n. 1; on motives for Reconstruction, 213

Beard, Charles, on Reconstruction, 213

Bingham, J. A., 58, 67, 70; on Committee of 15, 127–8, 133, 138–9, 142; opposes Stevens in 1866, 179–82, 188; offers amendments to military protection bill, 191–2; proposes a Reconstruction Bill, 192; actions on Reconstruction Bill, 197; and Second Reconstruction Act, 206; vote to sustain veto of Civil Rights Act, 254. as a prosecutor in impeachment, 261; on power of Supreme Court, 263–4; and civil rights, 288, 292

Blaine, James G., on House, 58; on influence of 'literary men', 66; on suffrage question in 1866, 172; proposes amendment to military protection bill, 192, 196; on negro suffrage, 297

Blow, Henry T., a member of Committee of 15, 129

Boutwell, George, 69; career of, 88; character, 127; on President Johnson, 108, 109; in Committee of 15, 123, 127; on power to amend, 266

Bryce, Lord, opinion on Congressmen, 49–50; on the Senate, 53; on the House, 58

Butler, B. F., career, 90–2; Greenback-Labor candidate, 13, 283; and cabinet office, 29 n. 1; letters to on conditions in the South, 34, 34 n. 1; letter to Wade, 42–3; letter to H. Wilson, 43; opponent of contraction, 220–1; on Grant's candidacy, 278; later career of, 283

Butler, G. B., views on the Supreme Court, 263

California, 73; in election of 1866, 154

Carey, Henry, economic views of, 235

Catell, Senator J., on protection, 230

Chandler, Senator Zachariah, 54; career of, 84–5

Chandler, W. E., 283

Chicago, 73

Cincinnati, 73

Civil Rights, 19; not guaranteed in 'ten-per-cent' plan, 23; in Johnson's policy, 45; proposals in Committee of 15, 131–132; concepts of, 287–93

Civil Rights Bill, provisions, 111–12; veto of, 113–14; passed over veto, 114

Clemenceau, Georges, 81 n. 1, 94

Clews, Henry, 239

Colfax, Schuyler, on Reconstruction, 44, 45; as Speaker, 59; career, 59 n. 1, 283 n. 1

Collamer, Senator J., 14

Committee of Fifteen, set up, 98; and the President, 99–100; character and purpose, 122; report, 122–3; collection of evidence, 123–4; membership of, 124–130; discussions in, 130 ff; and military protection bill, 190–1; adjournment *sine die*, 191

Congress, appointment of seats in, 21–2, 130–1; character of, Chapter III *passim*; Bryce on, 49–50; Godkin on, 51; powers of, Chapter VII *passim*; and national power, 299–301; and civil rights, 293

Congress: House of Representatives, character of, 55–9; procedure in, 60

Congress: Senate, character of, 52–5

Conkling, Roscoe, on Committee of Fifteen, 126–7; speech on 'centralism', 300

Connecticut, 70; Welles and election in, 116–17; in 1866 election, 154

Constitution of the United States, 5, 6; amendment to as a consequence of Republican policy, 22; effect of Reconstruction upon, Chapter VII *passim*; effect upon Reconstruction, 271–3; and national power, 298–9

Constitutional Amendments, *see* Thirteenth Amendment, Fourteenth Amendment, Fifteenth Amendment

Constitutional Theories on legislative supremacy, 254–6, 260; on presidential powers, 256–9, 260, 261; on Supreme Court, 262–4; on majority rule, 265–9; on equality and rights, 298–9; effect of on Reconstruction, 271

Contraction Bills, 217, 218–19

Cox, S. S., on power to amend, 266

Cullom, S. M., speech on currency, 218

Davis, Garrett, 54; on motives for Reconstruction, 212–13

Declaration of Independence, 5; Sumner on, 267–8; and concept of rights, 291

Democratic Party, 5–6; and 'Restoration' of Southern States, 22; character of, 63–5; and Reconstruction Bills 1867, 193, 196, 197; on economic questions, 241

Donnelly, Ignatius, *Diary*, 64 n. 1; on Democratic party, 64; on passage of Civil Rights Act, 114–15; supports lower tariffs, 234; on state of parties in 1870, 281; later career of, 283

Doolittle, Senator James W., on State Rights, 252; fails to carry Wisconsin for Johnson, 154

Douglass, Frederick, on negro rights, 47–48; on suffrage, 268

Dred Scott Case, 7

Du Bois, W. E. B., as a historian of Reconstruction, 275 n. 1

Ela, J. H., on effects of contraction, 219

Election of 1866, Republican majorities, 153–4; explanations for Republican success, 155–68 *passim*; negro suffrage and, 171–2; effect of upon Reconstruction, 168, 175

Emancipation Proclamation, 3

Equality, ideas on, 285–90

Fessenden, Senator W. P., 54, 74; career and influence, 125; in Committee of Fifteen, 103 n. 2, 104, 125, 134, 138; relations with Sumner, 103 n. 2, 110; interview with Johnson, 108, 136–8; and Second Reconstruction Act, 206–7; on constitutional power, 250; vote against impeachment, 262

Fifteenth Amendment, 7, 11; future of, 288; 'impartial' suffrage in, 297–8

Fourteenth Amendment, 7; evolution of, Chapter IV *passim*; form proposed by Owen, 139–41; suffrage in, 140–1; civil rights in, 142; political disabilities in, 142, 143–4; in Congress, 143–4; and admission of States, 145–6, 168–70, 180, 182; rejection in South, 170, 172, 173–4, 183; opposed by Johnson, 148, 173–4, 175 n. 1, 260–1; and impeachment, 260; later effect of, 288, 302

Freedmen's Bureau, 36

Freedmen's Bureau Bill, 1866, 105; veto of 105–6; and cotton production, 237–8

Freedmen's Bureau Act (1866), 144, 238

Garfield, James A., 58, 108; on duties of a Representative, 68; on Radicalism, 74; interviews with Johnson, 108, 109; on Reconstruction and suffrage, 172; letter to on impeachment, 260

Godkin, E. L., on Congressmen, 51

Grant, General U. S., report on South, 39; as candidate for the Presidency, 278–80

Greeley, Horace, letter from Lincoln, 3; proposes tests for suffrage, 47; 66

Grider, Henry, 129

Grimes, Senator J. W., 54; career of, 86; in Committee of Fifteen; on protection, 233–4; vote and argument against impeachment, 262

Harlan, James B., on President Johnson, 109 n. 3

Harris, Senator Ira, in Committee of Fifteen, 129, 142

Hayes, R. B., 58; quoted on Committee of Fifteen, 98

Hendricks, Senator T. A., 54; on Republican Senatorial caucus, 144

Hoar, G. F., on Republican party, 65–6; on Democratic party, 66; on H. Wilson

83–4; on lobbyists, 225; on Republicans, 276–7; on educational reform, 280; on education and Reconstruction, 294 n. 3

House of Representatives, see Congress: House of Representatives

Howard, Senator J. M., 54; career of, 85; a member of Committee of Fifteen, 129; on Thirteenth Amendment and national power, 253

Howe, Senator T., 54; career of, 85; on the cabinet and Tenure of Office Bill, 258–9

Illinois, parties in, 70; in election of 1866, 154

Indiana, parties in, 70; in election of 1866, 154

Iowa, parties in, 73; in election of 1866, 154

Jenckes, T. A., and civil service reform, 280

Johnson, President Andrew, character and career, 30–2; views on policy of Congress, 7, 18–19, 148; as governor of Tennessee, 17, 132; Reconstruction policy, 28, 32–4, 35, 39, 44, 96–7; relations with Congress, 29; and negro suffrage, 35, 48; and South in 1865, 32–3, 38; in 1866, 153; first message to Congress, 39; and Carl Schurz, 39–40; and Committee of Fifteen, 99–100, 108; veto of Freedmen's Bureau Bill, 105–6, 107 n. 1, 111, 133 n. 1; speech on 22 Feb, 110–11; veto of Civil Rights Bill, 113–14, 121; interview with Fessenden, 136–8; and Fourteenth Amendment, 148, 173–4, 175 n. 1; and New Orleans riot, 158–9; and National Union Movement, 160–2; and patronage 1865–6, 163–6; speaking tour 1866, 166–8; reaction to 1866 election, 172–3; veto of First Reconstruction Bill, 198–200; veto of Second Reconstruction Act, 207–8; impeachment of, 260–2, 277

Johnson, Senator Reverdy, career, 54 n. 2; on negro capabilities, 47; on Committee of Fifteen, 128–9; on consistency, 173; opposes veto of First Reconstruction Bill, 200–1; on consolidation and State rights, 251–2

Julian, G. W., career, 92–3; and negro suffrage, 13, 171–2; on Radicalism, 75; proposal for a military protection bill,

188–90; on Republican party, 281; and labour legislation, 283

Kansas, parties in, 73

Kelley, W. D.; career 58, 86–8; 'history is not repeating itself', 13; proposes a second Reconstruction Bill, 204; on prosperity in 1865, 213; opposes contraction bill, 216, 221; on Stevens and Legal Tender Act, 223; on protection, 230; on economic needs of the South, 243 n. 2

Kentucky, parties in, 70

Kuykendall, A. J., speech on currency, 217

Lincoln, President Abraham, on purpose of war, 2–3; on slavery and Union, 3; second inaugural, 12; and State rights, 22; proclamation of 8 Dec, 1863, 23; 'ten-per-cent' plan, 23; veto of Wade-Davis Bill, 24; last speech on Reconstruction, 26

Louisiana, Lincoln's speech on Reconstruction in, 26–7; 'black code' of, 36; in 1866, 159

Loyalty, 13–14; definition of, 269–70

McCulloch, Hugh, and policy of contraction, 215–16, 218

Maine, parties in, 70; in 1866 election, 153–4

Maryland, parties in, 70

Massachusetts, moderates and Radicals in, 70; in election of 1866, 154; Henry Wilson as Senator for, 83–4

Medill, Joseph, letter on tariffs, 234; on impeachment, 277

Michigan, parties in, 73; in election of 1866, 154

Milligan, ex parte, 7, 185–6; Stevens on, 186; and problem of legislative supremacy, 262–4

Minnesota, parties in, 73

Mississippi, 'black code' of, 36–7; report on in 1866, 184

Missouri, parties in, 70

Morrill, Justin M., 129; introduces contraction bill 1866, 216

Nation, The, on racial question, 4–5; on the Supreme Court, 262–3

National Union Movement, 161–2, 165

Negroes, emancipation of, 3; *The Nation* on, 4–5; suffrage, 19, 47–8, 67, 285–8, 293–4, 294–7; and 'black code', 36; Southern view of, 38; Reverdy Johnson on, 47; arguments on equality of, 285 ff

Newell, W. A., on national power, 251

New Hampshire, moderates and Radicals in, 70

New Jersey, parties in, 70; in election of 1866, 154

New Orleans, 17; 1866 riot, 158–9

New York, parties in, 70; in 1866 election, 154

New York City, 73

Ohio, parties in, 70; in 1866 election, 154

Opdyke, George W., letter on currency, 220

Owen, Robert Dale, proposes amendment to Stevens, 139–41

Pease, Governor, of Texas, and Welles, 187–8

Pendleton, on power to amend, 266

Pennsylvania, parties in, 70, 73

Philadelphia, 73

Phillips, Wendell, and labour, 13; on Johnson's policy, 43; as a spokesman of labour, 283

Poland, Luke, on constitutional power, 298–9

Press, the, and election of 1866, 156–7

Proclamation of Amnesty, 29 May, 1865, 32

Proclamation on North Carolina, 29 May, 1865, 32–3

Protection, attitudes towards, 228–35

Providence, 73

Racial equality, ideas on, 285–8

Radicalism, 10–11; geographical distribution of, 68–75; as an ideology, 248–9; apparent triumph of, 274; waning of, Chapter VIII *passim*

Radical Republicans, 13; reactions of Johnson's policy, 42–5; geographical distribution of, 70–3; on currency questions, 216–22; on monopolies, 233–4; on labour questions, 226–8; on tariffs, 228–35; economic views, 235–6

Raymond, Henry J., 58; on Reconstruction policy, 46, 99, 121; and election of 1866, 157; and National Union Movement, 161–2; abandons Johnson, 157

Reconstruction Acts: first act, Chapter V *passim*; final form of 192–7; veto of, 198–200; re-passage of, 201; R. Johnson on, 200–1; The *World* on, 203 n. 1; assessment of, 203: second act, 204–5, 206–7; veto of, 207–8: third act, 209–10

Reconstruction Bill (1866), in Owen's plan, 140; failure in Congress, 144–6

Reid, Whitelaw, 66; on Thaddeus Stevens, 80

Republicans; Radicals and moderates, geographical distribution of, 70–5; constituencies, 244–7; aims of, 65–9; and 'restoration', 22; after 1869, Chapter VIII *passim*

Republican party, 6, 7; character of, 8–9, 62–3, 65–7, 281; Radicals and moderates in, 70–5; and negro suffrage, 19, 67; economic views in, 242–3; social background of, 244–7; as an ideological party, 248–9; G. F. Hoar on, 276–7; B. F. Butler on, 281; changing character after 1869, Chapter VIII *passim*

Rhode Island, parties in, 70

Rogers, Andrew J., 129

St Louis, 73

Schenk, George W., opposes contraction, 221

Schurz, Carl, visit to the South, 39–40; report, 18, 40–2; on Democratic party, 64, 282; on currency, 222; and liberal Republicanism, 282

Senate, character of, 52–5

Seward, William H., and Johnson's policy, 118–21

Shellabarger, S., 58; proposes amendment to Reconstruction Bill, 196–7

Sheridan, General, report on conditions in Texas, 184

Sherman, Senator John, 54; on Johnson and Fourteenth Amendment, 175 n. 1; on Fifteenth Amendment and readmission of States, 182–3; presides over Senate Committee on Reconstruction Bill, 194; on Reconstruction Bill, 197; on disqualification under this Bill, 198 n. 1; on currency, 221; on Thirteenth Amendment and national power, 252; on Johnson's use of the appointing power, 256–7; proposes a tenure of office law, 258; on impeachment, 260–1

Sickles, General, report on South Carolina, 185

South Carolina, report on in 1866, 185

Spalding, R. G., on Radicalism, 74

Sprague, Senator W., on businessmen in Congress, 225; on benefits of industry, 230 n. 2; on protection, 229 n. 1

Stanton, Edward M., in cabinet, 208–9; and third Reconstruction Act, 209

State Rights, 20–1; Lincoln, Johnson and, 22; in veto of Freedmen's Bureau Bill, 106; in veto of Civil Rights Bill, 112–4; and concepts of national power, 250–4; Stevenson, 243 n. 1

Stephen, Leslie, on relationship of slavery to war, 4

Stephens, Alexander H., 36; examined by Committee of Fifteen, 123

Stevens, Thaddeus, character and influence, 58, 79–82; on Constitution, 6; on Southerners in Congress before 1861, 9; on character of war, 12 n. 1; on civil rights, 20, 291, 293; and 'ten-per-cent' plan, 24; Reconstruction policy, 27–8, 46, 98, 100–2, 149, 210; in Committee of Fifteen, 126, 131, 141, 191; interview with Owen, 139–41; on negro suffrage, 141, 150, 178–9, 295–6; and Fourteenth Amendment, 143; policy in 1867, 176–9; introduces military protection bill, 191; opposes Reconstruction Bill 1867, 192–193; introduces Third Reconstruction Act, 209; opposes contraction, 216–7; views on currency, 221–223; economic views, 243; on State Rights, 243 n. 1, national assistance, 270; death of, 281–2

Stewart, Alexander T., 239

Stewart, Senator W. M., career, 117; on war aims, 3; on Republican policy, 45, 67; plan for Reconstruction, 117–8, 139

Stockton, John P., deprived of Senatorship, 114 n. 1

Suffrage, negro, 19, 47–8, 67, 141, 150, 178–9; in election of 1866, 169–70; written into Reconstruction Bill, 196;

theoretical problems associated with, 285–8, 294–7; in Fifteenth Amendment, 297–8

Sumner, Charles, character and influence, 53, 54, 75–9; on Reconstruction, 5, 102–104; on 'duties of the hour, 13; on civil rights, 20, 291; on North Carolina Proclamation, 42; on negro suffrage, 48, 103, 131, 169 n. 1, 194; character of speeches, 53; and Fessenden, 103 n. 2; proposes Negro suffrage as a condition for Reconstruction, 194; proposes a second Reconstruction Bill, 204; views on Bill, 207; attempts to make free education without racial discrimination a condition for admission of States, 207 n. 2; on constitutional power, 250–1; on majority rule, 266 ff; on Declaration of Independence and Constitution, 267–8; on national existence, 270; approached by Schurz on Liberal Republicanism, 282

Supreme Court, 7; powers of, 262–4; deprived of appellate jurisdiction over military courts, 264 n. 1

Taylor, General Richard, description of Johnson, 31; interviews with Johnson, 109 n. 3; on the *N.Y. Times* in 1866, 157 n. 1

Tenure of Office Act, origin, 256–8; cabinet offices and, 258–9

Thirteenth Amendment, 12; and Civil Rights legislation, 112, 113, 252–4; and concept of national power, 252

Tennessee, 'ten-per-cent' plan in, 17; Republicanism in, 70; admission of, 98, 131, 132–4, 138–9, 144

Texas, report on in 1866, 184; Welles and Governor Pease, 187–8

Texas v. *White*, 264

Tobey, Edward, speech by, 237

Trumbull, Senator Lyman, 54, character 104–5; and Freedmen's Bureau Bill, 105–6; interviews with Johnson, 105, 108; and Civil Rights Act, 111–12; disappointment of, 116; opposes negro Suffrage, 194 n. 1; introduces Third Reconstruction Act, 209; on Thirteenth Amendment and national power, 252–3; proposes restraint on President's power to appoint, 257–8; votes against impeachment, 262; on civil rights, 292

Unionism, in the South, Northern view of, 17; effect of Johnson's policy on, 34; condition of 1866–7, 183–4

Vermont, parties in, 70; in election of 1866, 154

Wade, Senator B. F., career of, 54, 82–3; on influence of Radicals, 10; and Wade-Davis Bill, 24; correspondence with Butler on cabinet office, 29 n. 1; letter from Sumner, 42; letter from Butler, 42; on Fourteenth Amendment and admission of States, 169
Wade-Davis Bill, 24–6; compared with First and Second Reconstruction Acts, 205–6
War between the States, interpretation of, 11–12
Washburn, Elihu B., career of, 58, 89; on Southerners in Congress, 10; a member of Committee of Fifteen, 129; an opponent of monopolies, 224 n. 1; letters to, from S. Wilkinson, 15, from A. Badeau, 38, on contraction, 218, on impeachment, 277–8, on Grant's candidacy, 279 n. 3

Welles, Gideon, and the South in 1865, 38; on Radicals, 69; on B. F. Wade, 82–3; on Z. Chandler, 85 n. 1; on J. W. Grimes, 86; on W. D. Kelley, 87; influence upon Johnson, 107–8, 110; on use of patronage, 110, 163; and Connecticut election, 116–7; on 1866 election, 156
Wells, David A., on prosperity in 1867, 214
Wentworth, John, on lobbyists, 226
White, Horace, 66; on tariffs, 234
Wilson, Senator Henry, career of, 54, 83–84; on Radicalism, 10, 11; on 'black codes', 37, 252; letter from Butler, 43; on suffrage and Reconstruction, 194 n. 1; on 'the new danger', 224–5; on suffrage, 294 n. 1
Wilson, J. F., career of, 89–90; proposes amendment to Reconstruction Bill, 195; on *ex parte Milligan*, 262
Wilkinson, Sam, letter from on conditions for Reconstruction, 15
Williams, Senator G. H., 54; career of, 90; in committee of 15, 129; on Tenure of Office bill, 258 n. 3; on female suffrage, 294 n. 2
Wisconsin, parties in, 73; in election of 1866, 154
Wood, General, report on Mississippi, 184

PRINTED IN GREAT BRITAIN BY ROBERT MACLEHOSE AND CO. LTD
THE UNIVERSITY PRESS, GLASGOW